THE SUBJECTS AND SUBJECTIVITIES OF INTERNATIONAL CRIMINAL LAW

This book provides a critical introduction to the core elements of international criminal law. It does so by provoking thought on what international criminal law is, or could be, by contrasting the practice of widely recognised state-based actors and institutions such as the International Criminal Court with practices associated with non-state actors in particular citizens' tribunals.

International criminal law is now established as an essential legal and institutional response to atrocity. However, it faces a series of political and practical challenges. It is vital to consider its limits and potential, as well as the ways and extent to which those limitations might be addressed. Many actors with very different visions of its nature and parameters play a role in shaping the meaning of international criminal law whether that be in official or unofficial spaces. This book explores the principles and institutions of international criminal law alongside the alternative visions of it put forward by citizens' tribunals. In so doing it encourages reflection on that law's multiple meanings and usages in order to provoke consideration of what it means, and might mean, to deploy international criminal law today.

Kent Critical Law Series: Volume 1

Kent Critical Law

Series Editors: Nick Piška and Toni Williams

This series of short works is designed to provide students and scholars of law with the tools to enable critical engagement with the major fields of law and their historical, contemporary and future development. The series was conceived at Kent Law School to reflect its commitment to critical legal scholarship. The books offer original interdisciplinary examinations of the subjects commonly taught in universities and additional textbook reading for students seeking alternative approaches to otherwise familiar legal topics.

The Subjects and Subjectivities of International Criminal Law

A Critical Introduction

Emily Haslam

·HART·
OXFORD · LONDON · NEW YORK · NEW DELHI · SYDNEY

HART PUBLISHING

Bloomsbury Publishing Plc

Kemp House, Chawley Park, Cumnor Hill, Oxford, OX2 9PH, UK

1385 Broadway, New York, NY 10018, USA

29 Earlsfort Terrace, Dublin 2, Ireland

HART PUBLISHING, the Hart/Stag logo, BLOOMSBURY and the Diana logo are
trademarks of Bloomsbury Publishing Plc

First published in Great Britain 2024

A catalogue record for this book is available from the British Library.

Library of Congress Cataloging-in-Publication data

Names: Haslam, Emily, author.

Title: The subjects and subjectivities of international criminal law : a critical introduction / Emily Haslam.

Description: Oxford, UK ; New York, NY : Hart Publishing, 2024. |
Series: Kent critical law series; volume 1 | Includes bibliographical references and index. |
Summary: "This book provides students with a critical introduction to the core elements of international criminal
law. It does so by exploring the role that the law and practices of international criminal justice play in constructing
international subjects and objects, including victims, defendants, states and the international community.
International criminal law faces a series of challenges to its partiality and political bias. A central concern is
the construction of international subjectivity. It is clear that the law and practices of international criminal justice
play a crucial role in constructing international subjects and objects"—Provided by publisher.

Identifiers: LCCN 2023051583 (print) | LCCN 2023051584 (ebook) | ISBN 9781509973750 (hardback) |
ISBN 9781849467292 (paperback) | ISBN 9781509973736 (Epub) | ISBN 9781509973743 (ebook)

Subjects: LCSH: International criminal law. | Criminal liability (International law). |
Criminal justice, Administration of. | Subjectivity.

Classification: LCC KZ7050 .H379 2024 (print) | LCC KZ7050 (ebook) | DDC 345—dc23/eng/20231108

LC record available at https://lccn.loc.gov/2023051583

LC ebook record available at https://lccn.loc.gov/2023051584

ISBN: PB: 978-1-84946-729-2
       ePDF: 978-1-50997-374-3
       ePub: 978-1-50997-373-6

Typeset by Compuscript Ltd, Shannon

To find out more about our authors and books visit www.hartpublishing.co.uk. Here you will find extracts,
author information, details of forthcoming events and the option to sign up for our newsletters.

FOREWORD

This new series of short monographs was born out of research-led teaching at Kent Law School and the perceived need to supplement existing textbooks with challenging, interdisciplinary accounts of important legal subjects. It is primarily aimed at law students, both undergraduate and postgraduate, but will be of interest to researchers looking for alternative ways of considering the subject. The monographs will offer accessible but challenging accounts of important legal subjects, covering their subject's core principles and its key ideas, selected aspects of its legal and conceptual history and critical engagement with its future trajectory. The series' common themes reflect Kent Law School's foundational commitment to examining how shifting power relations shape legal rules, principles, and doctrine and build on the School's earlier pioneering contributions to critical legal education including *A Critical Introduction to Law* (first published in 1995) and two volumes *The Critical Lawyers' Handbook* (1992 and 1997).

We are delighted that Emily Haslam's *The Subjects and Subjectivities of International Criminal Law: a Critical Introduction* is the first book in the series. More often than not so-called foundational subjects of law (eg contract law, public law and national criminal law) form the core of a new series aimed at undergraduates, but international criminal law is an important subject of law and one in need of critical interrogation. In particular it draws attention to alternative ways of 'doing justice' on the international scene, ones more attuned to reconciliation processes, most notably 'citizens' tribunals'. In this way the book exemplifies the Kent tradition of questioning how law and justice are conceived and practiced, and shows how different approaches produce different legal subjectivities.

Since the series was commissioned in 2014, Professor Didi Herman, whose idea it was, has retired and stepped back from its editorship. We'd like to thank Didi for her enormous contribution over the years. Likewise we would like to thank Richard Hart for commissioning the series in the first place, Bill Asquith for his backing during its early days and especially Kate Whetter at Hart Publishing for her commitment to the series during the COVID years and her enthusiastic support and encouragement in getting this first book over the line.

Nick Piška and Toni Williams
Series Editors

ACKNOWLEDGEMENTS

This book is the product of many years teaching and researching international criminal law at Kent Law School, and prior to that at the University of Sussex. I have been fortunate to have benefited from countless stimulating interactions with colleagues, academic visitors and students over the years, which have enriched my approach to international law, specifically international criminal law. I would like to thank Donatella Alessandrini, Davina Cooper, Luis Eslava, Suhraiya Jivraj, Sara Kendall, Rose Parfitt, Josipa Šarić, Josephine Uwineza, Richard Vogler and Wade Mansell. My thoughts about victims in international criminal law were honed through previous rich collaborations with Marie-Bénédicte Dembour and Rod Edmunds. I am very grateful to Christine Schwöbel-Patel for her perceptive and helpful comments on the manuscript. Thanks go to Didi Herman, Nick Piška and Toni Williams for their enthusiasm for the project and their insightful comments, and to Marie Selwood for her excellent editing. Beth Ellis and Padmapriya Parthasarathy provided exemplary research assistance. I would also like to thank Kate Whetter at Hart Publishing for her supportive guidance, Catherine Minahan, Verity Stuart, Linda Goss and the production team at Hart Publishing, and Terry Gibson for his support.

CONTENTS

1

Introduction

I. Overview

International criminal law provides for the international and national prosecution of international crimes, that is crimes that are claimed to be of the most serious concern to the international community.[1] The orthodox understanding of these are the so-called core crimes, those that can be prosecuted by the International Criminal Court (ICC) in the Hague. These are genocide, war crimes, crimes against humanity and aggression. Since the 1990s, a plethora of international criminal institutions have been created, as a result of which there has been huge development of substantive and procedural international criminal law. Supporters variously argue that they have generated a culture of anti-impunity, delivered justice to victims and contributed to a historical record of atrocity (the absence of which tempers the achievement of justice and durable peace); in so doing they have also created a cadre of professional international criminal lawyers.[2] In a remarkably short space of time, international criminal law has come to provide the predominant legal, institutional and political response to atrocity at the international and national levels amongst state and non-state actors. It has become a central prism through which claims about suffering, harm and responsibility have come to be made and contested.[3]

In the early years of its post-Cold War revival, international criminal law generated high expectations. Amongst the claims its supporters made were that it could, variously, do justice, including to victims; contribute to reconciliation

---

[1] See, eg, Art 1, Rome Statute of the International Criminal Court A/CONF 183/9, 17 July 1998.

[2] PR Williams and K Larkin, 'Twenty-Four Years On: The Yugoslav and Rwanda Tribunals' Contributions to Durable Peace' in M Sterio and M Scharf (eds), *The Legacy of Ad Hoc Tribunals in International Criminal Law* (Cambridge University Press, 2019) 326 (discussing the International Criminal Tribunal for the Former Yugoslavia). Barrie Sander observes how international criminal tribunals 'have nurtured a growing sense of relevance among the international legal profession': B Sander, 'International Criminal Justice as Progress: From Faith to Critique' in M Bergsmo et al (eds), *Historical Origins of International Criminal Law*, vol 4 (Torkel Opsahl, 2015) 749, 773.

[3] See, eg, SMH Nouwen and WG Werner, 'Monopolizing Global Justice' (2015) 13 *Journal of International Criminal Justice* 157, 161, observing that 'in the past two decades complex questions of armed conflict, identity politics and wealth distribution have been redefined in the expert vocabulary of international criminal law'. MA Drumbl, *Atrocity, Punishment and International Law* (Cambridge University Press, 2007) 3 notes that 'the criminal law has gained ascendancy as the dominant regulatory mechanism for extreme evil'.

and the restoration and/or the maintenance of peace; and establish an undeniable and authoritative historical record of atrocity. However, the multiple and overlapping promises international criminal institutions held out have not always been matched by their impact in practice. For one, the purposes and practices of international criminal justice are riven with a series of tensions. These tensions require that choices are made between conflicting priorities and objectives (chapter 2), and as such, these choices are political in a broad sense.[4] For another, the formulation and practice of international criminal law reflects geopolitical realities. Like any law, international criminal law veers towards reflecting the interests of powerful actors, to a greater or lesser degree. This leaning is inevitable because international criminal law operates in a world of unequal sovereign states and in the context of deeply engrained structural inequalities. International criminal law is inevitably embedded in these power relations, even whilst those working within the field might desire and seek to transcend them. As a result of the above, international criminal law has been subject to multiple criticisms, including: its alleged partiality and political bias; its resulting focus on a restricted range of harms; its limited capacity to make a tangible difference to people's lives after large-scale atrocity; and its failure to deter crimes from occurring in the first place. Yet, for all that, the promise of international criminal law still strongly appeals to many states, academics, activists and communities, including in the global south.[5]

Against this background, then, it is essential to consider the limits and potential of international criminal law as well as the ways and extent to which these limitations might be challenged. This is the aim of this book. Thus, it offers a critical introduction to the core principles and institutions of international criminal law. It encourages consideration of how international criminal law reflects – or can be deployed by – the interests of powerful actors. It also emphasises practices that challenge these biases. Such practices take place in 'official' and 'unofficial' spaces, and are carried out by 'official' and 'unofficial' actors'.

States play the primary role in developing international law. For the most part it is states that negotiate and ratify international criminal conventions (which bind states that sign and ratify them) and participate in the formation of customary international law (international obligations that are driven by general and consistent state practice that is accepted as law (*opinio juris*)).[6]

---

[4] See further on the political choices inherent in international criminal law, D Robinson, 'Inescapable Dyads: Why the International Criminal Court Cannot Win' (2015) 28 *Leiden Journal of International Law* 323; Sander (n 2) 785.

[5] For further discussion see, eg, J Reynolds and S Xavier, '"The Dark Corners of the World": TWAIL and International Criminal Justice' (2016) 14 *Journal of International Criminal Justice* 959, 960, noting international criminal law's 'allure' and 'pitfalls'.

[6] See further on customary international law, eg, W Mansell and K Openshaw, *International Law: A Critical Introduction* (Hart Publishing, 2013) 19–25; J Klabbers, *International Law* (Cambridge University Press, 2020) 24–72.

However, multiple subjects, some with and some without formal international legal personality, also play a significant role in the development of international (criminal) law. Non-state actors, such as civil society groups for example, can help illuminate the 'blind-spots'[7] of international criminal law, provide valuable services to international criminal institutions, and connect courts and tribunals to local populations.[8] This book pays attention to a particular form of civil society activism, namely the establishment and operation of citizens' tribunals. Although in recent years increasing academic attention is being paid to them, citizens' tribunals are frequently overlooked in mainstream approaches to international criminal law. However, they offer a form of justice that draws on international criminal law (as well as human rights), and as such they function as a valuable mirror through which the limits and opportunities of 'official' international criminal law can be explored.

These non-state tribunals are variously called citizens' tribunals, Russell Tribunals (after the Bertrand Russell Peace Tribunal, the originator of the modern citizens' tribunal movement) or Permanent Peoples' Tribunals (PPTs) (established by the Permanent Peoples' Tribunal in Rome) amongst others. This book uses the term 'citizens' tribunal' to include all such bodies. Lelio Basso, who proposed the PPT as a permanent institution, rejected the term 'citizens' tribunal' considering it too bourgeois.[9] While acknowledging this criticism, this book uses the term because the idea of 'citizenship' brings important connotations about ownership,[10] and, as will become apparent, the ownership of law by the people is a key feature of citizens' tribunals.

While citizens' tribunals are not homogeneous, in general they do not just apply international law but also seek to critique and transform it.[11] Thus, they are a paradigmatic example of a critical approach to international criminal law. Section II sets this claim in context by considering what a critical approach to international criminal law looks like.

---

[7] On blind-spots in human rights law, see B Rajagopal, 'International Law and Social Movements: Challenges of Theorizing Resistance' (2003) 41 *Columbia Journal of Transnational Law* 397, 406.

[8] For a critical approach that explores how 'technologies of governmentality and government have fused local ownership to global governance', see V Nesiah, 'Local Ownership of Global Governance' (2016) 14 *Journal of International Criminal Justice* 985, 989. For critical discussion of the 'local' and 'global' categories in transitional justice, see L Ullrich, 'Beyond the 'Global-Local Divide Local Intermediaries, Victims and the Justice Contestations of the International Criminal Court' (2016) 14 *Journal of International Criminal Justice* 543.

[9] L Moita, 'Opinion Tribunals and the Permanent People's Tribunal' (2015) 6(1) *Janus.Net* 30, 41.

[10] See further in a different context, M Mamdani, 'Response' (2009) 3 *International Journal of Transitional Justice* 470, 471.

[11] A Byrnes and G Simm, 'Reflections on the Past and Future of International Peoples' Tribunals' in A Byrnes and G Simm (eds), *Peoples' Tribunals and International Law* (Cambridge University Press, 2019) 259, 262. U Dolgopol, 'Civil Society's Engagement with International Criminal Law: The Role of Peoples' Tribunals' in Bergsmo et al (eds) (n 2) 703.

II. What is a Critical Approach
to International Criminal Law?

This book draws on the ever-growing critical approaches to international criminal law.[12] There are different ways of understanding the term 'critical', but for the purposes of this book it represents a way of doing and thinking about law that emphasises law's multifaceted relations with power in its different forms. Different theoretical and methodological tools enable such an approach. Typically, these include feminism,[13] postcolonialism, Third World Approaches to International Law (TWAIL)[14] and critical race studies.[15] They also encompass other approaches, such as the use of art and critical interrogation of international criminal law's images.[16]

In essence, then, critical approaches to international criminal law are alert to the power biases inherent in existing international criminal law. Critical approaches take for granted that law – even apparently progressive law like international criminal law and human rights – tends to reflect, as Mansell and Openshaw explain, a 'particular distribution of power among states, and that this in turn dictates the interests that international law serves', even whilst it gains considerable power from its 'veneer of political neutrality'.[17] The sorts of questions that animate critical scholars do not just derive from concerns about the interpretation or application of the law. As McAuliffe and Schwöbel-Patel explain, critical

---

[12] See, eg, C Schwöbel, *Critical Approaches to International Criminal Law* (Routledge, 2014); C De Vos, S Kendall and C Stahn, *Contested Justice The Politics and Practice of International Criminal Court Interventions* (Cambridge University Press, 2015). See further, on the growth of critical voices in international criminal law, Sander (n 2) 753.

[13] See, eg, M Fineman, *Feminist Perspectives on Transitional Justice: From International and Criminal to Alternative Forms of Justice* (Intersentia, 2013); D Otto, 'Performing Legal Order: Some Feminist Thoughts on International Criminal Law' (2011) 11(3) *International Criminal Law Review* 409; R Rubio-Marin, *The Gender of Reparations: Unsettling Sexual Hierarchies while Redressing Human Rights Violations* (Cambridge University Press, 2009).

[14] See, eg, M Burgis-Kasthala, 'Scholarship as Dialogue? TWAIL and the Politics of Methodology' (2019) 14(4) *Journal of International Criminal Justice* 921; P Manirakiza, 'A Twail Perspective on the African Union's Project to Withdraw from the International Criminal Court' (2018) 23 *African Year Book of International Law* 391.

[15] RC DeFalco and F Mégret, 'The Invisibility of Race at the ICC: Lessons from the US Criminal Justice System' (2019) 7(1) *London Review of International Law* 55.

[16] See, eg, SM Wanjiru, *Black Iconography and Colonial (Re)production at the ICC: (In)depend-ence Cha Cha Cha?* (Routledge, 2022). For discussion of images and international criminal justice, see I Tallgren, 'Come and See? The Power of Images and International Criminal Justice' (2017) 17 *International Criminal Law Review* 259. See further, I Tallgren, 'Watching *Tokyo Trial*' (2017) 5(2) *London Review of International Law* 291.

[17] W Mansell and K Openshaw, *International Law* (Hart Publishing, 2013) 1. See further, eg, Krever, who observes that '[i]t is precisely in acting as *though* law were neutral that legal discourse operates *ideologically*, not merely masking social inequalities but making those inequalities appear the inevi-table concomitant to a neutral and impartial legal order': T Krever, 'International Criminal Law: An Ideology Critique' (2013) *Leiden Journal of International Law* 701, 705. See further P McAuliffe and C Schwöbel-Patel, 'Disciplinary Matchmaking Critics of International Criminal Law Meet Critics of Liberal Peacebuilding' (2018) 16(5) *Journal of International Criminal Justice* 985, 997.

approaches to international criminal law are not concerned with questions about the 'effectiveness' of law, but with broader questions about the taken-for-granted values underpinning it.[18] Critical approaches seek to identify who or what gains from international criminal law, and they interrogate the structures that underpin these respective benefits and burdens.[19] They are occupied with identifying the voices and perspectives that are glossed over, and with exploring how international criminal law represents its subjects.[20] In other words, they are concerned with identifying the stories law and legal processes tell, for example about race or gender, victims and perpetrators, and the global north and the global south.[21]

One central critical approach in international law is the body of scholarship known as TWAIL.[22] TWAIL scholars are diverse, but broadly they seek to illuminate the historical and continuing impact of the relationship between international law and colonialism and imperialism, and often to reimagine international law in more emancipatory ways. Although within TWAIL there are many different perspectives, TWAIL scholars typically adopt a broad understanding of violence, which includes, as Burgis-Kasthala explains, 'the everyday violence that results through neoliberal and neo-colonial forms of governance on the Global South whether realized as classic individual criminal harms or collective conditions such as poverty and racial inequality'.[23] In this way scholars challenge the representation of 'the causes of Third Word violence as indigenous' to the Third World, a representation that 'can serve as a powerful rhetorical device in affirming the need for ICL [international criminal law] deliverance to the Global South'.[24] They also focus

---

[18] McAuliffe and Schwöbel-Patel (n 17) 989–90.

[19] ibid 990.

[20] See further, eg, discussion in Reynolds and Xavier (n 5) 965–67.

[21] See further on the question of racism, particularly structural racism, racialisation and international criminal justice, DeFalco and Mégret (n 15) 80–81. See further on racialised representations of victims and defendants, eg, G Anders, 'Testifying about "Uncivilized Events": Problematic Representations of Africa in the Trial against Charles Taylor' (2011) 24(4) *Leiden Journal of International Law* 937; A Sagan, 'African Criminals/African Victims: The Institutionalised Production of Cultural Narratives in International Criminal Law' (2010) 39(1) *Millennium Journal of International Studies* 3; C Schwöbel-Patel, 'Spectacle in International Criminal Law: The Fundraising Image of Victimhood' (2016) 4(2) *London Review of International Law* 247.

[22] See further TV Ananthavinayagan, 'Panem et circences? People's Tribunals from TWAIL perspective' in RM Paulose (ed), *People's Tribunals, Human Rights and the Law Searching for Justice* (Routledge, 2020) 60; A Anghie and B Chimni, 'Third World Approaches to International Law and Individual Responsibility in Internal Conflict' (2004) 36 *Studies in Transnational Legal Policy* 185, 186; M Burgis-Kasthala, 'Scholarship as Dialogue? TWAIL and the Politics of Methodology' (2016) 14 *Journal of International Criminal Justice* 921; A Kiyani, 'International Crime and the Politics of Criminal Theory: Voices and Conduct of Exclusion' (2015) 48(1) *New York University Journal of International Law and Politic* 129; A Kiyani, J Reynolds and S Xavier, 'Foreword: Third World Approaches to International Criminal Law' (2016) 14 *Journal of International Criminal Justice* 915.

[23] Burgis-Kasthala (n 22) 935. For a similar argument, eg, Sehmi, who observes: 'Arguably, the ICC, as an integral part of the liberal peacebuilding agenda implicitly legitimates forms of structural violence stemming from neoliberal policies and liberal democracy in Africa'. A Sehmi, 'Judicializing Economic Violence as Means of Dismantling the Structural Causes of Atrocity in the Democratic Republic of Congo' (2020) 14 *International Journal of Transitional Justice* 423, 424.

[24] Burgis-Kasthala (n 22) 936.

on the people of the global south rather than just states or elites.[25] Many of these concerns also feature in the work of citizens' tribunals.

All this provokes a series of questions. For example, is it possible to marry a critical approach to law with a commitment to using the law to effect positive change, and is it possible to acknowledge law's limitations while believing in its ability to deliver justice after atrocity?[26] Does international criminal law need to be fundamentally rethought – and, if so, how? And how far can it be re-thought in the context of the existing international political and economic order? Scholars grapple with the extent to which a critical practice of international criminal law is realisable,[27] just as participants in citizens' tribunals debate how far they should adhere to existing or reimagined law to achieve their aims. Whatever conclusions are reached, these concerns show that any deployment of international criminal law, whether as student, researcher or practitioner, should be as alert as possible to disparities of power and their impact on the law. Adopting a critical approach means being up-front about the dilemmas inherent in international criminal justice and in attempts to mitigate its limitations. It means articulating the choices made in response to those quandaries, without assuming that these are inevitable, and recognising that critique is continuous.[28] Citizens' tribunals, while not without their problems, do just this and offer a paradigmatically critical approach to international criminal law. For this reason and for what they can offer to international criminal justice, this book emphasises their practice alongside that of official international criminal law.

III. What Role Do Citizens' Tribunals Play in a Critical Approach to International Criminal Law?

Citizens' tribunals provide a rich source for a critical approach to international criminal law.[29] As already mentioned, citizens' tribunals are diverse, but to a

---

[25] See, eg, A Kiyani, 'Group-Based Differentiation and Local Repression: the Custom and Curse of Selectivity' (2016) 14 *Journal of International Criminal Justice* 939, 941.

[26] See further Burgis-Kasthala (n 22), who describes a 'central tension animating TWAIL scholarship'. This lies in both a 'suspicion and faith in the possibility of transformation through international law': ibid 933. For discussion in the context of feminist engagements with international (criminal) law, see R Grey, K McLoughlin and L Chappell, 'Gender and Judging at the International Criminal Court: Lessons from 'Feminist Judgment Projects' (2021) 34 *Leiden Journal of International Law* 247, 255.

[27] See further, McAuliffe and Schwöbel-Patel (n 17) 1008.

[28] See further ibid 1009.

[29] See further, eg, D Otto, 'Impunity in a Different Register: People's Tribunals and Questions of Judgment, Law and Responsibility' in E Engle, Z Miller and DM Davis (eds), *Anti-Impunity and the Human Rights Agenda* (Cambridge University Press, 2016) 291; D Otto, 'Beyond Legal Justice: Some Personal Reflections on People's Tribunals, Listening and Responsibility' (2017) 5 *London Review of International law* 225, 226 and 248; and, in the context of transitional justice, M Zunino, 'Subversive Justice: The Russell Vietnam War Crimes Tribunal and Transitional Justice' (2016) 10 *International Journal of Transitional Justice* 211. For insider accounts of, and theoretical reflections about, people's tribunals see Paulose (n 22).

greater or lesser extent they adopt a trial form, albeit with varying approaches to the law, from a political to a more legalistic orientation.[30] Findings are pronounced not by judges but by a jury constituted by prominent intellectuals, public figures and activists. There are, however, key differences in the approach taken to 'judging' between citizens' tribunals and official institutions. Most obviously, citizens' tribunals have no enforcement power. Instead, as the Women's International War Crimes Tribunal observed of its judgment, they have 'significant moral force'.[31] They draw their legitimacy from an alternative legality, in which law 'belongs to the people'.[32] This approach enables them to put forward a vision of justice that could never come from official international criminal law in its current state-centric form.[33] As such, the practice of citizens' tribunals operates as a powerful critique of the limitations of official international criminal law and as a source of inspiration for alternative thinking about it. They also can deliver a form of justice when official institutions are silent. Citizens' tribunals do not just deal with international criminal law, however, but also, amongst others, with human rights law. This approach frees analyses of the causes and consequences of violations from a disciplinary straitjacket that can limit thinking about international law after atrocity.

Citizens' tribunals do not possess international legal personality.[34] While citizens' tribunals' pronouncements do not constitute sources of international law in the way that judgments of 'official' courts do (Article 38 of the Statute of the International Court of Justice),[35] this book reads them alongside official international criminal law. In that sense it reads formal and non-legal sources alongside each other without pointing to their different legal status at every juncture. However, it is important to remember that not only do citizens' tribunals not enjoy

---

[30] See further, eg, J Nayar, 'Taking Empire Seriously: Empire's Law, People's Law and the World Tribunal on Iraq' in A Bartholomew (ed), *Empire's Law The American Imperial Project and the 'War to Remake the World'* (Pluto Press, 2006) 313, 323–25. For a seminal account of the contestations within the WTI (World Tribunal on Iraq) and amongst WTI activists from variously 'legalist' and 'political' approaches, see further A Çubukçu, *For the Law of Humanity The World Tribunal on Iraq* (University of Pennsylvania Press, 2019), arguing for the importance of attending 'to persistent tensions between *legalist* and *political* imaginaries that animate rival visions of global peace and justice': ibid, 13. For the view that PPTs' use of 'certain legal descriptors' causes 'confusion and detract[s] from the critical conversations that are taking place', see RM Paulose, 'Can you hear the people sing? Victim/survivor rights in People's Tribunals' in Paulose (ed) (n 22) 2, 4. Also Otto, 'Beyond Legal Justice' (n 29) 233.

[31] Judgment of Women's International War Crimes Tribunal, 4 December 2001, PT-2000-1-T, para 485 at https://archives.wam-peace.org/wt/wp-content/uploads/2020/03/Judgement.pdf.

[32] See, eg, R Falk, 'Opening Speech on Behalf of the Panel of Advocates' in MG Sökmen (ed), *World Tribunal on Iraq: Making the Case against War* (Olive Branch Press, 2008) 5, 7.

[33] For discussion of the Women's Court in Bosnia and its distinctively feminist approach to international criminal law, see K Campbell, *The Justice of Humans Subject, Society and Sexual Violence in International Criminal Law* (Cambridge University Press, 2022) 230, arguing that 'the Women's Court builds a new paradigm of justice'. See further more generally, B Duerr, 'Political will and the people's will: The role of People's Tribunals in international justice' in Paulose (ed) (n 22) 22, 30–31.

[34] Duerr (n 33) 24.

[35] For the argument that PPTs are 'a contribution towards a new facet of the formation of *opinio juris communis*', see Ananthavinayagan (n 22) 68.

the same legal status as official bodies, their very legitimacy is based on an alternative authority. They do not seek to acquire the same legal status as official bodies. In emphasising the work of citizens' tribunals alongside that of official criminal institutions, this book encourages a broader approach to international criminal law and its legal toolkit. However, it does not seek to suggest that these sources should be treated equally; rather, that each source tells us something different about the law, and its possibilities.

To summarise, this book introduces the key principles and institutions of international criminal law. It also encourages reflection on the worldview that supports the study and practice of international criminal law and the international criminal legal methods used. It encourages acknowledgement of the power relations that underpin contemporary international criminal law and institutions, and a consideration of how those power relations are and may be challenged in formal and informal spaces. There are many excellent texts on international criminal law that examine doctrine in more depth, some of which also include contributions from key practitioners in the field.[36] This book supports a more overtly political and ethical position towards international criminal law by encouraging reflection on how one might position oneself within a critical international criminal legal practice or research.[37] More recently, there has been increasing recognition that citizens' tribunals offer a productive provocation to international law.[38] By reading the work of citizens' tribunals alongside that of more orthodox international law, this book encourages substantive critical reflection about the theory and practice of international criminal law. Thus it encourages reflection about the taken-for-granted choices that underpin international criminal law and its practice, and their consequences. To that end, chapter 2 explores different approaches to international criminal law and their implications.

---

[36] See, eg, R Cryer, D Robinson and S Vasiliev, *An Introduction to International Criminal Law and Procedure* (Cambridge University Press, 2019); R O'Keefe, *International Criminal Law* (Oxford University Press, 2017); W Schabas, *International Criminal Law* (Cambridge University Press, 2016). For critical approaches to international criminal law, see, eg, C Schwöbel, *Critical Approaches to International Criminal Law* (Routledge, 2014); C Stahn, *A Critical Introduction to International Criminal Law* (Cambridge University Press, 2019); and P Kastner (ed), *International Criminal Law in Context* (Routledge, 2017).

[37] See further, on critical teaching of international law, L Eslava, 'The Teaching of (Another) International Law: Critical Realism and the Question of Agency and Structure' (2020) 54(3) *The Law Teacher* 368.

[38] See eg, Duerr (n 33) 35, arguing that they can 'fill gaps and give victims a forum to tell their story' and 'highlight short-comings of the formal international legal system and contribute to its development and advancement'; R Rogo, 'People's Tribunals and truth commissions' in Paulose (ed) (n 22) 40, 43. In contrast, however, see the concern that PPTs 'are in danger of becoming yet another routine enterprise, a part of the *status quo* that they were designed to revolt against': S Sadr, 'From painkillers to cures: Challenges and future of Peoples Tribunals' in Paulose (ed) (n 22) 177, 182.

Further Reading

G Bass, *Stay the Hand of Vengeance: The Politics of War Crimes Tribunals* (Princeton University Press, 2000).

K Campbell, *The Justice of Humans Subject, Society and Sexual Violence in International Criminal Law* (Cambridge University Press, 2022).

AJ Klinghoffer and JA Klinghoffer, *International Citizens' Tribunals: Mobilizing Public Opinion to Advance Human Rights* (Palgrave, 2002).

RM Paulose (ed), *People's Tribunals, Human Rights and the Law Searching for Justice* (Routledge, 2020).

2

What is International Criminal Law?

I. Introduction

This book began by explaining that international criminal law provides for the national or international prosecution of crimes considered to be of the most serious concern to the international community. Although correct, this is a rather limited understanding of the discipline. Definitions matter, and the boundaries of international criminal law are far from fixed. International criminal justice, Barrie Sander explains, 'is a field whose identity is subject to continual contestation'.[1] How international criminal law is approached plays a key role in determining how we see the discipline's scope and potential. This chapter, then, adds to the understanding of international criminal law set out in the previous chapter with alternative approaches towards its study and practice. It considers international criminal law as a set of institutions; a group of crimes; a strategic legal toolkit; as politics; and as contestation.

These approaches are not exhaustive, and they overlap. Each of these approaches to international criminal law reflects a different set of preoccupations and gives rise to different questions. One approach may particularly resonate but, irrespective of whether this is the case, it is important to ask another question: what is excluded when, or what is the 'cost' of, approaching international criminal law from each of these different perspectives? In other words, what are the politics of knowledge production in the way the field is – and might be – defined?

II. International Criminal Law as a Set of Institutions

One way in which we might understand international criminal law is through its institutions, for example the international criminal courts that provide for the international criminal prosecution of individuals at the international level. These institutions and their historical development are examined in more detail in chapter 4. They include the ad hoc International Criminal Tribunal for the former Yugoslavia (ICTY), the International Criminal Tribunal for Rwanda (ICTR), the

---

[1] B Sander, 'International Criminal Justice as Progress: From Faith to Critique' in M Bergsmo et al (eds), *Historical Origins of International Criminal Law*, vol 4 (Torkel Opsahl, 2015) 749.

Special Court for Sierra Leone (SCSL) and the permanent International Criminal Court (ICC). Understanding the achievements and limitations of these bodies typically forms a central part of the study of the discipline. However, a preoccupation with institutions also tends to result in narratives of legal change that leave unaddressed – or pushed to the periphery – broader structural issues that underpin the commission of international crimes and that limit the response to them. Such institutional narratives can position the 'blind-spots' of the current law (that is the injustices the law fails to see and acknowledge) as unfortunate by-products of otherwise progressive institutional change.[2] Moreover, when international criminal law is understood through the prism of its institutions, the institutions themselves can become the symbol or object of justice. In other words, it can become difficult to separate the institutional interests from those of (or claimed in the name of) international criminal justice. These tendencies are of course all predispositions, not inevitabilities. We could, for example, expand our approach to international criminal institutions by including the work of citizens' tribunals more firmly as a mirror, a critical practice and a source of alternative justice.

III. International Criminal Law as a Set of International Crimes

Closely related to the above is an approach that associates international criminal law with the most serious crimes of international concern, that is crimes against humanity, genocide, war crimes and aggression. This approach also has its shortcomings. Despite claims that international crimes 'shock the conscience of mankind', there is no clearly agreed rationale for identifying an international crime or its consequences.[3] Fundamental to citizens' tribunals in contrast is the so-called 'crime of silence' (chapter 5). International crimes are often distinguished from transnational crimes, such as trafficking offences, money laundering, organised crime and corruption, but the distinction between transnational and international crimes is not inevitable or self-evident. Further, whilst it is invidious to compare one atrocity or form of suffering with another, the conscience of mankind has been triggered in partial ways, so that there are forms of violence and types of harms that do not fall within the remit of international criminal law. Critical legal scholars challenge the law's focus on the 'spectacular' at the expense of structural

---

[2] On 'blind-spots' in international human rights law, see B Rajagopal, 'International Law and Social Movements: Challenges of Theorizing Resistance' (2003) 41 *Columbia Journal of Transnational Law* 397, 406. For a critique of progress narratives in international law, see T Skouteris, *The Notion of Progress in International Law Discourse* (TMC Asser Press, 2010); and in international criminal law more specifically, Sander (n 1).

[3] See, eg, C Stahn, *A Critical Introduction to International Criminal Law* (Cambridge University Press, 2019) 18.

violence, for example.[4] As will become apparent, citizens' tribunals seek, in contrast, to address forms of structural violence typically overlooked by 'official' international criminal law. Associating international criminal law with a limited (albeit important) set of international crimes can present the reach of international criminal law – and the world order it reflects – as self-evident and uncontroversial. The question of the actual, optimum and potential reach of international criminal law is, however, more contested than the above list of international crimes suggests and is a question about which reflection is encouraged throughout the book.

Both the approaches to international criminal law outlined above – that is international criminal law as a set of institutions and as a set of crimes – conceive of international criminal law as identifiable and bounded, with events, individuals and conduct falling within or outside it. The following approaches in contrast are more pragmatic or even ambivalent towards international criminal law and what it encompasses.

IV. International Criminal Law as a Toolkit

More pragmatically, we might see international criminal law as a legal toolkit. The legal 'tools' international criminal law makes available include international criminal prosecution and universal jurisdiction (chapter 7). Thinking of international criminal law as a toolkit entails considering what the tools can achieve in any one instance. It also requires asking to what extent the contents of this toolkit are universally shared. Thus, international criminal law has been criticised for embodying a western liberal legal subjectivity.[5] For example, individual criminal responsibility, one of the hallmarks of international criminal law, is seen to reflect a conception of individuals as rational autonomous actors and, as such, has been described as a 'classically liberal project'.[6] Thinking of international criminal law as a toolkit requires consideration of the relationship between international criminal legal and other responses. It also requires asking what is at stake in a predominantly retributive approach to atrocity, and suggests a contextual, case-by-case approach to international criminal justice that locates international criminal law within a broader set of international and national legal responses. Overall, this approach encourages a pragmatic response to international criminal law and its possibilities, including through the consideration of the potential strategic effects

---

[4] See, eg, I Kalpouzos and I Mann, 'Banal Crimes Against Humanity: The Case of Asylum Seekers in Greece' (2015) 16 *Melbourne Journal of International Law* 1; A Kiyani, 'International Crime and the Politics of Criminal Theory: Voices and Conduct of Exclusion' (2015) 48(1) *New York University Journal of International Law and Politic* 129, 137.

[5] MA Drumbl, *Atrocity, Punishment, and International Law* (Cambridge University Press, 2007) 5.

[6] P McAuliffe and C Schwöbel-Patel, 'Disciplinary Matchmaking Critics of International Criminal Law Meet Critics of Liberal Peacebuilding' (2018) 16(5) *Journal of International Criminal Justice* 985, 988. See further, Drumbl (n 5) 5.

of international criminal litigation across a range of fora. As already mentioned, this book emphasises that the extension of international criminal law's legal toolkit to include citizens' tribunals might be more widely recognised.[7]

V. International Criminal Law as Politics/Political

International crimes and international criminal law take place in a highly charged political context. As Pre-Trial Chamber 1 of the ICC observed regarding the situation in Palestine:

> It should however be noted that, by the very nature of the core crimes under the Rome Statute, the facts and situations that are brought before the Court arise from controversial contexts where political issues are sensitive and latent. Accordingly, the judiciary cannot retreat when it is confronted with facts which might have arisen from political situations and/or disputes, but which also trigger legal and juridical issues.[8]

Moreover, in a profoundly unequal geo-political order, international criminal law cannot escape questions of power politics.[9] This becomes evident in this book, particularly in the context of international criminal jurisdiction (chapter 7).

However, for critical lawyers, international criminal law is political in an additional way. This is because, like all law, it involves choices.[10] For example, for Barrie Sander, writing of the ICC, the 'question is not *whether* the Prosecutor is acting politically, but rather *what kind of politics* is being manifested in practice'.[11] Critical approaches to international criminal law illuminate these choices and the assumptions that underpin them.

We might understand international criminal law as politically contingent at macro and micro levels. At the macro level, international criminal law is a

---

[7] Dolgopol makes a similar argument in relation to citizens' tribunals 'that do attempt to engage seriously with the principle of law adopted by the international community'. See U Dolgopol, 'Civil Society's Engagement with International Criminal Law: The Role of Peoples' Tribunals' in Bergsmo et al (eds) (n 1) 703, 712.

[8] Decision on the 'Prosecution Request Pursuant to Article 19(3) for a Ruling on the Court's Territorial Jurisdiction in Palestine', 5 February 2021, ICC-01/18, para 55. It continued, at para 57, 'the fact that the present decision on the Prosecutors' Request might entail political consequences shall not prevent the Chamber from exercising its mandate'.

[9] See further SMH Nouwen and W Werner, 'Doing Justice to the Political: the International Criminal Court in Uganda and Sudan' (2011) 21(4) *European Journal of International Law* 941.

[10] D Robinson, 'Inescapable Dyads: Why the International Criminal Court Cannot Win' (2015) 28 *Leiden Journal of International Law* 323, 346. Robinson draws on M Koskenniemi, *From Apology to Utopia: The Structure of Legal Argument* (Cambridge University Press, 2006). See further on different understandings of political, Nouwen and Werner (n 9) 944–45; Sander (n 1) 785–98.

[11] Sander (n 1) 798; See also McAuliffe and Schwöbel-Patel (n 6) 990; Nouwen and Werner (n 9) 964; F Mégret, 'Beyond "Gravity": For a Politics of International Criminal Prosecution' (2013) 107 *Proceedings of the Annual Meeting of the American Society of International Law* 428, 431: 'A realistic politics of international criminal justice can emerge, but in order to do so it needs to be verbalized, contestable, and contested.'

historically and politically contingent response to atrocity. Sander notes how 'international criminal courts are the product of a particular time and place: secular, rationalist, Western, capitalist and modern'.[12] From this perspective, then, it is important to consider the conditions that led to the dominance of international criminal law as a response to (some forms of) atrocity, and the extent to which those conditions – and therefore international criminal law as we know it – are stable, permanent or mutable. It is also important to consider whether international criminal law can be universal if it is also historically and politically contingent. Finally, and as already mentioned, it is also vital to explore whether the dominance of international criminal law limits the space for alternative approaches towards justice after atrocity.[13] This, then, is what Frédéric Mégret has described as the 'opportunity costs' of international criminal justice,[14] or what Sarah Nouwen and Wouter Werner describe as its 'monopolizing' tendencies.[15]

International criminal law is historically contingent at the micro level too. The complex context in which international criminal law operates, together with the ambitious aims that have been claimed for it (explored in more detail in chapter 3), requires a series of well-documented tensions to be navigated. These include tensions between peace and justice, the demands of history and the demands of an international criminal trial, and the rights of victims and defendants, to name but a few. The mediation of these tensions in any one situation or case is ultimately a political process in the sense already mentioned, that a series of choices must be made, the outcome of which is not inevitable but, instead, is the product of time, people and place. A key consideration here is who or what gets to participate in these processes, and whose interests get reflected in, or excluded from, their outcomes.

VI. International Criminal Law as Contestation

International criminal law can also be understood as a framework for, or a language of, contestation[16] – a space for a series of claims and counterclaims. Understood as a language of contestation, international criminal law is politically neutral in the sense that it may be deployed progressively or regressively. This then requires consideration of how progressive deployments of international criminal law can

---

[12] Sander (n 1) 819.

[13] See, eg, Drumbl (n 5) 122; SMH Nouwen and W Werner, 'Monopolizing Global Justice' (2015) 13 *Journal of International Criminal Justice* 157; Sander (n 1) 82; F Mégret, 'What Sort of Global Justice is "International Criminal Justice"?' (2015) 13(1) *Journal of International Criminal Justice* 77, 96.

[14] Mégret (n 13) 84; See further I Kalpouzos, 'International Criminal Law and the Violence against Migrants' (2020) 21 *German Law Journal* 571, 596.

[15] Nouwen and Werner (n 13) 163.

[16] See, eg, McAuliffe and Schwöbel-Patel (n 6) 987, noting that 'critical approaches to international criminal law provide a platform for a distinct way of thinking about international criminal law as a field of contestation over meaning, methods and solutions'.

be distinguished from regressive ones, a question that is even more acute against the backdrop of populist movements. Jayan Nayar, writing of the People's Law Programme, concludes it has the right

> to apply an interrogation of the 'justice-cause' of a people's mobilisation in determining support. Justice-denying mobilisations which seek the denigration of suffering, which proclaim the priority of rights to violence, which assert the individuality of political visions that possesses no cross-mobilisation of solidarities of suffering, none of these would fit within the Programmes vision of actors contributing to a more humane realisation of politics and governance.[17]

Although he was writing about the People's Law Programme, Nayar provides an important and productive starting point from which to distinguish regressive from progressive uses of international criminal law more generally in the context of thinking about international criminal law as contestation. Building on and drawing from this is the potential importance of practices of solidarity, as found in resistance practices,[18] as a potential central mediating principle in thinking about how to distinguish repressive and progressive deployments of international criminal law.

VII. Conclusion

The above approaches overlap, and none on its own explains or identifies international criminal law comprehensively. However, articulating these approaches points to different ways of seeing international criminal law and its role in the world, as well as the limitations and opportunities of each perspective. In so doing, it opens up different questions about international criminal law and what can be expected of it. How the essence of international criminal law is viewed by any individual may change over time and depending on context. I tend to think of international criminal law as a legal toolkit and a language of contestation, as I see these as constants in international criminal law. Which starting point is adopted will determine the kinds of questions asked about international criminal law and the responses to questions others ask. In chapter 3, we turn to consider in more detail what we might expect from international criminal law.

---

[17] J Nayar, 'Thinking the "Impossible": People's Law' (2003) 1 *Law, Social Justice and Global Development* at https://warwick.ac.uk/fac/soc/law/elj/lgd/2003_1/nayar2/.

[18] On the role of solidarity in the anti-apartheid movement, see H Thörn, *Anti-Apartheid and the Emergence of a Global Civil Society* (Palgrave Macmillan, 2006).

Further Reading

C De Vos, S Kendall and C Stahn, *Contested Justice The Politics and Practice of International Criminal Court Interventions* (Cambridge University Press, 2015).

M Koskenniemi, 'Between Impunity and Show Trials' (2002) 6 *Max Planck Yearbook of United Nations Law* 1.

F Mégret, 'What Sort of Global Justice is "International Criminal Justice"?' (2015) 13(1) *Journal of International Criminal Justice* 77.

SMH Nouwen and W Werner, 'Doing Justice to the Political: the International Criminal Court in Uganda and Sudan' (2011) 21(4) *European Journal of International Law* 941.

3

The Aims and Objectives
of International Criminal Law

I. Introduction

This chapter explores the series of aims that have been attributed to international criminal law. Most obviously, international criminal trials are directed at retribution and deterrence. However, supporters of international criminal justice typically claim more expansive aims for it, including reconciliation, justice for victims, the establishment of a historical record and the restoration or maintenance of peace.[1] Tribunals also emphasise their 'legacy', that is the advancement of the rule of law at a more local level, including through enhancing local capacity.[2] Increasingly, attention has focused on the expressive or symbolic functions of international criminal trials, with some considering that the expressive function is now one of the main aims of international criminal justice.[3]

The achievement of such wide-ranging, loosely defined and potentially contradictory aims was always going to be fraught and raise the potential for disappointed expectations amongst various constituencies, and it is doubtful that the ultimately narrow focus of international criminal law could satisfy such ambitious objectives.[4] A central question that runs through this book, then, is: what

---

[1] See further United Nations (UN), *Report of the Secretary-General on the Rule of Law and Transitional Justice in Conflict and Post-Conflict Societies*, UN Doc S/2004/616 (2004) 38.

[2] See further M Scharf and M Sterio, 'Introduction' in M Sterio and M Scharf (eds), *The Legacy of Ad Hoc Tribunals in International Criminal Law* (Cambridge University Press, 2019) 3.

[3] See, eg, M Aksenova, *Complicity in International Criminal Law* (Hart Publishing, 2019) 243 and 250. See further, for an extensive discussion of expressivism in international criminal law, B Sander, 'The Expressive Turn of International Criminal Justice: A Field in Search Of Meaning' (2019) 32 *Leiden Journal of International Law* 851, distinguishing between instrumental, interpretive, critical and strategic expressivism.

[4] M Burgis-Kasthala, 'Scholarship as Dialogue? TWAIL and the Politics of Methodology' (2016) 14 *Journal of International Criminal Justice* 921, 928, noting that 'the promise of ICL is radically overambitious in the way it seeks to realize (a particularized) "global justice" for humanity, while adopting a radically narrow practice … to achieve such a goal'; F Mégret, 'What Sort of Global Justice is "International Criminal Justice"?' (2015) 13 *Journal of International Criminal Justice* 77, 96. See further I Tallgren, 'The Sensibility and Sense of International Criminal Law' (2002) 13(3) *European Journal of International Law* 561, 593, observing 'that an overwhelming majority of the crucial problems of the societies concerned are not adequately addressed by criminal law'; MA Drumbl, *Atrocity, Punishment and International Law* (Cambridge University Press, 2007) 36, noting that '[i]n the end, the law is overambitious by claiming such a transformative role, but then underambitious by involving only a handful of characters'.

can international criminal law – and a critical practice thereof – realistically and appropriately achieve at normative, expressive and material levels? To that end this chapter interrogates some of the central claims made on behalf of international criminal law.

II. Retribution, Deterrence and a Fair Trial

Most immediately, international criminal hearings aim to hold individuals accountable for wrongdoing after a fair trial and to deter international crimes,[5] although it might be thought that prosecution is a limited understanding of justice. There are, however, some significant challenges in achieving these aims. For one, punishment will only ever be 'a distant second-best to preventing atrocities',[6] and it is difficult to see how punishment can ever be, in the words of Hannah Arendt (writing of Nazi crimes), 'severe enough'.[7] For another, the retributive approach to justice is also undermined because international criminal law is inevitably and necessarily selective. International criminal law in practice has characteristically focused its retributive gaze on non-western actors, with crimes of the west typically going unprosecuted.[8] International criminal law has typically overlooked structural and so-called 'slow violence' and the victims of such violence, a tendency that citizens' tribunals challenge. International criminal justice then has been described as a 'justice of exception' and, as such, 'a form of distributive justice'.[9] Additionally, while a fair trial is vital to the legitimacy of international criminal law, as well as to the achievement of justice, concerns have been raised about international criminal courts' ability to deliver it in full, despite the fact that the relevant instruments of international courts and tribunals contain important provisions about the rights of the defence. Finally, international criminal law's capacity to act as a deterrent in this context may be limited. The last two concerns are explored in more depth below.

Concerns have been raised about international criminal courts' ability to ensure a fair trial. The often difficult political contexts in which complex international crimes are prosecuted would likely challenge the capacity of any court. International criminal courts have faced additional challenges, particularly in their

[5] See further AKA Greenawalt, 'International Criminal Law for Retributivists' (2014) 25 *University of Pennsylvania Journal of International Law* 969.

[6] T Adami, '"Who Will Be Left to Tell the Tale?" Recordkeeping and International Criminal Jurisprudence' (2007) 7 *Archives and Museum Informatics* 213, 214, although he acknowledges that it is still imperative.

[7] Cited in P Akhavan, 'Is Grassroots Justice a Viable Alternative to Impunity? The Case of the Iran People's Tribunal' (2017) 39 *Human Rights Quarterly* 73, 97.

[8] See further A Jones, *Genocide, War Crimes and the West* (Zed Books, 2004).

[9] Mégret (n 4) 81.

early days: specifically, the need to develop and then apply an international criminal procedural law at varying stages of its development, amongst a body of legal
professionals who hail from different legal systems with varying approaches to key
issues. Moreover, the paramount right of the defendant to a fair trial can rub up
against international criminal courts' other aims and objectives, for example the
delivery of justice to victims. The Covid-19 pandemic also gave rise to additional
concerns about fair trials in the context of international criminal prosecution.[10]
Finally, despite international criminal tribunals' including provisions on fair trial,
there has been criticism that, at least in the early days of the post-Cold War resur-
gence of international criminal law, the defence as an institution was marginalised
to some extent, with an additional challenge being that civil society activism and
scholarship tended to be victim- and prosecution-focused.[11] To the extent that this
book does not contain a specific chapter on fair trials, it could also be criticised
for marginalising the defence. At the same time, fair trial considerations should
be embedded at every stage of the international criminal process. More recent
law-making efforts have reflected this, by embedding concerns about fair treatment in the 2019 Draft Articles on Prevention and Punishment of Crimes against
Humanity (Article 11) for example.[12]

Considerations of fairness to the accused at a general level are evident in discussion about modes of liability (chapter 6) and victims' rights (chapter 8). There is
also further literature to explore on fair trials in international criminal law.[13]

Citizens' tribunals also raise due process concerns and have been criticised for
being one-sided (a criticism official international criminal institutions have also
been unable to avoid). For Bertrand Russell, the one-sided nature of non-state
tribunals did mean they were not impartial.[14] An insistence on dual responsibility, that is demanding that citizens' tribunals address the responsibility of actors
on all sides, fails to acknowledge that citizens' tribunals are focused on injustices
that mainstream law overlooks. Arundhati Roy, President of the unofficial World

---

[10] See, eg, Defence Submissions on the Scheduled Oral Hearing *Prosecutor v Bosco Ntaganda*,
5 May 2020, ICC-01/04-02/06. Compare, however, H Abtahi, 'The International Criminal Court
during the Covid-19 Pandemic' (2020) 18(5) *Journal of International Criminal Justice* 1069. See
further, International Criminal Court, 'Guidelines for the Judiciary Concerning the Holding of Court
Hearings during the COVID-19 pandemic' (23 June 2020) at www.icc-cpi.int/sites/default/files/
itemsDocuments/200623-guidelines-for-court-proceedings-covid-19-eng.pdf.
[11] JK Cogan, 'International Criminal Courts and Fair Trials: Difficulties and Prospects' (2002) 27 *Yale
Journal of International Law* 111, 112. See further, on the defendant and on fair trial in international
criminal law, Anonymous, 'Developments in the Law – International Criminal Law: III. Fair Trials and
the Role of the International Criminal Defence' (2001) 114 *Harvard Law Review* 1982; F Mégret, 'Bring
Forth the Accused: Defendant Attitudes and the Intimate Legitimacy of the International Criminal
Trial' (2019) 36(3) *Arizona Journal of International and Comparative Law* 397.
[12] Draft Articles on Prevention and Punishment of Crimes against Humanity 2019 A/74/10 (2019) II
Yearbook of the International Law Commission.
[13] See, eg, B Elberling, *The Defendant in International Criminal Proceedings* (Hart Publishing, 2012).
[14] AJ Klinghoffer and JA Klinghoffer, *International Citizens' Tribunals: Mobilizing Public Opinion to
Advance Human Rights* (Palgrave, 2002) 7.

Tribunal on Iraq, addressed criticism that the tribunal was one-sided in her opening statement at Istanbul in the following way:

> Now this view seems to suggest a touching concern that in this harsh world, the views of the US government and the so-called Coalition of the Willing headed by President George Bush and Prime Minister Tony Blair have somehow gone unrepresented. That the World Tribunal on Iraq isn't aware of the arguments in support of the war and is unwilling to consider the point of view of the invaders. If in the era of the multinational corporate media and embedded journalism anybody can seriously hold this view, then we truly do live in the Age of Irony, in an age when satire has become meaningless because real life is more satirical than satire can ever be.[15]

Even so, most citizens' tribunals offer 'the accused' – whether that be an organisation, a state or on rare occasions an individual – a chance to answer the case. For example, although not specifically about international criminal law, during the hearings of the Permanent Peoples' Tribunal (PPT) on the Global Garment Trade, some major companies exercised their right to a defence in writing or orally, whereas others refused to do so, with some citing concerns about the approach of the tribunal.[16] Citizens' tribunals do not always decide against the 'defendant'. For example, the PPT on Global Corporations and Human Wrongs 2000 (again focusing on human rights rather than international criminal law specifically)[17] decided it had not heard sufficient evidence to recommend the indictment of Rio Tinto in contrast to other corporations.[18] Where an 'accused' opts not to present a defence, an amicus curia is often appointed. In any case, citizens' tribunals have no enforcement power: as the Women's International War Crimes Tribunal (WIWCT), established to consider the crimes against the euphemistically called 'comfort women' (approximately 200,000 women forced into sexual slavery for the Japanese Imperial Army between 1932 and 1945), explained:[19]

> The extent of process rights is contingent on the potential prejudice to the individual whose rights are affected. This is a Peoples' Tribunal that has no power to impose any criminal sanctions or civil penalties on the accused, nor any power to compel testimony or production of evidence.[20]

---

[15] A Roy, 'Opening Speech of the Spokesperson of the Jury of Conscience' in MG Sökmen (ed), *World Tribunal on Iraq: Making the Case against War* (Olive Branch Press, 2008) 2, 3.

[16] PPT, 'Workers and Consumers Rights in the Garment Industry' (PPT & International Clean Clothes Campaign, 1998) 6–9 at http://permanentpeoplestribunal.org/wp-content/uploads/2016/07/Diritti-dei-lavoratori_ENG.pdf.

[17] PPT, 'Global Corporations and Human Wrongs' (PPT March 2000) at https://warwick.ac.uk/fac/soc/law/elj/lgd/2001_1/ppt/. Its purpose was to 'decide whether there was sufficient evidence to indict the alleged violators and ask them to show cause why they were not guilty of committing the violations concerned': para 2.4.2.

[18] ibid para 1.5.1.

[19] A Lynch, 'Comfort Women' *Encyclopedia Britannica* (15 February 2023) at www.britannica.com/topic/comfort-women.

[20] Judgment of Women's International War Crimes Tribunal, 4 December 2001, PT-2000-1-T, para 484 at https://archives.wam-peace.org/wt/wp-content/uploads/2020/03/Judgement.pdf.

Finally, as regards deterrence, despite optimism otherwise,[21] international criminal law does not seem to have reduced the incidence of international crime, although it is difficult – if not impossible – to measure this empirically. It may well be that the failure to prosecute encourages impunity.[22] It is to be hoped that trial and imprisonment – or the threat thereof – might prevent an individual from committing (further) crime, although it has been observed that deterrence may be less effective where individuals act out of 'blind hatred' or where they consider themselves dedicated to a broader cause.[23] The hope is that international criminal law inculcates certain moral values in individuals.[24] However, for reasons explored in chapter 6, the achievement of this may be limited in the context of international crimes.[25] More generally, the focus on individual criminal responsibility overlooks the conditions underpinning – and broader contributions to – the commission of international crime, thereby limiting the law's potential to prevent it.[26] One response to the limitations of deterrence in this context is to argue that the net of international criminal responsibility should be cast more widely. However, broadening the scope of responsibility raises a practical question about overreach. It also raises a more theoretical question: how far can a system built on individualised responsibility account for collective actors and the wider context within which international crimes take place? An alternative response to the above difficulties might be to deprioritise the international criminal legal response, recognising that other processes may be better able to address the collective nature of atrocity. Here again, the practice of citizens' tribunals offers a fertile source for thinking about responsibility within and outside the formal frameworks of the law (chapter 6).

Another way in which international criminal law might address both the conditions underpinning international crime and more effective deterrence is by using international criminal law to generate resistance to international

---

[21] See, eg, Luis Moreno-Ocampo, former Chief Prosecutor at the ICC, 'putting an end to impunity for the perpetrators of the most serious crimes … can and will contribute to the prevention of such crimes, thus having a deterrence effect', cited in T Krever, 'International Criminal Law: An Ideology Critique' (2013) 26(3) *Leiden Journal of International Law* 701, 710. See further on deterrence J Meernik, 'The International Criminal Court and the Deterrence of Human Rights Atrocities' (2015) 17 *Journal of Civil Wars* 318.

[22] P Akhavan, 'Are International Criminal Tribunals a Disincentive to Peace?: Reconciling Judicial Romanticism with Political Realism' (2009) 31(3) *Human Rights Quarterly* 624, 629.

[23] B Sander, 'International Criminal Justice as Progress: From Faith to Critique' in M Bergsmo et al (eds), *Historical Origins of International Criminal Law*, vol 4 (Torkel Opsahl, 2015) 749, 809. See further, on the debate about deterrence, BJ Appel, 'In the Shadow of the International Criminal Court: Does the ICC Deter Human Rights Violations?' (2018) 62(1) *Journal of Conflict Resolution* 3.

[24] See Tallgren (n 4) 570–77, for discussion of general and specific deterrence in international criminal law.

[25] See ibid 575.

[26] See, eg, A Anghie and BS Chimni, 'Third World Approaches to International Law and Individual Responsibility in International Conflict' (2004) 36 *Studies in Transnational Legal Policy* 185, 198. See also Sander (n 23) 813.

crime and the conditions that underpin it.[27] Deploying international criminal law to generate resistance implicates a wider range of individuals, including bystanders, than deterrence, which typically focuses on defendants or potential defendants. There are a number of ways in which resistance to international crime might be encouraged. For example, resistance might be acknowledged in judgments;[28] resistance to international crime might be encouraged in definitions of crime;[29] and it might be reflected in standards of culpability. As will become clear throughout this book, the alternative didacticism of citizens' tribunals provides a useful starting point for thinking about resistance in international criminal law.

At the least, citizens' tribunals can mobilise more quickly than official international legal bodies. For example, in 2019, The Gambia instituted proceedings against Myanmar at the International Court of Justice, alleging violation of the Genocide Convention. In November 2019, the ICC Prosecutor was authorised to investigate the Situation in the People's Republic of Bangladesh/Republic of Myanmar.[30] However, as the unofficial PPT on State Crimes Allegedly Committed in Myanmar against the Rohingyas, Kachins and Other Groups noted, the PPT had been concerned with the situation since 2013, 'at a time when Myanmar's (already ongoing) violations were hardly considered, and even less well known on the world stage'.[31] Citizens' tribunals can therefore provide some sort of accountability for conduct and actors who fall outside of the attention of 'official' international criminal law.

III.   Truth-Telling and the Construction of History

International criminal tribunals have generated an enormous archive of atrocity.[32] For example, in addition to their trial records, the freely accessible websites of the ICTR and the ICTY include films aiming in the case of the ICTY to make

---

[27] See further, eg, B Leebaw, 'Justice and the Faithless: The Demand for Disobedience in International Criminal Law' (2018) 24(2) *European Journal of International Relations* 344, 345 on the 'pedagogical role of exemplary disobedience'.

[28] LE Fletcher, 'From Indifference to Engagement: Bystanders and International Criminal Justice' (2005) 26 *Michigan Journal of International Law* 2013; Leebaw (n 27).

[29] See, in the context of aggression, MA Drumbl, 'The Push to Criminalize Aggression: Something Lost Amid the Gains' (2009) 41 *Case Western Reserve Journal of International Law* 291, 316.

[30] Decision Pursuant to Art 15 of the Rome Statute on the Authorisation of an Investigation into the Situation in the People's Republic of Bangladesh/Republic of the Union of Myanmar, 14 November 2019, ICC-01/19-27.

[31] See PPT, 'State Crimes Allegedly Committed in Myanmar against the Rohingyas, Kachins and Other Groups' (University of Malaya 2017) 5 at http://permanentpeoplestribunal.org/wp-content/uploads/2017/11/PPT-on-Myanmar-Judgment-FINAL.pdf.

[32] See further, eg, Adami (n 6) 220; S Stolk, 'The Record on Which History Will Judge Us Tomorrow: Auto-History in the Opening Statements of International Criminal Trials' (2015) 28 *Leiden Journal of International Law* 993.

its work 'more visible and comprehensive',[33] and a powerful online exhibition, 'A Glimpse into the Archives' of the records of the ICTY and ICTR, which incorporates physical artefacts used in trials.[34] The truth-telling functions of international criminal trials are often considered to contribute to justice, reconciliation and conflict resolution.[35] Indeed, the importance of judicial archives is recognised in the 2005 shortlisting of the ICTR judicial archives for the United Nations Educational, Scientific and Cultural Organization (UNESCO) Jikji Memory of the World Prize,[36] a prize the purpose of which is 'to reward efforts contributing to the preservation and accessibility of documentary heritage as a common heritage of humanity'.[37] However, the archival functions of international criminal tribunals and their associated history-writing functions are not straightforward and can be controversial.

For one thing, scholars emphasise the need to find a 'proper balance between too much forgetting and too much remembrance'.[38] Even assuming the importance of remembering, the construction of history – and memory creation – is never a wholly neutral exercise. The failure of the ICTR to prosecute Rwandan Patriotic Front members, for example, is widely criticised for having resulted in a one-sided historical account, which 'may have marginalized stories of moderate Hutu victims who were also targeted by Hutu extremists'.[39] Historians may baulk at the idea of international proceedings creating 'official history', given history's contested nature.[40] Moreover, while the historical record produced by a trial can reduce 'the space for denial',[41] or 'false moral equivalencies',[42] trials have not in practice always prevented historical revisionism in the way their supporters have hoped.[43] The demands of history and the demands of a trial may conflict. Legal tests of admissibility affect the history a trial produces, as does its jurisdictional

---

[33] UN ICTY Documentaries at www.icty.org/en/outreach/documentaries.

[34] UN International Residual Mechanism for Criminal Tribunals, Online Exhibition: A Glimpse into the Archives, at irmct.org/specials/glimpse-into-the-archives/index.html. See further the archive of the Residual SCSL at www.scsldocs.org/.

[35] See further, eg, B Bevernage, 'Transitional Justice and Historiography: Challenges, Dilemmas and Possibilities' (2014) 13 *Macquarie Law Journal* 7, 8.

[36] Adami (n 6) 217; ICTR Newsletter, March 2005, 5 at https://unictr.irmct.org/sites/unictr.org/files/news/newsletters/mar05.pdf. See further I Vukušić, 'The Archives of the International Criminal Tribunal for the Former Yugoslavia' (2013) 98 *History* 623.

[37] UNESCO/Jikji Memory of the World Prize at www.unesco.org/en/prizes/jikji.

[38] Bevernage (n 35) 13. Remembrance has also been described as a western value: ibid 14, referring to the work of Ashis Nandy.

[39] PR Williams and K Larkin, 'Twenty-Four Years On: The Yugoslav and Rwanda Tribunals' Contributions to Durable Peace' in M Sterio and M Scharf (eds), *The Legacy of Ad Hoc Tribunals in International Criminal Law* (Cambridge University Press, 2019) 326, 349.

[40] See further, eg, Bevernage (n 35) 10.

[41] J Trahan, 'Examining the Benchmarks by Which to Evaluate the ICTYs Legacy' in Sterio and Scharf (eds) (n 39) 25, 37.

[42] Williams and Larkin (n 39) 326.

[43] See, eg, in the context of the Tokyo Tribunal, M Ediger, 'Prosecuting the Crime of Aggression at the International Criminal Court: Lessons from the Tokyo Tribunal' (2018) *New York University Journal of International Law and Politics* 179, 181. See further M Milanovic, 'Establishing the Facts about Mass

scope. Thus, a trial may produce a particular kind of truth. It excludes the role of actors over whom it has no jurisdiction, including the international community more generally. Koskenniemi has observed:

> It often seems that the memory for which the trial in the Hague is staged is not the memory of Balkan populations but that of an 'international community' recounting its past as a progress narrative from 'Nuremberg to the Hague', impunity to the Rule of Law.[44]

Thus, while an international criminal trial can create an authoritative historical record, the 'history' it produces is neither complete nor uncontested. Moreover, once delivered, courts have little control over how their judgments and archives are received over time.

Citizens' tribunals also play an important role in creating an archive of harm and responsibility.[45] This is evident in a response to a question to the British Foreign Office regarding the implications of the 2021 judgment of the Uyghur Tribunal, a recent citizens' tribunal established to consider allegations of international crimes against Uyghur and Kazakh ethnic minorities in Xinjiang region.[46] The response was as follows:

> The Government notes the findings of the Uyghur Tribunal and welcomes its contribution to building the international awareness and understanding of the human rights violations occurring in Zinjiang.[47]

That citizens' tribunals are not without effect can also be seen from the impact of a PPT on Armenia in 1984, which Klinghoffer and Klinghoffer note is often considered to have contributed to the acknowledgement by some states and others of the crimes committed against the Armenians in 1915 and 1916 as genocide.[48]

However, the histories that emanate from citizens' tribunals often differ markedly from those that 'official' international criminal courts produce. Typically, citizens' tribunals contextualise harms broadly; expose the complicity of officials and often the international community; and memorialise resistance in ways that seek to encourage solidarity. This alternative narrative framing gives much needed attention to voices that official international criminal law overlooks,[49] and is aimed at a different political end from that of official trials.

Atrocities: Accounting for the Failure of the ICTY to Persuade Target Audiences' (2016) 47 *Georgetown Journal of International Law* 1321.

[44] M Koskenniemi, 'Between Impunity and Show Trials' (2002) 6 *Max Planck Yearbook of United Nations Law* 1, 34.

[45] See further in the context of the WIWCT, U Dolgopol, 'Civil Society's Engagement with International Criminal Law: The Role of Peoples' Tribunals' in Bergsmo et al (eds) (n 23) 703, 709.

[46] Uyghur Tribunal Judgment (Church House Westminster, 9 December 2021) at https://uyghurtribunal.com/wp-content/uploads/2022/09/UYGHUR-TRIBUNAL-Judgment-2022.09.20.pdf.

[47] J Curtis and T Robinson, 'The Uyghur Tribunal' (House of Commons Library, 18 January 2022) 17 at https://researchbriefings.files.parliament.uk/documents/CDP-2022-0009/CDP-2022-0009.pdf.

[48] Klinghoffer and Klinghoffer (n 14) 173.

[49] See, eg, D Otto, 'Beyond Legal Justice: Some Personal Reflections on People's Tribunals, Listening and Responsibility' (2017) 5 *London Review of International Law* 225, 235; see further G Simm,

IV. Peace and Reconciliation

It is often argued that there can be 'no peace without justice'. However, the relationship between peace and justice is complex and contested, especially where conflict is ongoing and where an institution's jurisdictional scope is limited, as it inevitably will be.[50] In addition to which, the understanding of peace is itself contested.

The link between peace and justice operates at a normative as well as institutional level. Institutionally, the link between justice and international peace is evident in the fact that the UN ad hoc tribunals for the former Yugoslavia and Rwanda were established by a Chapter 7 UN Security Council Resolution (see chapter 4).[51] At one level this institutional link was a necessary device to trigger the Security Council's power to issue a binding resolution under Chapter 7. However, it gave rise to questions as to the potential influence of the UN Security Council (the body in the UN with primary responsibility for the maintenance of international peace and security) in the life of the tribunal, risking the (appearance of) politicisation of international criminal justice. As will become apparent, the ICC also retains a controversial role for the Security Council (chapter 7). Of the Security Council's 15 member states, five permanent members (the United Kingdom, United States, Russia, China and France) enjoy the legal privilege of the veto, which can work to insulate them or their allies from international criminal jurisdiction where it is empowered or disempowered by a Security Council resolution.

Concerns have also been raised that the prospect of international criminal prosecution may encourage belligerents to prolong conflict,[52] although this has also been disputed. Thus, Akhavan, reviewing the situation in Cote d'Ivoire, Uganda and Darfur, has argued that judicial intervention can contribute to achieving peace even in situations where arrest warrants are not executed.[53] Finally, the dominant understanding of peace that underpins international criminal law is negative peace (the absence of direct violence). An alternative understanding of peace, namely positive peace, can be found in the seminal work of John Galtung. Positive peace encompasses the absence of indirect violence, that is structural violence (in other words, social injustice).[54] One of the key criticisms that critical

---

'The Paris Peoples' Tribunal and the Istanbul Trials: Archives of the Armenian Genocide' (2026) 29 *Leiden Journal of International Law* 245, 247–50.

[50] See further, eg, Sander (n 23) 799. See further, M Kersten, 'No Justice Without Peace, But What Peace is on Offer? Palestine, Israel and the International Criminal Court' (2020) 18(4) *Journal of International Criminal Justice* 1001.

[51] Art 39 of the UN Charter states 'The Security Council shall determine the existence of any threat to the peace, breach of the peace, or act of aggression and shall make recommendations, or decide what measures shall be taken in accordance with Articles 41 and 42, to maintain or restore international peace and security.'

[52] Sander (n 23) 809.

[53] Akhavan (n 22).

[54] J Galtung, 'Violence, Peace and Peace Research' (1969) 6(3) *Journal of Peace Research* 167.

international criminal lawyers make about international criminal law is its failure to address structural violence,[55] something that many citizens' tribunals attempt to redress.

Reconciliation is related to peace. However, whether it is appropriate or realistic for tribunal goals to include reconciliation is disputed.[56] Reconciliation is a complex socio-political process at both individual and collective levels, and we lack sufficient empirical evidence for a link between international criminal trials and reconciliation, and the circumstances in which a trial may be more or less likely to contribute to reconciliation and over what time period. In their seminal edited collection, *My Neighbor, My Enemy*, based on empirical research, Stover and Weinstein suggest 'that there is no direct link between criminal trials … and reconciliation, although it is possible this could change over time'.[57] Indeed, they observe that criminal trials 'often divided small multi-ethnic communities by causing further suspicion and fear'.[58] Moreover, they observed, survivors typically viewed reconciliation as an individual rather than collective matter.[59] It is important then to think about the conditions and circumstances in which international criminal hearings are more or less likely to contribute to reconciliation and, critically, how that can be measured.

V. Expressivism

Increasingly, as already mentioned, attention has been paid to the expressive potential of international criminal law. As Drumbl explains, expressivism focuses on 'the messaging value of punishment to affirm respect for law, reinforce a moral consensus, narrate history, and educate the public'.[60] The expressive function of international criminal law has considerable appeal. However, it is not neutral. As Immi Tallgren has asked, 'whose symbols, standing for what?'[61] Moreover, there

---

[55] For discussion of slow and structural violence, see Burgis-Kasthala, 'Scholarship as Dialogue?' 936–37. See further A Sehmi, Judicializing Economic Violence as Means of Dismantling the Structural Causes of Atrocity in the Democratic Republic of Congo' (2020) 14 *International Journal of Transitional Justice* 423.

[56] JN Clark, 'The Impact Question: The ICTY and the Restoration and Maintenance of Peace' in B Swart et al (eds), *The Legacy of the International Criminal Tribunal for the Former Yugoslavia* (Oxford University Press, 2011) 55. See further, on the relationship between the Special Court for Sierra Leone and the Truth and Reconciliation Commission, WA Schabas, 'Conjoined Twins of Transitional Justice? The Sierra Leone Truth and Reconciliation Commission and the Special Court' (2004) 2 *Journal of International Criminal Justice* 1082.

[57] E Stover and HM Weinstein, 'Conclusion: A common objective, a universe of alternatives' in E Stover and HM Weinstein (eds), *My Neighbor, My Enemy: Justice and Community in the Aftermath of Atrocity* (Cambridge University Press, 2004) 323.

[58] ibid.

[59] ibid.

[60] Drumbl (n 4) 12.

[61] Tallgren (n 4) 581. See further LG Minkova, 'Expressing What? The Stigmatization of the Defendant and the ICC's Institutional Interests in the Ongwen Case' (2021) 34(1) *Leiden Journal of International Law* 223.

may be a divergence between the ways in which legal professionals understand the symbolism of the trial and how others do.[62] Despite these difficulties, the more official institutions come to rely on the expressive functions of international criminal law, the more difficult it may be to overlook the work of citizens' tribunals, which depend entirely on their expressive potential.

VI. Ideology

Running through international criminal law may be another, albeit unarticulated, rationale. Tallgren offers the insightful provocation about international criminal law that

> [p]erhaps its task is to naturalize, to exclude from the political battle, certain phenomena which are in fact the pre-conditions for the maintenance of the existing governance; by the North, by wealthy states, by wealthy individuals, by strong states, by strong individuals, by men, especially white men and so forth.[63]

From this perspective, international criminal law can contribute to buttressing a profoundly unequal status quo. Critics see this in its failure to account for structural harms and the structural underpinnings of the crimes it does focus on, especially where accounting for them could implicate powerful (often economic) actors located in the global north. The practice of citizens' tribunals challenges the particular ideology underpinning international criminal law. It does more than that: by articulating an overtly political vision of law, it foregrounds the issue of ideology in law more generally.[64]

VII. Conclusion: Going Forward

How should we respond to the inevitable tensions and contradictions in the practice of international criminal law, some of which have been outlined in this chapter? One way would be to seek a 'scaled-back' vision of international criminal law, in other words to expect international criminal law to focus on prosecuting individuals and recognise that individual criminal prosecution is just one of several potential responses to atrocity. However, it may be difficult to justify the enormous resources spent on international criminal law without attributing to it more ambitious aims, which then in turn generate expectations that risk being disappointed. On the other hand, and more optimistically, the necessary

---

[62] N Sekhon, 'Complementarity and Post-Coloniality' (2013) 27 *Emory International Law Review* 799, 814.

[63] Tallgren (n 4) 594–95. See further Krever (n 21) 703.

[64] On the professed neutrality of law, see further Krever (n 21) 705; W Mansell and K Openshaw, *International Law: A Critical Introduction* (Hart Publishing, 2013) 1.

navigation and negotiation between the several objectives claimed for international criminal law might allow for a contextual nuanced response to atrocity in individual cases and situations. Even if that were the case, we are still left with the dilemma of how to assess the balancing of these different aims and objectives in any one situation or case. In other words, by what standard should we assess whether international criminal justice has been done? Ultimately, then, this requires us to be realistic about what we might expect of and from international criminal law. The question of what international criminal law can reasonably deliver runs through this book. First, however, we turn to the history of international criminal law. Just as it is vital to understand the different ways in which we might identify international criminal law and its objectives, it is also important to be alert to the choices, and consequences thereof, of the different ways in which international criminal legal histories are – and might otherwise be – narrated. This is the twofold aim of chapter 4.

Further Reading

N Chazal, *The International Criminal Court and Global Society Control International Criminal Justice in Late Modernity* (Routledge, 2018).

MA Drumbl, *Atrocity, Punishment and International Law* (Cambridge University Press, 2007).

C Schwöbel-Patel, *Marketing Global Justice The Political Economy of International Criminal Law* (Cambridge University Press, 2021).

G Simpson, Law, *War and Crime War Crimes Trials and the Reinvention of International Law* (Polity Press, 2007).

SM Wanjiru, *Black Iconography and Colonial (Re)production at the ICC: (In)dependence Cha Cha Cha?* (Routledge, 2023).

4

The Histories of International Criminal Law

I. Introduction

This chapter outlines the development of international criminal law over the past century, but it diverges from more orthodox international criminal legal histories because it includes citizens' tribunals. As already mentioned, citizens' tribunals offer an alternative vision of international criminal law and an additional potential tool in international criminal law's toolbox. They evidence the power of international criminal law amongst multiple constituencies, the limits of contemporary international criminal law, and the opportunities and challenges inherent in a critical approach to international criminal law and practice. For these reasons, citizens' tribunals should form part of the history of international criminal law.

However, the focus of this chapter is not just to explore the development of the law, but also to emphasise that history writing is never a value-free activity. How we frame historical developments, for example by inserting or excluding citizens' tribunals in histories of international criminal law, involves important but often unarticulated choices. Thus, the chapter encourages consideration of how histories of international criminal law might be written and to what ends. It is important, therefore, to be alert to the politics, in the broad sense alluded to previously (chapter 2), behind the construction and use of international criminal legal histories. It is to this that the chapter first turns.

II. International Criminal Legal History and International Criminal Law

It is a truism that our perceptions about the past influence our understanding of the present; and, conversely, that our feelings about the past are influenced by, and reflect, concerns that we have about the present.[1] To illustrate, Bassiouni observes that the abortive attempts to prosecute the German Kaiser and officers that occurred after the First World War (explored further below) were in time

---

[1] For a seminal examination in the context of the Haitian Revolution, see further D Scott, *Conscripts of Modernity: The Tragedy of Colonial Enlightenment* (Duke University Press, 2004) 97. See further E Haslam, 'Archived Bodies: The Transatlantic Slave Trade and Abolition' in D Herman

transformed into a partially valid precedent because that was what was needed to justify the rising expectations of the international society. And so it was also for the post-World War II precedent, whose weaknesses were omitted in favour of the positive aspects that international society wanted to buttress.[2]

History is an important tool for (critical) approaches to (international criminal) law, but the way histories are written is neither fixed nor self-evident. Different historical narratives perform different functions. It is in this sense that history writing is political.[3] Critical approaches to international legal histories, like critical approaches to international criminal law more generally, seek to make these standpoints more explicit. In so doing they emphasise silences in dominant legal histories, perspectives that have been overlooked and the choices behind how they should be written back in.

It follows that one way of approaching international criminal legal histories critically is to reflect upon how international criminal law might look were different historical starting points adopted, or different events emphasised. Given that the Nuremberg and Tokyo Tribunals delivered the first international criminal prosecutions of individuals, it seems common sense to think of them as the root of modern international criminal law, as histories of international criminal law typically do. However, this focus leaves out other important histories, most notably perhaps the transatlantic slave trade (and colonialism).[4] One response to this particular gap is to emphasise international criminal law's failure to criminalise the transatlantic slave trade, and the effects of that failure on the shape and politics of contemporary international criminal law, as I have sought to do elsewhere.[5] Another response is to make the slave trade more present in our understanding of international legal development. Jenny Martinez, for example, traces the early uses of the phrase 'crime against humanity' to the transatlantic slave trade.[6] Whether we emphasise the absence or presence of the slave trade (or indeed any overlooked history) in international criminal law will depend partly on how we wish to deploy the past in the present. Thus, the past can be used to legitimate

---

and C Parsley (eds), *Interdisciplinarities Research Process, Method, and the Body of Law* (Palgrave Macmillan, 2022) 9; E Haslam, *The Slave Trade, Abolition and the Long History of International Criminal Law: The Recaptive and the Victim* (Routledge, 2020) 121–22.

[2] MC Bassiouni, 'World War I: The War to End All Wars and the Birth of a Handicapped International Criminal Justice System' (2002) 30 *Denver Journal of International Law and Policy* 244, 291.

[3] See further discussion in Haslam, *The Slave Trade* (n 1) 2–3.

[4] ibid 5–6. On the limitations of international criminal law in relation to colonial injustices, see C Stahn, 'Confronting Colonial Amnesia' (2020) 18 *International Journal of Transitional Justice* 793. For discussion of multiple potential historical precursors to international criminal law, see G Simpson, 'The Conscience of Civilisation, and its Discontents: A counter history of international criminal law' in P Kastner (ed), *International Criminal Law in Context* (Routledge, 2017) 11. On including the slave trade in international criminal legal histories, see E Haslam, 'Writing More Inclusive Histories of International Criminal Law: Lessons from the Slave Trade and Slavery' in I Tallgren and T Skouteris, *New Histories of International Criminal Law* (Oxford University Press, 2019) 130.

[5] See further Haslam, *The Slave Trade* (n 1) 8–9, 54–55, 58–59.

[6] JS Martinez, *The Slave Trade and the Origins of International Human Rights Law* (Oxford University Press, 2012); For further discussion, see Haslam, *The Slave Trade* (n 1) 6–7.

contemporary developments, because the past can be considered to lend them some 'authority' or weight.[7] In contrast, the past can lend a more critical perspective to a contemporary situation. For example, scholars who take a TWAIL stance (see chapter 1) trace the colonial and imperial origins of international law and their multiple influences today.[8] The past might also reveal ideas that have been overlooked, from which we might usefully draw inspiration in the present.[9]

To illustrate, we might think about how to respond to the criticism that international law, and more specifically international criminal law, is western. Historically, western states and activists have had a disproportionate influence on the development of international criminal law as it is currently understood and framed. A history might be written, then, that criticises the ways in which the contributions of non-western actors have been glossed over in the development of international criminal law. Alternatively, a history might seek to excavate the contributions of non-western actors to the development of international criminal law or perhaps to an alternative vision of it. Although these two approaches are not necessarily mutually exclusive, the narrative that results from each performs different functions in the present. So, when reading, researching or writing international criminal legal history, it is important to be alert to the particular politics behind the writing of history – whether articulated or not – because it is not possible to simply restate what happened in the past. All of this is good news for anyone interested in further research. There are multiple histories and their consequences waiting to be thought through. However, this does not mean that history writing is an entirely subjective exercise. It must still be informed by careful consideration of sources, whether legal doctrinal, archival or otherwise.

This chapter considers the development of international criminal law, incorporating citizens' tribunals. Excluding citizens' tribunals from international criminal legal histories seems a lost opportunity. Aside from the justice they can deliver in any one situation, citizens' tribunals provide important critiques of international criminal law and inspiration for alternative thinking about it. They also provide some indication of the way 'people' (some people at least) view the promises and limitations of international criminal law. This knowledge is precious as we seek to navigate international criminal law's contemporary challenges.

III. Nuremberg and Tokyo and the 'Origins' of International Criminal Law

As mentioned, the origins of modern international criminal law are typically traced to the Nuremberg and Tokyo Tribunals that took place at the end of the

---

[7] Haslam, *The Slave Trade* (n 1) 121–22.
[8] See, eg, A Anghie, *Imperialism, Sovereignty and the Making of International Law* (Cambridge University Press, 2005). See further, Haslam, *The Slave Trade* (n 1) 121–22.
[9] Haslam, *The Slave Trade* (n 1) 121–22.

Second World War. If Nuremberg and Tokyo are widely seen as the foundational moment of international criminal law, perceptions of their legacy are nevertheless mixed. Thus, over the years, interpretations of Nuremberg and Tokyo have varied, from those who, as Schwarzenberg observes, 'consider Nuremberg a landmark ... , as the expression of the moral conscience of organized mankind', to others in contrast who view it as a 'symptom of the hypocrisy of their leaders'.[10]

The United States (US) had been reluctant to support prosecutions for crimes against humanity and peace after the First World War. Although the Allies had wished to hold the Kaiser legally responsible, the US considered that he enjoyed sovereign immunity.[11] As a compromise, Article 227 of the Treaty of Versailles innovatively provided for the former Kaiser's arraignment 'for a supreme offence against international morality and the sanctity of treaties'. This offence did not satisfy the double criminality requirement for extradition (that is the requirement that the offence must be a crime in both the state that requests extradition and the state from which extradition is requested). This is one reason why Bassiouni suggests that it 'was not actually intended to produce a trial'.[12] In the end, the neutral Netherlands, where the Kaiser remained until he died in 1941, refused to extradite him and no trial took place. Allied attempts to secure the extradition of individuals following the provisions of Article 228 of the Treaty of Versailles, which were extremely unpopular in Germany, also did not go as planned.[13] Concerned about the rise of Bolshevism and growing instability in Germany, the Allies accepted a German offer to try suspects before the Supreme Court at Leipzig, as a result of which very few German officers were tried and even fewer convicted.[14]

By the end of the Second World War, the US position had changed. By 1943, the Allies had committed to returning suspects to be tried in the places where they allegedly perpetrated their crimes. However, they disagreed about what should happen to those whose offences were not geographically circumscribed (the so-called 'major war criminals'). At least initially, the British Prime Minister favoured their summary execution, because of concerns about the length, legality and cost of trials.[15] However, on 8 August 1945, the US, United Kingdom, France and the Soviet Union, amongst others, signed the London agreement for the International Military Tribunal for the 'trial of war criminals whose offences have no particular geographical location'. The timing of signature was inauspicious, being two days after the first atomic bomb was dropped on Hiroshima and

---

[10] G Schwarzenberger, 'Judgment of Nuremberg' (1946–47) 21 *Tulane Law Review* 329, 361.

[11] In contrast to the recommendation of the Commission on the Responsibility of the War and Enforcement of Penalties. See further, M Lippman, 'Nuremberg: Forty Five Years Later' (1991) 7 *Connecticut Journal of International Law* 1, 7–8.

[12] Bassiouni (n 2) 271.

[13] The German Government recognised in Art 228 of the Treaty of Versailles 'the right of the Allied and Associated Powers to bring before military tribunals persons accused of having committed acts in violation of the laws and customs of war'.

[14] Bassiouni (n 2) 282; Lippman (n 11) 10.

[15] Lippman (n 11) 20–21.

one day before the second fell on Nagasaki. On 19 January 1946, General Douglas MacArthur established the International Military Tribunal for the Far East (IMTFE) by Special Proclamation. These efforts were complemented by national prosecutions and by zonal prosecutions under the authority of occupying powers, including 12 major US trials in Nuremberg.

Nuremberg was far from a universal tribunal, but it was an international one:

> The making of the Charter was the exercise of the sovereign legislative power by the countries to which the German Reich unconditionally surrendered; and the undoubted right of these countries to legislate for the occupied territories has been recognized by the civilized world.[16]

Thus, the Allies did 'together what any one of them might have done singly; for it is not to be doubted that any nation has the right thus to set up special courts to administer law'.[17] Twenty-two defendants were indicted, including on novel charges of conspiracy, crimes against humanity and crimes against peace. Proceedings lasted 10 months; 12 individuals received the death sentence; seven were sentenced to terms of imprisonment; three were acquitted; and three organisations were declared criminal according to Article 9 of the Charter of the International Military Tribunal.

The Tokyo Tribunal essentially followed the legal approach of Nuremberg. Twenty-eight individuals, excluding the Japanese Emperor, were initially indicted for crimes against peace and war crimes; seven were sentenced to death and 18 to terms of imprisonment.[18] Proceedings generated powerful separate and dissenting opinions, perhaps most famously from Judge Pal of India.[19] Amongst his concerns was that the IMTFE's mandate was too limited, that charges were retroactive, and that the Hiroshima and Nagasaki attacks had been excluded.[20] By 1955, 14 of those imprisoned had been granted parole, some of whom went on to become politically powerful once more.[21]

The Nuremberg and Tokyo Charters and judgments were legally innovative, at least regarding the law they applied to the Axis Powers. They affirmed individual criminal responsibility at the international level, with the judgment at Nuremberg famously proclaiming that 'only by punishing individuals who commit such crimes can the provisions of international law be enforced.'[22] The Nuremberg Charter affirmed the irrelevance of official position (Article 7) and superior orders (unless

---

[16] International Military Tribunal (Nuremberg), Judgment and Sentences, 1 October 1946 (1947) 41 *AJIL* 172, 216.

[17] ibid.

[18] M Ediger, 'Prosecuting the Crime of Aggression at the International Criminal Court: Lessons from the Tokyo Tribunal' (2018) *New York University Journal of International Law and Politics* 179, 188.

[19] See further, and for a discussion of the controversial legacy and memorialisation of Pal, MA Drumbl, 'Memorializing Dissent: Justice Pal in Tokyo' (2020) *American Journal of International Law Unbound* 111.

[20] ibid 112–13.

[21] Ediger (n 18) 194–95.

[22] International Military Tribunal (Nuremberg), Judgment and Sentences (n 16) 221.

as mitigation of punishment (Article 8)). However, both Nuremberg and Tokyo have been criticised for being retroactive, especially as regards crimes against peace, conspiracy and crimes against humanity. The Nuremberg Tribunal considered the principle *nullum crimen sine lege* (no punishment without a prior law) 'a principle of justice', so that

> [t]o assert that it is unjust to punish those who in defiance of treaties and assurances have attacked neighboring states without warning is obviously untrue, for in such circumstances the attacker must know that he is doing wrong, and so far from it being unjust to punish him, it would be unjust if his wrong were allowed to go unpunished.[23]

Both tribunals only tried the defeated side. Robert Jackson, Chief Prosecutor, famously said:

> If certain acts in violation of treaties are crimes, they are crimes whether the United States does them or whether Germany does them, and we are not prepared to lay down a rule of criminal conduct against others which we would not be willing to have invoked against us.[24]

However, he also observed that the military nature of the tribunal was designed to avoid any 'precedent-creating effect'.[25] No one from Allied nations was tried for the carpet-bombing of Dresden, nor for the dropping of atomic weapons on Japan. Amongst his many concerns, as already mentioned, Judge Pal also criticised the double standards of the Allies.[26] This avowedly new international criminal legal order that the trials represented was conducive to western interests. For example, Lippman argues that the focus of the post-Second World War trials on individual criminal responsibility enabled West Germany to be 'comfortably' brought into 'the Cold War combat against the Soviet Union'.[27] Moreover, he opines that the 'portrayal of the Nazi leadership as "monsters" resulted in the Nuremberg precedent losing much of its import in contemporary political discourse and debate', giving the example that 'allegations that the policies pursued by seemingly responsible and "normal" officials of the United States in Southeast Asia or in Central America constitute Nuremberg crimes are dismissed as hyperbole'.[28]

The framing of the trials was problematic in several other ways too. Lippman observes that '[t]he Tribunal ... viewed Nuremberg primarily as a trial of those who had initiated and waged an aggressive war, and had little inclination to establish minimum international standards for regimes' domestic treatment of their

[23] Judgment ibid 217.
[24] International Conference on Military Trials, London, 1945 (Department of State Publication No 3080, 1949) 330.
[25] H Ehard, 'The Nuremberg Trial against the Major War Criminals and International Law' (1949) 43 *American Journal of International Law* 223, 242–43.
[26] S Kopelman, 'Ideology and International Law: Dissent of Indian Justice at the Tokyo War Crimes Trial' (1991) 23 *New York University Journal of International Law and Politics* 373, 423–24.
[27] Lippman (n 11) 40.
[28] ibid 41.

citizens'.[29] Thus, for Felman it was the trial of Adolf Eichmann in Jerusalem in 1961 (discussed further in chapter 7) that established the Holocaust as a collective narrative of 'a crime against the Jewish people independently from the political and military story of the Second World War'.[30] Nuremberg and Tokyo's neglect of sexual and gender-based violence (SGBV) was also striking. Sexual violence was not included as a war crime or crime against humanity at Nuremberg, although it was prosecuted at Tokyo as a war crime. However, the Tokyo Tribunal neglected crimes against the so-called 'comfort women', a travesty that the non-governmental WIWCT addressed in 2000.

The legal legacy of Nuremberg and Tokyo is thus mixed and contested. Debates about the interpretation of Nuremberg can be seen in a particular aspect of the post-Second World War trials that has attracted attention recently, that is, their treatment of economic actors. These debates also illustrate the points made in section II about history and the use made of it in the present.

Trials of economic actors were consigned to prosecution by the occupying authorities under Control Council Law No 10.[31] How these trials can and should be interpreted today comes into sharp relief in the context of contemporary debates about the responsibility of corporate actors and corporate criminal responsibility for international crimes (chapter 6), as Grietje Baars has so powerfully shown.[32] Some commentators turn to the prosecution and conviction of industrialists after the Second World War to draw inspiration and legitimacy for contemporary attempts to extend corporate criminal responsibility, or to provide impetus for contemporary tribunals to address economic actors more fully. Baars has drawn instead on the post-Second World War history of trials of industrialists to make a powerful critique of the relationship between international criminal law and capitalism.[33] For example, she shows how, with the advent of the Cold War, the Allies turned attention from prosecutions of economic actors to the reconstruction of the German economy,[34] with the result that national military tribunals took a 'generous' approach to defendants during trial and even after conviction.[35] Consequently, she argues that

---

[29] ibid.

[30] S Felman, *The Juridical Unconscious: Trials and Traumas in the Twentieth Century* (Harvard University Press, 2002) 128.

[31] See further L Bryk and M Saage-Maass, 'Individual Criminal Liability for Arms Exports under the ICC Statute' (2019) 17 *Journal of International Criminal Justice* 117, 119–20 on the ideological difficulties for the Allies of trying economic actors.

[32] G Baars, 'Law(yers) congealing capitalism: On the (im)possibility of restraining business in conflict through international criminal law' (PhD Thesis, UCL, 2012). See further, G Baars, 'Capitalism's Victor's Justice? The Hidden Stories behind the Prosecution of Industrialists Post-WWII' in K Heller and G Simpson (eds), *The Hidden Histories of War Crimes Trials* (Oxford University Press, 2013) 163, 179.

[33] Baars, 'Capitalism's Victor's Justice?' (n 32) 164.

[34] ibid 174.

[35] ibid 179.

rather than suggesting 'corporate accountability in ICL' is a real possibility, the hidden history of Nuremberg may give us cause to investigate more deeply exactly how and why international criminal law constructs de facto 'corporate impunity' as a necessary ingredient of today's capitalist imperialism.[36]

Baars' provocation challenges us to reflect on the deeper causes of corporate impunity. It also illustrates the multiple possible interpretations of historical precedents and how they are mediated by the view we take of the present to which they speak.

Finally, and more generally, the Nuremberg and Tokyo trials can be thought of more symbolically, that is from the perspective of what they have come to mean beyond their strict legal precedents. Schwarzenberger, writing in the 1940s, suggests:

> Whether the 'idealists' or 'realists' are right can only be determined in retrospect. Both camps, however, may find common ground in the proposition that the Judgment of Nuremberg should not primarily be thought of as a matter of the past. It presents a challenge which has to be accepted in its full magnitude ... If the present cosmic rearmament race ... is permitted to reach its wont culmination, it will matter little whether the victor ... will consider the Judgment of Nuremberg a valuable precedent. The constructive task ahead consists in making a Judgment of Washington or Moscow unnecessary.[37]

The idea that Nuremberg poses a 'challenge' or provocation has been taken up, for example, by some civil society actors (explored more in chapter 6), who claim a right from Nuremberg to enforce the law when the state fails to do so.[38] While this claim is not without its problems, it illustrates that legal legacies and meanings are negotiated amongst a wide range of actors. It also illustrates the powerful provocation that Nuremberg and Tokyo present.

Citizens' tribunals too draw on the legacies of Nuremberg and Tokyo, aiming to keep a particular vision of them alive. We can trace their birth in contemporary form to the Cold War period, and this is another area ripe for reconsideration in international criminal legal history.

IV. The Cold War

Accounts of international criminal law during the Cold War period mostly emphasise how super-power rivalry halted the further development of international criminal legal instruments and institutions. However, this period is not without significance for international criminal law. The broader understanding of international crimes seen in this period provides the springboard for thinking about the directions that international criminal law did not take but might

[36] ibid 192 (footnote excluded).
[37] Schwarzenberger (n 10) 361; see further, Lippman (n 11), calling for the principles to be 'revitalized'.
[38] See further, Lippman (n 11) 52–57.

have taken. Moreover, the period also saw the criminalisation of apartheid and, as already mentioned, and of particular significance for this book, the origins of modern citizens' tribunals, which contributed to keeping a distinctive vision of the promise of Nuremberg and Tokyo alive, by subjecting it to counter-hegemonic interpretations.

On 21 November 1947, General Assembly Resolution 177(II) mandated the International Law Commission (ILC) to prepare a draft code on offences against the peace and security of mankind, and to formulate the international legal principles set forth in the Nuremberg Charter and judgment, the latter of which the ILC finalised in 1950. In 1951 and 1954, the ILC produced texts of the Draft Code of Crimes.[39] Without progress on a definition of aggression, work on the Draft Code of Crimes halted in 1954,[40] but it began again in the 1980s, with further drafts in 1991 and 1996.

Notably, the 1991 draft incorporated a broad set of crimes, including colonialism, apartheid, foreign intervention and terrorism. By 1996, the list of 12 categories of crimes had been significantly reduced. 'Colonial domination and other forms of alien domination' and apartheid were removed, but crimes against UN and associated personnel were retained in order to obtain the broadest possible acceptance amongst states.[41] The now removed draft Article 19 on the responsibility of states for internationally wrongful acts contained a similarly broad conceptualisation of international crime. These articles are directed at state (not individual criminal) responsibility, and therefore do not strictly speaking fall within international criminal law, and the draft Article 19 (on state criminal responsibility) of the previous draft was not included in the final Articles on state responsibility.[42] However, it is interesting to refer to this Article in this discussion because it defined 'international crime' broadly, albeit for the purposes of state responsibility, as follows: 'an internationally wrongful act' resulting 'from the breach by a State of an international obligation so essential for the protection of fundamental interests of the international community that its breach is recognized as a crime by that community as a whole'. This included 'a serious breach of an international obligation of essential importance for safeguarding the right of self-determination of people' – for example, the 'establishment or maintenance by force of colonial domination' – and 'a serious breach of an international obligation – of essential importance for the

---

[39] See further, eg, J Allain and JRWD Jones, 'A Patchwork of Norms: A Commentary on the 1996 Draft Code of Crimes against the Peace and Security of Mankind' (1997) 1 *European Journal of International Law* 100; DHN Johnson, 'The Draft Code of Offences against the Peace and Security of Mankind (1955) 4 *International and Comparative Law Quarterly* 455.

[40] UN GA Resolution [1954] UNGA 37 A/RES/897 (IX) 4 December 1954.

[41] KM Clarke, *Fictions of Justice: The International Criminal Court and the Challenge of Legal Pluralism in Sub-Saharan Africa* (Cambridge University Press, 2009) 57–59, Allain and Jones (n 39) 114. See further, KM Clarke, AS Knottnerus and E de Volder (eds), *Africa and the ICC Perceptions of Justice* (Cambridge University Press, 2016) 12–13.

[42] Responsibility of States for Internationally Wrongful Acts 2001, annexed to GAR 56/83 12 December 2001.

safeguarding and preservation of the human environment' – for example, 'those prohibiting massive pollution of the atmosphere or of the sea'.[43]

It was primarily due to western state opposition that the definition of 'international crime' was significantly reframed in these different ILC drafts. The Draft Code on the Peace and Security of Mankind in the end implemented what Kiyani describes as 'Western interpretations of Nuremberg'.[44] How might this shift be interpreted? It might be seen as confirming the western nature of international criminal law. At the same time, though, the ILC's unanimous agreement on the nature of the establishment or maintenance by force of colonial domination, for example,[45] is not without legal significance. This agreement may be seen as evidence of a potentially wider range of international crimes in customary international law than the Rome Statute currently reflects. A slight digression is in order here to elaborate this point, and it relates to the sources of international criminal law.

Broadly speaking, the two main sources of international (criminal) law of relevance here are treaties (which bind only those states that have signed and ratified them) and customary international law. Customary international law is made up of state practice and so-called *opinio juris*, that is, the belief on the part of a state that it is behaving in a particular way because it is legally obliged to do so. If the behaviour of states reveals a sufficiently generalised and consistent practice and evidence of *opinio juris*, it may signify a binding rule of customary international law. Customary international law is not without its conceptual and practical problems. For example, it is not always possible to identify the exact moment when a customary international law rule emerges, a potentially critical issue in the context of international criminal law, where certainty is required for the application of the principle of legality. Moreover, customary international law reflects the practice of states. As such, despite the formal equality of states, it can give more emphasis to the practice of powerful states.[46] To return to the definition of international crimes discussed above, the ICC must follow the provisions of its founding treaty, the Rome Statute. However, treaties and customary international law have an independent and separate existence. Thus, customary international law may diverge from the rather narrow formulation of international crimes as set out in the Rome Statute (chapter 5). The question then is whether it is possible to return to previous occasions when the international community took a broader approach to international crime as the basis for a more encompassing understanding of international criminality, or whether the narrowing of crimes since (albeit

---

[43] Draft Articles on State Responsibility with Commentaries Thereto Adopted by the International Law Commission on First Reading, January 1997 97-02583, Art 19.

[44] A Kiyani, 'International Crime and the Politics of Criminal Theory: Voices and Conduct of Exclusion' (2015) 48(1) *New York University Journal of International Law and Politics* 129, 150.

[45] See Commentary to Art 19 (n 43) note 42, 131, para 69.

[46] See further, for an extensive discussion on the relationship between power and custom, M Byers, 'Custom, Power and the Power of Rules' (1995) 17(1) *Michigan Journal of International Law* 109, 144.

in the context of international institutions) affirms a narrower understanding of international crime. This is a doctrinal question, and the latter view would have more support. Beyond the question of law, however, this history provides inspiration for alternative formulations of international criminal law. In sum, this period offers a provocation in different registers to the current framing of international criminal law.

A further significant development during this time was the criminalisation of apartheid as a crime against humanity. Described by one commentator as the 'first truly postcolonial crime', the International Convention on the Suppression and Punishment of the Crime of Apartheid 1973[47] remains unratified by major western states,[48] although apartheid has been included as a crime against humanity at the ICC under Article 7(2)(h) of the Rome Statute. Its inclusion in the Rome Statute is important, because the applicability of the Apartheid Convention beyond the South African context has been disputed. The Apartheid Convention was significant for several reasons, including its encompassing of structural violence[49] and its application to 'individuals, members of organizations and institutions and representatives of the State' (Article III). It was, however, controversial. Lingaas observes '[n]ot only was the treaty said to be a Russian conspiracy against the West, several states also feared indictment for aiding and abetting the South African regime'.[50]

Interestingly, however, whilst anti-apartheid activism ensured the criminalisation of apartheid, the establishment of a truth and reconciliation commission in South Africa provides an exception to the trajectory of (international) prosecution, although this approach did not go unchallenged.[51] Even while there is not space to do so here, it is productive to reflect further on the advantages and disadvantages of a truth and reconciliation response to atrocity and the extent to which the dominance of international criminal prosecutions limits recourse to it.

Another key development during this period was the establishment of citizens' tribunals. Within the non-state tribunal movement two organisations are noteworthy for the influence they have exerted: the Bertrand Russell Peace Foundation (BRPF) and the Permanent Peoples' Tribunal (PPT). Tragically prefiguring Nuremberg, in 1934 the American Federation of Labour and the American Jewish Congress had already organised a mock trial of Hitler, which found him guilty of

---

[47] Kiyani (n 44) 156; International Convention on the Suppression and Punishment of the Crime of Apartheid 1973, GAR 3068 (XXVIII) (adopted 30 November 1973, entered into force 18 July 1976) 1015 UNTS 243.

[48] Kiyani (n 44) 138.

[49] See, eg, Art II(c), International Convention on the Suppression and Punishment of the Crime of Apartheid 1973. See further, Stahn (n 4) 796. Kiyani (n 44).

[50] C Lingaas, 'The Crime Against Humanity of Apartheid in a Post-Apartheid World' (2015) 2 *Oslo Law Review* 86, 89.

[51] See, eg, *Azanian Peoples Organisation (AZAPO) and Others v President of the Republic of South Africa* (Constitutional Court, 27 July 1996) CCT 17/86. See further S Garkawe, 'The South African Truth and Reconciliation Commission: A Suitable Model to Enhance the Role and Rights of the Victims of Gross Violations of Human Rights' (2003) 27 *Melbourne University Law Review* 334, 348–49.

crimes against civilisation.[52] The Dewey Commission of Inquiry into the Charges Made against Leon Trotsky in the Moscow Trials was another significant influence on the Russell Tribunal.[53] In 1966, Bertrand Russell organised the Russell Tribunal to hear allegations of war crimes carried out by the US and its allies in Vietnam. He claimed that 'with the exception of the extermination of the Jews … everything that the Germans did in Eastern Europe has been repeated by the US in Vietnam on a scale which is larger and with an efficiency which is more terrible and more complete'.[54] Hearings aimed, in the words of its philosopher President, Jean-Paul Sartre, 'to reintroduce the juridical notion of international crime'.[55] Amongst its findings over multiple sessions, the Tribunal concluded that the US had committed acts of aggression against Vietnam and Laos and genocide against the Vietnamese. It also criticised third states for complicity. The Russell Tribunal drew damaging evidence to the public's attention, including on the use of fragmentation bombs. While the US Government did not take part, it did respond to some of the claims and admitted it had used defoliants.[56] Numerous citizens' tribunals followed, including those organised by the PPT.

The establishment under the auspices of the Lelio Basso Foundation of the PPT in 1978 and the associated development of so-called 'peoples' law' have been central to the citizens' tribunal movement. This permanent 'court for the dispossessed' is made up of about 60 individuals, from amongst whom smaller panels are drawn for particular hearings.[57] Around 50 per cent of tribunal members are lawyers.[58] It has held 49 sessions at the time of writing.[59] Proceedings of the PPT are based on the Rules of Procedure contained in its updated 1979 Statute,[60] and verdicts, which are final, are presented to 'interested parties, to the Secretary General of the United Nations, to the competent international bodies, to the concerned governments, to the media'.[61]

For PPTs (and other non-state tribunals), 'law belongs to the people'. In his opening statement to the World Tribunal on Iraq (WTI) in Istanbul, Richard Falk observed that the United Nations (UN) Charter

> confirmed in its opening words that it is the peoples of the world and not the governments or even the UN that have been entrusted with the ultimate responsibility for

---

[52] AJ Klinghoffer and JA Klinghoffer, *International Citizens' Tribunals Mobilizing Public Opinion to Advance Human Rights* (Palgrave, 2002) 48–49.

[53] AW Blaser, 'How to Advance Human Rights without Really Trying: An Analysis of Nongovernmental Tribunals' (1992) 14 *Human Rights Quarterly* 339, 340.

[54] As quoted in Klinghoffer and Klinghoffer (n 52) 106.

[55] ibid 124.

[56] ibid 126.

[57] Blaser (n 53) 347. See further the Permanent Peoples' Tribunal at http://permanentpeoplestribunal.org/?lang=en.

[58] Blaser (n 53) 354.

[59] Permanent Peoples' Tribunal (n 57).

[60] New Statute of the Permanent Peoples' Tribunal, updated December 2018 at http://permanentpeoplestribunal.org/wp-content/uploads/2019/05/Statute-of-the-PPT_ENG_FINAL.pdf.

[61] Art 22, New Statute of the Permanent Peoples' Tribunal.

upholding this renunciation of war: 'We the peoples of the United Nations determined to save succeeding generations from the scourge of war ...' that set forth the duties of states in the United Nations Charter.[62]

Permanent Peoples' Tribunals draw on the 1976 non-governmental Universal Declaration of the Rights of Peoples (the Algiers Declaration).[63] Described by Jayan Nayar as 'perhaps, the highwater mark of the anti-imperial conceptualisation of human rights struggles', its seven operative sections reject an 'individualistic, legalistic and segregationist' interpretation of human rights[64] For example, Article 18 states that economic development should be coordinated 'with solidarity amongst all peoples of the world'. Permanent Peoples' Tribunals have since adopted other similar instruments.[65] The 1976 Brussels Women's Tribunal presaged the subsequent Courts of Women Project, established in 1992, by the Asian Women's Human Rights Council. Emanating from the global south, over 40 such World Courts of Women have been held.[66]

The Cold War period offers a rich practice that sheds light on alternative possibilities and formulations of the practice and discipline of international criminal law. In the case of citizens' tribunals, it is the origins of a rich movement. Revisiting this period is vital for thinking about the ways in which international criminal law might have developed but did not, and the conditions of possibility that led to the directions it eventually took.

---

[62] R Falk, 'Opening Speech on Behalf of the Panel of Advocates' in MG Sökmen (ed), *World Tribunal on Iraq: Making the Case against War* (Olive Branch Press, 2008) 5, 7.

[63] Preamble to the Universal Declaration of the Rights of People, Algiers, 4 July 1976 (Algiers Declaration) at http://permanentpeoplestribunal.org/wp-content/uploads/2015/01/Carta-di-algeri-EN-1.pdf.

[64] J Nayar, 'A People's Tribunal Against the Crime of Silence? The Politics of Judgement and an Agenda for People's Law' (2001) (2) *Social Justice and Global Development* at https://warwick.ac.uk/fac/soc/law/elj/lgd/2001_2/nayar/nayar.rtf. See further S Fraudatario and G Tognoni, 'The Participation of People and the Development of International Law: The Laboratory of the Permanent Peoples' Tribunal' in A Byrnes and G Simm, *Peoples' Tribunals and International Law* (Cambridge University Press, 2018) 133, 138; D Otto, 'Impunity in a Different Register: People's Tribunals and Questions of Judgment, Law and Responsibility' in E Engle, Z Miller and DM Davis (eds), *Anti-Impunity and the Human Rights Agenda* (Cambridge University Press, 2016) 291, 304.

[65] See further, eg, the Charter on Industrial Hazards and Human Rights 1996 and the Charter of Health, Safety and Environmental Rights of Workers and Communities 1994; Permanent People's Tribunal on Global Corporations and Human Wrongs 2000 (2001) 1 *Law Social Justice and Global Development Journal* at www2.warwick.ac.uk/fac/soc/law/elj/lgd/2001_1/ppt.

[66] CM Chinkin, 'Peoples' Tribunals: Legitimate or Rough Justice' (2006) 24(2) *Windsor Yearbook of Access to Justice* 201, 212; D Otto, 'Beyond Legal Justice: Some Personal Reflections on People's Tribunals, Listening and Responsibility' (2017) 5 *London Review of International Law* 225, 227; Otto (n 64) 305–08. For discussion of the Bosnian Women's Court and a feminist approach to international criminal justice, see K Campbell, *The Justice of Humans Subject, Society and Sexual Violence in International Criminal Justice* (Cambridge University Press, 2022). See further N Tromp, 'The right to tell: The Sarajevo Women Court in search for a feminist approach to justice' in RM Paulose, (ed), *People's Tribunals, Human Rights and the Law Searching for Justice* (Routledge, 2020).

V. Post-Cold War Reassertion of International Criminal Justice

In 1989, Trinidad and Tobago tried to initiate dialogue about a permanent international criminal court during the Special Session of the General Assembly on narcotic drugs. The response, Immi Tallgren observed, 'ranged from caution to fatherly amusement full of pessimism'.[67] Yet within 10 years, international criminal courts and tribunals were proliferating,[68] a body of substantive and procedural international criminal law had been established, and some states had experimented with expansive provisions on universal jurisdiction (chapter 7). However, the optimism of the 1990s has given way to hard realism about the limits of international criminal justice. Concerns have been raised about the ICC's effectiveness and its inability to insulate itself fully from the political context in which it finds itself.

The end of the Cold War enabled permanent Security Council member states to agree (at least for a short period) to measures that previously would have been impossible. Early on they were also faced with crimes in the Former Yugoslavia. Hazan observes that states were reluctant to agree to military intervention but at the same time could not 'tolerate the nature and magnitude of the crimes committed without denying their own fundamental morality and policy'.[69] The result was the unprecedented establishment by the Security Council under Chapter 7 of the UN Charter of the ICTY. Its task was to prosecute 'persons responsible for serious violations of international humanitarian law committed in the territory of the Former Yugoslavia since January 1, 1991'. Having established the ICTY, it would have been very difficult for the Security Council not to establish a tribunal for Rwanda (as it did by Security Council Resolution 955, 8 November 1994), the Security Council's having withdrawn most of its UN peacekeeping troops on the outbreak of the genocide there. Both tribunals have been described as 'acts of political contrition'.[70] Although the Rwandan Government had requested the establishment of such a tribunal, it voted against its founding resolution. Amongst its objections were the tribunal's restricted temporal jurisdiction, its location outside Rwanda and its inability to order the death penalty. Rwandan local courts also adjudicated over accused, alongside 'gacaca', a modified traditional justice mechanism.[71]

---

[67] I Tallgren, 'The Sensibility and Sense of International Criminal Law' (2002) 13(3) *European Journal of International Law* 561, 563.

[68] Along with other international institutions, including the International Tribunal for the Law of the Sea and the Appellate Body of the World Trade Organization; R Goldstone, 'Foreword' in M Sterio and M Scharf (eds), *The Legacy of Ad Hoc Tribunals in International Criminal Law* (Cambridge University Press, 2019) xv.

[69] P Hazan, *Justice In A Time of War* (Texas A&M University Press, 2004) 19.

[70] R Zacklin, 'The Failings of Ad Hoc International Tribunals' (2004) 2 *Journal of International Criminal Justice* 541, 542.

[71] A Kiyani, 'Group-Based Differentiation and Local Repression: the Custom and Curse of Selectivity' (2016) 14 *Journal of International Criminal Justice* 939, 945–46; N Palmer, *Courts in Conflict: Interpreting the Lawyers of Justice in Post-Genocide Rwanda* (Oxford University Press, 2015).

Neither the ICTY nor the ICTR started auspiciously. As former ICTY Judge and President Gabrielle Kirk McDonald observed, 'we had no premises, no permanent staff and, critically, we had no legal framework to guide the work of the prosecution staff and the Judges'.[72] The support the international community lent to the ICTY varied over its lifetime. Critically, the Dayton Peace Accords marginalised the ICTY, and some commentators have argued that 'the ICTY indictments tended to reflect the shifts in US alignments in the region'.[73] However, by the time both institutions closed their operations, in 2017 and 2015 respectively (with ongoing essential tasks now performed by the Mechanism for International Criminal Tribunals), they had made enormous strides in the development of substantive and procedural international criminal law, some of which this book examines.

The legality of the establishment by the Security Council of an international criminal tribunal was unsuccessfully challenged early in the life of the ICTY in the *Tadić* case.[74] Legality and legitimacy are not the same, however. The ICTR was set up by the Security Council to adjudicate the genocide in which the Security Council is widely criticised for having failed to intervene.[75] Moreover, the ICTR has been criticised for one-sided prosecutions.[76] The failure of the ICTY to investigate allegations of war crimes on the part of the North Atlantic Treaty Organization (NATO) also challenged its legitimacy. Former Prosecutor Carla Del Ponte observed:

> I quickly concluded that it was impossible to investigate NATO, because NATO and its member states would not cooperate with us … I understood that I had collided with the edge of the political universe in which the tribunal was allowed to function.[77]

Both tribunals have been criticised for being distant from the communities at which their work was directed. Alongside cost, this was one of the reasons for the development of mixed or hybrid jurisdictions.[78] Hybrid tribunals seek to marry the professed expertise and independence of the 'international' alongside the legitimacy and contextual understanding of the 'local'. In other words, they are constituted by a mix of international and national personnel, and apply a mix of international and national law. Such institutions, it is hoped, have a greater potential for capacity

---

[72] GK McDonald, 'Problems, Obstacles and Achievements of the ICTY' (2004) 2 *Journal of International Criminal Justice* 558, 558.

[73] J Graubart and L Varadarajan, 'Taking Milosevic Seriously: Imperialism, Law and the Politics of Global Justice' (2013) 27(4) *International Relations* 439, 449.

[74] *Prosecutor v Tadić*, Decision on the Defence Motion for Interlocutory Appeal on Jurisdiction, 2 October 1995, IT-94-1-AR72.

[75] The failures of the UN during the genocide are widely documented. See further R Dallaire, K Manocha and N Degnarain, 'The Major Powers on Trial' (2005) 3 *Journal of International Criminal Justice* 861; I Carlsson, 'The UN Inadequacies' (2005) 3 *Journal of International Criminal Justice* 837.

[76] See further L Reydams, 'The ICTR Ten Years On: Back to the Nuremberg Paradigm?' (2005) 3 *Journal of International Criminal Justice* 977.

[77] C Del Ponte and C Sudetic, *Madame Prosecutor: Confrontations with Humanity's Worst Criminals and the Culture of Impunity* (Other Press, 2009) 60.

[78] Together the ad hoc tribunals cost $3.8 billion; M Scharf and M Sterio, 'Conclusion' in M Sterio and M Scharf (eds), *The Legacy of Ad Hoc Tribunals in International Criminal Law* (Cambridge University Press, 2019) 357.

building and resonance with local populations. They include the SCSL, the Special Tribunal for Lebanon (STL), the Extraordinary Chambers in the Courts of Cambodia (ECCC) and the Special Panel for Serious Crimes in Dili, East Timor. Each of these is distinctive in its constitution, the balance between the national and the international law that is applied, and the legal and political challenges it faces. Many have faced significant resource challenges. This model is likely to continue, however, as can been seen from the 2015 establishment of the Special Criminal Court within the justice system of the Central African Republic. Faced with Security Council paralysis regarding Syria, the UN General Assembly established the International, Impartial and Independent Mechanism to Assist in the Investigation and Prosecution of those responsible for the most serious crimes under international law committed in the Syrian Arab Republic since March 2011,[79] also indicative of the continuing need for special bodies. Several proposals argue for the creation of an international or hybrid tribunal to try the crime of aggression' (over which the ICC has no jurisdiction) and other international crimes committed in Ukraine.[80]

Ad hoc and hybrid tribunals are by their nature temporary. However, their existence indicated the need for – and the possibility of – a more permanent institution, and thus gave renewed impetus to the development of a permanent international criminal court. The adoption by 120 states of the Rome Statute on 17 July 1998, and the coming into force of the Statute in July 2002 with the deposit of the 60th instrument of ratification, represented a high point of optimism in the international criminal justice story.[81] Over 20 years later, however, this optimism has been tempered. Two concerns marred the operation of the ICC in its early years: its apparent focus on African situations and the challenge of ensuring the accountability of actors from powerful states.

A. The ICC and Africa

By 2009, the African Union had decided not to cooperate with the ICC;[82] and in 2016, Burundi became the first state to announce its intention to withdraw from the Rome Statute. Dersso observes:

---

[79] GAR 71/248. See further A Whiting, 'An Investigation Mechanism for Syria: The GA Steps into the Breach' (2017) 15(2) *International Journal of Criminal Justice* 231.

[80] See further, OA Hathaway, 'The Case for Creating an International Tribunal to Prosecute the Crime of Aggression against Ukraine' *Just Security* (20 September 2022) at www.justsecurity. org/83117/the-case-for-creating-an-international-tribunal-to-prosecute-the-crime-of-aggression-against-ukraine/. See further Public International Law and Policy Group's Draft Law for a Domestic Ukrainian High War Crimes Court at www.publicinternationallawandpolicygroup.org/draft-law-ukrainian-high-war-crimes-court.

[81] See further, eg, M Glasius, 'Expertise in the Cause of Justice: Global Civil Society Influence on the Statute for an International Criminal Court' in M Glasius, M Kaldor and HK Anheier (eds), *Global Civil Society Yearbook 2002* (Oxford University Press, 2002) 137. For critical reflection, see I Tallgren, 'We Did It? The Vertigo of Law and Everyday Life at the Diplomatic Conference on the Establishment of an International Criminal Court' (1999) 12 *Leiden Journal of International Law* 683.

[82] SA Dersso, 'The ICC's Africa Problem: A Spotlight on the Politics and Limits of International Criminal Justice' in Clarke, Knottnerus and Volder (eds) (n 41) 61, 63.

Notably, for the very first time in the history of the international relations, countries outside of the traditional power centre of the international legal order threatened the very survival of an international institution embodying a significant component of international law, namely international criminal law.[83]

The ICC's focus on Africa is sometimes explained through the observation that Africa as a continent has generated the most ratifications of the Rome Statute, although concerns have also been expressed that ratification may have resulted from pressures of foreign aid and the need to satisfy good governance conditions.[84] However, African leaders have also sought to use the ICC to their strategic advantage (chapter 7).[85] While the African Union has been critical of the ICC, noteworthy is that important international criminal legal innovations have emanated from the African continent. For example, the African Union Model Law on universal jurisdiction innovatively extends universal jurisdiction (see further chapter 7) to include narcotics trafficking and terrorism, and the 2014 Malabo Protocol, if it enters into force, will expand the jurisdiction of the African Court of Justice and Human Rights to include international criminal jurisdiction. Article 28A of the accompanying Statute of the African Court of Justice and Human and Peoples' Rights (also not in force) incorporates a much wider range of crimes than does the Rome Statute, encompassing unconstitutional change of government, money laundering and corruption, and a range of trafficking offences, including trafficking in hazardous wastes and the illegal exploitation of natural resources.[86] This broader approach to international crimes and responsibility (the Protocol, unlike the Rome Statute, includes corporate criminal responsibility) promises to address some of the conditions underpinning violence and the commission of international crime on the African continent.[87] However, controversy has also attached to the express inclusion of immunity for heads of states and governments (Article 46A*bis*). Views differ on the Protocol. Mutua describes it as an attempt 'to sabotage the ICC by establishing a toothless body'.[88] Knottnerus and de Volder, on the other hand, consider it to be 'a protest *for* international criminal justice' because 'it articulates a regional vision on its future', one that is 'shaped by African perceptions of justice'.[89]

The 'African' position on the ICC is not homogeneous, and some criticism of the ICC – wherever and from whomever it emanates – may be expedient.[90]

---

[83] ibid 64.

[84] Kiyani (n 44) 178.

[85] See further P Clark, *Distant Justice: The Impact of the International Criminal Court on African Politics* (Cambridge University Press, 2018).

[86] Protocol on Amendments to the Protocol on the Statute of the African Court of Justice and Human Rights, 27 June 2014 at https://au.int/en/treaties/protocol-amendments-protocol-statute-african-court-justice-and-human-rights.

[87] AS Knottnerus and E de Volder, 'International Criminal Justice and the Early Formation of an African Criminal Court' in Clarke, Knottnerus and Volder (eds) (n 41) 376, 388.

[88] MW Mutua, 'Africans and the ICC Hypocrisy, Impunity, and Perversion' in Clarke, Knottnerus and Volder (eds) (n 41) 47, 52.

[89] Knottnerus and de Volder (n 87) 394.

[90] See, eg, Mutua (n 88) 56.

This raises the question of how to approach these developments from a critical perspective, which requires an alertness to the multiple ways in which power operates. One response to this dilemma is to explore the ways in which knowledge is produced about these developments and by whom. Thus, we might consider who is speaking, taking into account that the voices of elite actors may not necessarily represent people's perspectives.[91] Another is to consider the extent to which the Malabo Protocol promises to address some of the blind-spots in international criminal law more generally. It might be explored whether these moves seem to affirm or challenge existing inequalities in the international legal order, considering the 'African' critique of the ICC alongside another issue, which is the ICC's limitations in addressing powerful actors in powerful states, in particular the US.[92]

B. The ICC and the US

While the US has played a key role in the development of international criminal law, it has also sought to ensure an exceptional place for American citizens at the ICC. On 31 December 2000, then US President Clinton signed the Rome Statute. A 2002 note from the administration of President George W Bush to the UN Secretary General made it clear that the US would not ratify the Rome Statute, thereby freeing the US from the obligation not to defeat the Rome Statute's object and purpose pending ratification. Since then, several US governments have taken measures that to a greater or less extent have undermined the ICC.[93] For example, the Bush administration negotiated over 100 so-called bilateral immunity agreements by which states agreed not to transfer US citizens to the ICC. Former President Obama was also opposed to the ICC's exercise of jurisdiction over US nationals, although general relations between the ICC and the US were more cordial. They deteriorated significantly with former President Trump's administration.[94] In particular, the authorisation of the investigation into Afghanistan in 2019 was politically highly controversial and provoked fierce backlash from the US Government at the time.[95]

---

[91] See, eg, ibid 47 and 56. For analyses of various perspectives on the ICC from Africa, see Clarke, Knottnerus and Volder (eds) (n 41).

[92] See further, eg, Mutua (n 88) 56.

[93] See further, eg, The American Service-Members Protection Act 2002, which, *inter alia*, prohibited cooperation with the ICC, affirms US policy to 'seek permanent exemption from the ICC for US troops in every UN peacekeeping operation authorization', and authorised the President to 'use all means necessary and appropriate to bring about the release of any US or allied personnel being detained by, on behalf, of or at the request of the International Criminal Court'.

[94] Including through the imposition by the then US Government of sanctions (now lifted) against the ICC Prosecutor.

[95] Just before the April 2019 decision, the US revoked the ICC's Chief Prosecutor's visa. See further, Center for Constitutional Rights Complaint against the United States of America: Interference with Judicial Proceedings at the International Criminal Court to the UN Special Rapporteur of the Human Rights Council on the Independence of Judges and Lawyers, 5 June 2019 at https://ccrjustice.org/sites/default/files/attach/2019/06/5%20June%202019_Special%20Rapp%20letter%20ICC_final.pdf.

VI. Conclusion

The proliferation of international tribunals and the operation of a permanent international criminal court has not quelled the demand for citizens' tribunals, which continue to multiply. Amongst the most well-known post-Cold War citizens' tribunals are the WIWCT for the Trial of Japan's Military Sexual Slavery 2000 and the WTI 2003–05.[96] On 9 December 2021, the Uyghur Tribunal delivered its judgment.[97] Earlier that same year, China had imposed sanctions on, amongst others, Sir Geoffrey Nice QC, its chair.[98]

Although unofficial bodies, scholars observe how citizens' tribunals have taken up issues that 'would later become paradigmatic for transitional justice'.[99] Terrell notes that the Global Tribunal on Violations of Women's Human Rights 1993 considered that SGBV (see section III) could constitute torture and crimes against humanity, well in advance of the ground-breaking ICTR judgment in *Akayesu*, which held that rape could constitute genocide.[100] It has also been claimed that the WIWCT enhanced the attention given to SGBV and its prosecution in conflict.[101] Citizens' tribunals have also sought to engage with the ICC, for example by addressing the Prosecutor.[102]

The continued establishment of citizens' tribunals raises the question of how the ongoing call for justice in these unofficial fora might be read. It might be seen variously as: an affirmation of the ideal of international criminal justice; a parallel space for a different form of justice; evidence of the hegemony of the language and form of international criminal law; or as a call to, and inspiration for, an alternative form of international criminal justice. It might also be seen as any combination of these. Citizens' tribunals also demonstrate how the subjects and subjectivities of international criminal law are related. In other words, international criminal

---

[96] See further, Otto, 'Impunity in a Different Register' (n 64) 298–302; Chinkin (n 66); U Dolgopol, 'Civil Society's Engagement with International Criminal Law: The Role of Peoples' Tribunals' in M Bergsmo et al (eds), *Historical Origins of International Criminal Law*, vol 4 (Torkel Opsahl, 2015) 703. See further on the WTI, A Çubukçu, *For the Love of Humanity: The World Tribunal on Iraq* (University of Pennsylvania Press, 2019).

[97] Uyghur Tribunal Judgment (Church House Westminster, 9 December 2021) at https://uyghurtribunal.com/wp-content/uploads/2022/09/UYGHUR-TRIBUNAL-Judgment-2022.09.20.pdf.

[98] Ministry of Foreign Affairs of the People's Republic of China, Foreign Ministry Spokesperson Announces Sanctions on Relevant UK Individuals and Entities, 26 March 2021 at www.fmprc.gov.cn/mfa_eng/xwfw_665399/s2510_665401/2535_665405/202103/t20210326_9170815.html. J Curtis and T Robinson, 'The Uyghur Tribunal' (House of Commons Library, 18 January 2022) 3 at Https://researchbriefings.files.parliament.uk/documents/CDP-2022-0009/CDP-2022-0009.pdf.

[99] M Zunino, 'Subversive Justice: The Russell Vietnam War Crimes Tribunal and Transitional Justice' (2016) 10 *International Journal of Transitional Justice* 211, 227.

[100] *The Prosecutor v Jean-Paul Akayesu*, 2 September 1998, ICTR-96-4-T; F Terrell, 'Unofficial Accountability: A Proposal for the Permanent Women's Tribunal on Sexual Violence in Armed Conflict' (2005) 15 *Texas Journal of Women and the Law* 107, 119.

[101] Terrell (n 100) 133.

[102] See, eg, rec 9.1.3, Permanent Peoples' Tribunal, 'Free Trade, Violence, Impunity and Peoples' Rights in Mexico (2011–2014)' (PPT November 2014), Ruling at http://permanentpeoplestribunal.org/wp-content/uploads/2016/07/FINALVERDICTMEXICO.pdf.

law has multiple meanings and forms depending on who is speaking and enacting it. How international criminal law is viewed in official and unofficial forms will depend on how its promises, potential and limitations are seen. Judgments about this will be partly influenced by understandings of international criminal legal history, bearing in mind that international criminal legal history can be read and written in many ways. How international criminal law is seen will also be influenced by the view taken of current international criminal law. To that end, the following chapters provide an introduction to key aspects of contemporary international criminal law, starting with the core crimes under the Rome Statute.

Further Reading

KJ Heller, *The Nuremberg Military Tribunals and the Origins of International Criminal Law* (Oxford University Press, 2012).

KJ Heller and G Simpson, *The Hidden Histories of War Crimes Trials* (Oxford University Press, 2013).

I Tallgren and T Skouteris, *The New Histories of International Criminal Law: Retrials* (Oxford University Press, 2019).

5

Whose Conscience?
International Crimes

I. Introduction

International criminal law is said to deal with the most serious crimes of international concern. The so-called core crimes, namely those that fall within the jurisdiction of the ICC, are crimes against humanity (widespread or systematic attacks against a civilian population), genocide (an attack against a specific group with the intention to destroy that group), war crimes and aggression (essentially a leadership and interstate crime). Noteworthy is that the Malabo Protocol encompasses a broader range of criminal activity.[1] While the core crimes undoubtedly shock the 'conscience of mankind' (as General Assembly Resolution 96(1) observed in relation to genocide[2]), the conscience of humanity, as has been widely observed, has also been triggered in partial ways.[3] The identification of international criminal conduct plays a key role in determining the scope and potential of international criminal law. Yet there is not one single rationale that is accepted as a means of identifying what conduct falls within the category of an international crime.[4] A fair dose of historical contingency has played a role in determining whether conduct is classified as an international crime (as opposed to, for example, a transnational crime). As a result, international crimes can be criticised for reflecting the interests of powerful actors in several and sometimes subtle ways. At the same time, this contingency means that other approaches are imaginable, as the work of citizens' tribunals demonstrates. This chapter therefore provides an introduction to the main elements of the core crimes in international law, and encourages reflection on potential alternative formulations and what they might offer.

---

[1] Including unconstitutional change of government, money laundering and corruption, and a range of trafficking offences, including trafficking in hazardous wastes and the illegal exploitation of natural resources. Protocol on Amendments to the Protocol on the Statute of the African Court of Justice and Human Rights, 27 June 2014.

[2] UNGA Res 96(1) (11 December 1946) UN Doc A/RES_96(1).

[3] For example, Reynolds and Xavier ask 'why is the victim of child solider recruitment constructed as more deserving than the child victim of structural adjustment?': S Reynolds and J Xavier, 'The Dark Corners of the World' (2016) 14 *Journal of International Criminal Justice* 958, 981.

[4] See further, C Stahn, *A Critical Introduction to International Criminal Law* (Cambridge University Press, 2019) 416.

There is much to be said about the scope and application of international crimes. There is only enough space in this chapter to provide a brief introduction to each. It is suggested that this chapter be read in three parts: first, the definition of international crimes at a conceptual level; second, genocide and crimes against humanity; and, third, international criminal law and armed conflict.

II. What Is – And What Might Be – An International Crime?

As already mentioned, there is no clear agreement on how to identify an international crime or its consequences. Carsten Stahn observes that '[o]ne of the striking features of international criminal justice is that it does not contain a fully developed theory of international crimes'.[5] International crimes are typically assumed to attract universal jurisdiction and international criminal responsibility, and to be triable before an international criminal tribunal. But this is not always the case. The crime of genocide, for example, does not attract universal jurisdiction under the 1948 Genocide Convention but only in customary international law. One approach would be to adopt a purely positivist approach towards identifying international crimes. In other words, it is possible simply to ask whether international law criminalises certain conduct.[6] However, this might feel overly state-centric and problematic, not least because, despite formal equality, the processes of international law-making do not even out power differences between states.[7] Alternatively, a more normative perspective might be followed, such as is reflected in the statement that international crimes 'shock the conscience of mankind' and the 'legal fiction' that international criminals are *hostis humani generis*, namely, the 'enemies of mankind'.[8] However, one problem with the specific claim that international crimes shock the conscience of mankind is that it can detract attention from the actual victims of international crime. As Mégret has observed, 'it is unclear that international crimes truly "shock the conscience of mankind" in some recognizably sociological way or that such a thin reality is any match for the actual, targeted, intensely felt trauma of actual victims'.[9] Moreover, whatever the phrase the 'enemies of mankind' means today, historically the concept denoted not so much heinousness as the need for self-defence.[10]

---

[5] ibid 18.

[6] See further, eg, ibid 20.

[7] See, eg, M Byers, 'Custom, Power, and the Power of Rules' (1995) 17(1) *Michigan Journal of International Law* 109, 114–16.

[8] See further on *hostis humani generis* as a legal fiction, E Kontorovich, 'The Piracy Analogy: Modern Universal Jurisdiction's Hollow Foundation' (2004) 45(10) *Harvard International Law Journal* 183, 235.

[9] F Mégret, 'What Sort of Global Justice is "International Criminal Justice"?' (2015) 13 *Journal of International Criminal Justice* 77, 87. See further also MA Drumbl, *Atrocity, Punishment and International Law* (Cambridge University Press, 2007) 3.

[10] See further Kontorovich (n 8) 186; M Garrod, 'Piracy, the Protection of Vital State Interests and the False Foundations of Universal Jurisdiction in International Law' (2014) 25 *Diplomacy and Statecraft*

Another way to think about international crimes is to reflect on the values that the law protects through the designation of conduct as internationally criminal. These values may include or range from human dignity to (international) peace and security.[11] A values-based approach allows for a more ready expansion of the categories of international crime, but key to this approach is the identification of avowedly universal and fundamental values and those by whom they are held. The identification of such values is not problem-free. The history (and present) of international criminal law is replete with examples where certain harms have been overlooked. For example, international criminal law has historically failed to protect against sexual and gender-based violence (SGBV), a position that started to change only in the 1990s and that owes a considerable debt to women's activism. As already emphasised, a key concern of critical legal scholars is that international criminal law typically excludes structural violence. Mégret, for example, has observed that 'it is entirely logically possible that the worst international offence would be the fact of "deliberately tolerating conditions of relievable poverty"'.[12] Another example is the minimal protection international criminal law has accorded to the environment, and then typically only in the context of armed conflict.[13] In 2016, the ICC Office of the Prosecutor (OTP) raised the prospect of prosecuting environmental damage, land-grabbing and the illegal exploitation of natural resources.[14] However, this does not appear to have had a significant impact

---

195; J Greene, 'Hostis Humani Generis' (2008) 34(4) *Critical Inquiry* 638; E Haslam, *The Slave Trade, Abolition and the Long History of International Criminal Law* (Routledge, 2020) 66–71.

[11] Stahn (n 4) 16.

[12] Mégret (n 9) 80–81. See further I Kalpouzos and I Mann, 'Banal Crimes against Humanity: The Case of Asylum Seekers in Greece' (2015) 16(1) *Melbourne Journal of International Law* 1, 1–2, comparing 'spectacular examples of "radical evil"' with less apparent so-called 'banal international crimes', which they describe as 'normalized occurrences, understood as rooted in social and economic process rather than in politics'. See further RC DeFalco, *Invisible Atrocities: The Aesthetic Biases of International Criminal Justice* (Cambridge University Press, 2022).

[13] See, eg, Art 8(2)(b)(iv), Rome Statute. See further ILC Draft Articles on the Protection of the Environment in Relation to Armed Conflict 2019 A/CN4/L937. See further, on environmental crimes, ecocide and campaigns for a crime of ecocide, Stop Ecocide Foundation, *Independent Expert Panel for the Legal Definition of Ecocide* (2 June 2021) at www.stopecocide.earth/legal-definition; J Durney, 'Crafting a Standard: Environmental Crimes as Crimes Against Humanity under the International Criminal Court' (2018) 24 *Hastings Environmental Law Journal* 41; F Mégret, 'The Problem of an International Criminal Law of the Environment' (2011) 36 *Columbia Journal of Environmental Law* 195; R Pereira, 'After the ICC Office of the Prosecutor's 2016 Policy Paper on Case Selection and Prioritisation: Towards an International Crime of Ecocide?' (2020) 31 *Criminal Law Forum* 179, 180–81; M Colacurci, 'The Draft Convention Ecocide and the Role for Corporate Remediation: Some Insights from the Monsanto Tribunal and a Recent Research Proposal' (2021) 21(1) *International Criminal Law Review* 154; S Mehta and P Merz, '"Ecocide – A New Crime against Peace" (2015) 17(1) *Environmental Law Review* 3; A Greene, 'The Campaign to Make Ecocide an International Crimes: Quixotic Quest or Moral Imperative' (2019) 30(3) *Fordham Journal of International Law* 1.

[14] OTP, Policy Paper on Case Selection and Prioritisation (15 September 2016) para 14. See further Global Diligence LLP, Communication under Article 15 of the Rome Statute of the International Criminal Court: The Commission of Crimes Against Humanity in Cambodia July 2002 to Present (2014) alleging, inter alia, widespread and systematic land grabs, at https://static1.squarespace.com/static/5bf447e7365f02310e09e592/t/5eb178be2da21b0620c19194/1588689097212/executive_summary-ICC.pdf.

on practice.[15] It is undoubtedly the case that the ICC cannot cover all international crimes. Nevertheless, as critical scholarship emphasises, by glossing over particular kinds of harm, international criminal law buttresses and reflects a world view that perceives of certain kinds of suffering as less serious and/or unavoidable, rather than a preventable outcome of human decision-making.

Citizens' tribunals adopt an alternative approach to the identification of 'crime' through their central concept of the 'crime of silence'. Bertrand Russell declared to the first meeting of members of the war crimes tribunal:

> Our mandate is to uncover and tell all. My conviction is that no greater tribute can be provided than an offer of the truth, born of intense and unyielding inquiry. May this Tribunal prevent the crime of silence.[16]

The crime of silence, according to the PPT on Global Corporations and Human Wrongs 2000, is 'the silence which refuses to name the violence that is inflicted upon marginalized populations as a crime', and the role of PPTs is to contribute 'to peoples' struggle to find the words to name this violence'.[17] Structural injustices are very often key to the crime of silence. For example, Article 1 of the New Statute of the PPT lists crimes within its competence as genocide, crimes against humanity, war crimes, ecological crimes, economic crimes and systemic crimes.[18]

The limited scope of 'official' international crimes raises the question: What might international criminal law look like if it acknowledged a broader range of harms, such as structural violence? And how might it do so within its current framework? And should it? Alternatively, given that international criminal law has been indelibly shaped by the absence of structural violence, does it need a more fundamental reimagining to be able to encompass it? From within the current framework of international criminal law it might be argued that severe violations of social and economic rights should be criminalised (to the extent that they are not already), or that international criminal law should more explicitly acknowledge the economic and social processes that underpin the commission of many international crimes. Going further, it could be argued that some forms of structural harm should be international crimes. This requires a more fundamental shift in thinking, including about responsibility, as Article 7 of the New Statute of the

---

[15] Pereira (n 13).

[16] K Coates, P Limqueco and P Weiss (eds), *Prevent the Crime of Silence: Reports from the Sessions of the International War Crimes Tribunal Founded by Bertrand Russell* (Penguin Press, 1971) 59.

[17] Permanent Peoples' Tribunal, 'Permanent Peoples' Tribunal on Global Corporations and Human Wrongs, University of Warwick, 22–25 March 2000, Findings and Recommended Action' (2001) (1) *Law, Social Justice and Global Development Journal* at www2.warwick.ac.uk/fac/soc/law/elj/lgd/2001_1/ppt/.

[18] New Statute of the PPT at http://permanentpeoplestribunal.org/wp-content/uploads/2019/05/Statute-of-the-PPT_ENG_FINAL.pdf. See further Art 5 on environmental crimes and Art 6 on economic crimes.

PPT, which accords the PPT jurisdiction over so-called system crimes, shows. Article 7 describes system crimes in the following way:

'System crimes' are crimes considered in articles 5 and 6 that are not imputable to specific persons, but of which it is possible to identify the causes as being not natural, but political or economic, in the functioning of legal and social systems.

System crimes cause serious injury to the fundamental human rights of entire communities by depriving them of access to food, water, medicine, housing, work, ultimately to human dignity. These effects that do not derive from natural catastrophes but *rather by a sum of decisions adopted over the years, often in different countries and therefore they are not easily imputable to identified persons, states or companies.*[19]

A number of issues arise when considering the potential incorporation of structural harms into international criminal law. One question is whether expanding the scope of international crimes might infringe the principle of legality and therefore a fair trial. However, concerns about the principle of legality go to the issue of retrospective punishment but not to progressive legal development. There is also an issue of potential overreach from both institutional and normative aspects. From an institutional aspect, overreach raises questions about the ability of an international criminal court faced with an expanded list of international crimes to function efficiently, and the risk of disappointing victims' and others' expectations if it does not. From a normative perspective, the risk of overreach requires consideration of how to maintain the exceptional nature of international crimes and international criminality.[20] However, it is doubtful that there is always universal agreement about what is exceptionally harmful conduct. Alternatively, a more pragmatic approach might be taken. This simply asks whether an international criminal legal response offers a useful solution to structural violence in terms of its ability to contribute to the reduction of (human) suffering.[21] In other words, it asks what the international criminal legal toolbox has to offer to counteract structural harm. From this perspective, there may be expressive value in designating conduct as internationally criminal, thus giving out a message about the gravity of its harm and more specifically responsibility for it.

---

[19] ibid (emphasis added). For further discussion, see, eg, L Smith and C Friedlaender, 'Collective Agent and Global Structural Injustice: An Introduction to the Special Issue' (2021) 38(1) *Journal of Applied Philosophy* doi:10.1111/japp.12489.

[20] See, eg, Kress, who asks: 'Is international criminal law (*stricto sensu*) not an instrument for exceptionally grave assaults upon the international legal order to be applied with utmost restraint? An expansionist resort to international criminal law must lead to its trivialization.' C Kress, 'Time for Decision: Some Thoughts on the Immediate Future of the Crime of Aggression: A Reply to Andreas Paulus' (2010) 20 *European Journal of International Law* 1129, 1142.

[21] For a provocation in relation to animals and international criminal law, see, eg, M Lostal, 'De-Objectifying Animals: Could They Qualify as Victims before the International Criminal Court' (2021) 19(3) *Journal of International Criminal Justice* 583. See further D Legge and S Brooman, 'Reflecting on 25 Years of Teaching Animal Law: Is It Time for an International Crime of Animal Ecocide?' (2020) 41 *Liverpool Law Review* 201.

Ultimately, the question is whether structural violence can (and should) be incorporated into existing law and whether it requires minor or major modification to do so. And, if it is incorporated, will that result in a transformation of either international criminal law and/or the lived conditions of people's lives? The response to these questions then depends upon the reader's view about what international criminal law can achieve. On the one hand, then, the incorporation of system crimes into citizens' tribunals, and with that the provocation to incorporate them in some way into 'official' international criminal law, may be seen as a progressive move. On the other hand, the absence of structural violence from international criminal law may be seen as a stark reminder that we should not claim too much for international criminal law in the first place.[22] With these thoughts in mind, we now turn to the core crimes in international criminal law.

III. Genocide

The term 'genocide' was developed by Polish Jewish refugee lawyer and professor of international law, Raphael Lemkin. Lemkin, who lost 49 members of his family in the Holocaust, published *Axis Rule in Occupied Europe* in 1944,[23] in which he developed the term 'genocide', merging the Greek '*genos*' (race or tribe) with the Latin '*cide*' (killing). Genocide was not prosecuted as such at Nuremberg, although it did feature in the indictment. However, in 1946, General Assembly Resolution 96(1) affirmed that genocide was an international crime.[24] This was followed by the 1948 Convention on the Prevention and Punishment of Genocide (in force 12 January 1951).[25] Although a post-Second World War international legal development, the commission of genocide pre-dates the twentieth century. As the Preamble to the Genocide Convention recognises, 'at all periods of history genocide has inflicted great losses on humanity'.

Key to the prohibition of genocide is the protection of human diversity. As General Assembly Resolution 96(1) had recognised:

> Genocide is a denial of the right of existence of entire human groups, as homicide is the denial of the right to live of individual human beings; such denial of the right of existence shocks the conscience of mankind, results in great losses to humanity in the form of cultural and other contributions represented by these human groups ...[26]

---

[22] See further, eg, I Kalpouzos, 'International Criminal Law and the Violence against Migrants' (2020) 21(3) *German Law Review* 571 discussing at 595–97 the 'fetishization of international criminal law'.

[23] R Lemkin, *Axis Rule in Occupied Europe* (Carnegie Endowment for International Peace, Division of International Law, 1944).

[24] UNGA Res 96(1) (n 2). See further R Lemkin, 'Genocide as a Crime under International Law' (1947) 41(1) *American Journal of International Law* 145.

[25] Convention on the Prevention and Punishment of the Crime of Genocide 9 December 1948, GAR 260 A(III).

[26] See further *The Prosecutor v Krstić*, 19 April 2004, Judgment, ICTY IT-98-33-A, para 36: 'Those who devise and implement genocide seek to deprive humanity of the manifold richness its nationalities,

The Genocide Convention affirms that genocide is an international crime (Article I) and obliges contracting parties to prevent and punish it in peace and war. However, Article II defines genocide restrictively, which limits the application of the Genocide Convention in many situations that would be seen as genocidal from a non-legal or sociological perspective. In other circumstances, its application is assured only with some significant legal gymnastics. As the report of the Independent International Commission of Inquiry on the Syrian Arab Republic observed:

> It is worthy of note that 'genocide' as it exists in the public imagination often departs from the legal definition. The colloquial use of the term 'genocide', steeped in images of the Holocaust and the Rwandan genocide, has tended to signify the organised extermination of masses of civilians, regardless of the specific intention behind the killings. This is not, however, the legal definition of the crime of genocide. Whether a genocide has occurred, by a mass killing or not, hinges upon the existence in the perpetrator's mind, at the time of the commission of the prohibited act, of a specific intent to destroy, in whole or in part, a protected group by one of the specified methods, alongside the intent to commit the specified act.[27]

A finding of genocide – as opposed to a crime against humanity, for example – does not influence sentencing, nor does it determine the relative gravity of the conduct. However, there is expressive value in acknowledging a situation as genocidal, thus ensuring that the label given adequately captures the offence. For the PPT on Sri Lanka:

> The recognition that the Tamil people of Sri Lanka were persecuted, harassed and killed not just as individuals but as a group with its own identity, is fundamental in any attempt to confront the genocidal objectives of identity destruction and it is also a way to ratify the right of self-determination of any people.[28]

The distinction between genocide and other international crimes may also be critical in the context of states' obligations to prevent genocide, because this obligation is expressly included in the Genocide Convention, whereas it has only been included in the *draft* articles on the Prevention and Punishment of Crimes against Humanity 2019.[29]

As already noted, the key to distinguishing genocide from other international crimes lies in its distinctive mens rea, that is the 'intent to destroy, in whole or

---

races, ethnicities and religions provide. This is a crime against all humankind, its harm being felt not only by the group targeted for destruction, but by all of humanity.'

[27] Independent International Commission of Inquiry on the Syria Arab Republic, 'They Came to Destroy': ISIS Crimes Against the Yazidis, 15 June 2016, A/HRC/32/CRP2, para 13.

[28] PPT, *Peoples' Tribunal on Sri Lanka*, 7–10 December 2013 (PPT 2014) 15 at www.ptsrilanka.org/wp-content/uploads/2017/04/ppt_final_report_web_en.pdf.

[29] Art 4, ILC Draft Articles on Prevention and Punishment of Crimes against Humanity 2019 A/74/10, *Yearbook of the International Law Commission* 2019, vol II, available at https://legal.un.org/ilc/texts/instruments/english/draft_articles/7_7_2019.pdf.

in part, a national, ethnical, racial or religious group as such', and an apparently exhaustive list of actus rei in Article II:

(a)   Killing members of the group
(b)   Causing serious bodily or mental harm to members of the group;
(c)   Deliberately inflicting on the group conditions of life calculated to bring about its physical destruction in whole or in part;
(d)   Imposing measures intended to prevent births within the group;
(e)   Forcibly transferring children of the group to another group.

Notably, this list does not include SGBV (unlike the comparable provision in the Malabo Protocol). It was not until the ground-breaking judgment in the *Akayesu* case at the ICTR that it was held that rape and sexual violence could be genocidal. This finding was serendipitous because, although victim-witnesses testified to rape during their examination-in-chief and in response to questions from Judge Pillay, the sole female judge on the Bench, rape had not originally been charged in the indictment.[30]

Two aspects of genocide have proved particularly problematic. The first is the distinctive mens rea, that is, the intention to destroy in whole or in part a national, ethnical, racial or religious group; and the second is the limited groups that the Genocide Convention protects.

The specific intent can be difficult to prove and may be problematic in the collective context in which genocide occurs. Courts have responded to the challenge of establishing genocidal intent by inferring specific intent. A paradigmatic example is the *Akayesu* case:

> The Chamber considers that intent is a mental factor which is difficult, even impossible, to determine. This is the reason why, in the absence of a confession from the accused, his intent can be inferred from a certain number of presumptions of fact. The Chamber considers that it is possible to deduce the genocidal intent inherent in a particular act charged from the general context of the perpetration of other culpable acts systematically directed against that same group, whether these acts were committed by the same offender or by others. Other factors, such as the scale of atrocities committed, their general nature in a region or a country, or furthermore, the fact of deliberately and systematically targeting victims on account of their membership of a particular group, while excluding the members of other groups, can enable the Chamber to infer the genocidal intent of a particular act.[31]

---

[30] The subsequent amendment of the indictment paved the way for its normatively historic judgment that rape and sexual violence could constitute genocide: *Prosecutor v Jean-Paul Akayesu*, 2 September 1998, ICTR-96-4-T. After this decision, a number of indictments were amended to include charges of sexual violence and rape, but commentators have criticised subsequent practice at the ICTR for insufficient attention to SGBV. See, eg, B Norwojee, '"Your Justice is Too Slow" Will the ICTR Fail Rwanda's Rape Victims?' United Nations Research Institute for Social Development Occasional Paper (United Nations Research Institute for Social Development, 2005) at www.unrisd.org/80256B3C005BCCF9/ (httpPublications)/56FE32D5C0F6DCE9C125710F0045D89F?OpenDocument. See further, eg, KD Askin, 'Gender Crimes Jurisprudence in the ICTR' (2005) 3 *Journal of International Criminal Justice* 1007; S Balthazar, 'Gender Crimes and the International Criminal Tribunals' (2006) 10 *Gonzaga Journal of International Law* 42; R Copelon, 'Gender Crimes as War Crimes: Integrating Crimes against Women into International Criminal Law' (2000) 46 *McGill Law Journal* 217.

[31] *Prosecutor v Jean-Paul Akayesu* (n 30) para 523.

However, inferring specific intent in this way is controversial. Some commentators have advocated instead an approach that distinguishes between the intention required at the individual (or micro) level on the one hand, and the collective (or macro) level on the other, and between the intention required for top-, mid- and low-level perpetrators.[32] Individuals have also been charged instead with aiding and abetting genocide or joint criminal enterprise, rather than as direct perpetrators (see chapter 6).

Second, the Genocide Convention is criticised for the limited groups that it protects. General Assembly Resolution 96(1) acknowledged that genocides had taken place against 'racial, religious, *political and other groups*'.[33] While early drafts of the Genocide Convention included physical, biological and cultural genocide, as well as genocide against political groups, the drafting process that led to the adoption of the Convention limited the protected groups against which genocide could be committed and the means by which genocide could take place. Whether the Genocide Convention should encompass political and cultural genocide was controversial. The Soviet Union was amongst the states that objected to the inclusion of political groups. The US, which did not ratify the Genocide Convention until 1988, was amongst those, including colonial, former colonial and settler states, opposed to the inclusion of cultural genocide.[34] Moreover, despite arguments for the inclusion of economic genocide by Latin American states and Saudi Arabia, this was also excluded.[35] The exclusion of these groups, coupled with problems tribunals face in defining racial and ethnic groups in particular, potentially restricts the application of the Genocide Convention.[36] To take just one example, approximately 1.7 million Cambodians were killed between 1975 and 1979 under the Pol Pot regime. However, the ECCC only charged genocide in Case 002/02 in respect of acts against the Vietnamese and Cham minorities.[37] The Cambodian citizens targeted were members of political, economic or social groups, and therefore

---

[32] For further discussion, see, eg, T Williams and D Pfeiffer, 'Unpacking the Mind of Evil: A Sociological Perspective on the Role of Intent and Motivations in Genocide' (2017) 11(2) *Genocide Studies and Prevention: An International Journal* 72, 73. For discussion of knowledge and purpose-based approaches to the specific intent of genocide, see AKA Greenawalt, 'Rethinking Genocidal Intent: the Case for a Knowledge-Based Interpretation' (1999) 99 *Columbia Law Review* 2259.

[33] UNGA Res 96(1) (n 2) (emphasis added).

[34] See further, YK Tefferi, 'The Genocide Convention and the Protection of "Political Groups" against the Crime of Genocide' (2017) 5 *Mekelle University Law Journal* 29, 32–33, 37–41. For an extensive discussion on the drafting history, see WA Schabas, *Genocide in International Law* (Cambridge University Press, 2009).

[35] PS Morris, 'Economic Genocide under International Law' (2018) 82(1) *Journal of Criminal Law* 18, 19.

[36] See further, on the difficulties of defining such groups, C Lingaas, 'The Elephant in the Room: The Uneasy Task of Defining "Racial" in International Criminal Law' (2015) 15 *International Criminal Law Review* 485; C Lingaas, 'Imagined Identities: Defining the Racial Group in the Crime of Genocide' (2016) 10(1) *Genocide Studies and Prevention: An International Journal* 79; A Szpak, 'National, Ethnic, Racial and Religious Groups Protected against Genocide in the Jurisprudence of the Ad Hoc International Criminal Tribunals' (2012) 23(1) *European Journal of International Law* 155.

[37] Nuon Chea and Khieu Samphan were convicted of genocide of the Vietnamese as an ethnic, racial and national group, and Nuon Chea was found guilty of genocide of the Cham as an ethnic and religious

did not fall within the definition of genocide under the Genocide Convention. Some national jurisdictions have adopted a broader definition of the protected groups but, even so, the identification of recognised groups remains problematic.

Tribunals have struggled to objectively identify distinct racial and ethnic groups, categories that may also intersect. It is now widely recognised that race is 'socially constructed' rather than biologically determined.[38] DeFalco and Mégret observe 'that international crimes such as genocide have their origins in outdated notions of race as an actual biological reality that have long been discredited'.[39] In *Akayesu*, the Trial Chamber was faced with the question of how to define an ethnic group. It drew on the *travaux préparatoires* to affirm that the Genocide Convention protected groups that were 'stable' and 'permanent', unlike economic and political groups.[40] As a result, it found that the Tutsi were a protected ethnic group within the Genocide Convention, even though they shared the same language and culture with the Hutu, with the differences between them driven mainly by social status.[41] The reasoning of the Court – although not the finding that the Tutsi were a distinct ethnic group – has since been criticised, with subsequent decisions typically focusing case by case on the subjective perceptions of perpetrators (mainly) as to the existence of a protected group, alongside more objective criteria, although there are continued differences in approaches amongst and within relevant tribunals.[42]

The challenge of identifying ethnic groups arose in the context of Sudan. The ICC Pre-Trial Chamber in *Prosecutor v Al Bashir* took the view that there were reasonable grounds to believe the Fur, Masalit and Zaghawa were 'distinct ethnic groups as each of them has its own language, its own tribal customs and its own traditional links to their lands'.[43] This was a departure from the approach of the UN Commission on Darfur, which had considered that '[t]hose tribes in Darfur who support rebels have increasingly come to be identified as "African" and those supporting the government as the "Arabs"', continuing:

> The Arab-African divide has also been fanned by the growing insistence on such divide in some circles and in the media. All this has contributed to the consolidation of the

group. *Co-Prosecutors v Nuon (Chea) and Khieu (Samphan)* Case No 002/02 19-09-2007/ECCC/TC, 16 November 2018. The conviction of Samphan was affirmed on appeal, while Nuon Chea died before an appeal. See further, Lingaas, 'Imagined Identities' (n 36) 85.

[38] Lingaas, 'The Elephant in the Room' (n 36) 485–86.

[39] RC DeFalco and F Mégret, 'The Invisibility of Race at the ICC: Lessons from the US Criminal Justice System' (2019) 7(1) *London Review of International Law* 55, 61.

[40] *Prosecutor v Jean-Paul Akayesu* (n 30) para 516, although national and religious groups are not necessarily permanent and stable.

[41] Szpak (n 36) 160.

[42] See further Lingaas, 'The Elephant in the Room' (n 36) 509–10. And, although not a tribunal, see also International Commission of Inquiry on Darfur, Report to the United Nations Secretary-General Pursuant to SCR 564 of 18 September 2004, 25 January 2005, paras 509–10 at www.legal-tools.org/doc/1480de/pdf/.

[43] *Prosecutor v Omar Hassan Ahmad Al Bashir*, Second Decision on the Prosecution's Application for A Warrant of Arrest, 12 July 2010, ICC-02/05-01/09-94, para 9 (referring to the first decision on the arrest warrant).

contrast and gradually created a marked polarisation in the perception and self-perception of the groups concerned.[44]

The need to identify distinct racial groups can further 'the perpetuation of the categorisation of people'.[45] It can feed into simplistic portrayals of conflicts, particularly in Africa, as ethnic or tribal, and gloss over more complex causes. Identifying groups based on subjective criteria can temper these pitfalls to some extent. Schabas has observed that '[t]rying to find an objective basis for racist crimes suggests that the perpetrators act rationally, and this is more credit than they deserve'.[46] The subjective approach, then, can affirm that discrimination has no rational basis. For example, as the ICTR observed:

> In the early 1930s, Belgian authorities introduced a permanent distinction by dividing the population into three groups which they called ethnic groups … In line with this division, it became mandatory for every Rwandan to carry an identity card mentioning his or her ethnicity.[47]

A subjective approach can open a space for a longer-term historical account of the origins of, and processes behind, such perceptions.

Another challenge that has arisen from the conceptualisation of genocide as an attack against protected groups is that the distinct harm that an individual suffers can become subsumed within the attack against the protected group itself. This is a risk with all crimes of a collective nature, but it is of particular concern in the context of SGBV. The concern is that the need to identify the relevant protected group precludes the recognition that SGBV is intersectional. In other words, that victims are targeted on multiple grounds.[48] As the Commission on the Yazidi Women recognised:

> Yazidi women and girls are not, however, simply vessels through which ISIS seeks to achieve the destruction of the Yazidi religious group. Rape and sexual violence, when committed against women and girls as part of a genocide, is a crime against a wider protected group, but it is equally a crime committed against a female, as an individual, on the basis of her sex. … In treating the trauma arising from their sexual enslavement, care must be paid to the fact that Yazidi women and girls have been doubly victimized, on the basis of their religion and their sex.[49]

One response to the limitations of the Genocide Convention has been for commentators to call for a widening of the scope of genocide, including broadening the categories of groups against whom genocide can be committed. However, even if

---

[44] Report of the International Commission of Inquiry on Darfur (n 42) para 510. See further Lingaas, 'Imagined Identities' (n 36) 98, who notes that 'The Darfur Commission finds that the protected groups of genocide are social constructs rather than social facts.'

[45] Lingaas, 'The Elephant in the Room' (n 36) 488.

[46] Schabas (n 34) 128, as cited in Lingaas, 'The Elephant in the Room' (n 36) 512.

[47] *Prosecutor v Jean-Paul Akayesu* (n 30) para 83.

[48] See further, eg, AM Beringola, 'Intersectionality: A Tool for the Gender Analysis of Sexual Violence at the ICC' (2017) 9(2) *Amsterdam Law Forum* 84.

[49] Independent International Commission of Inquiry on the Syria Arab Republic (n 27) para 124.

the definition of genocide is widened through the addition of more groups, there will likely remain groups that are omitted. Without the requirement for a protected group, the crime becomes more like a crime against humanity than genocide (see section IV).

To varying degrees, citizens' tribunals have gone further in their approach to genocide, applying it in what Fraudatario and Tognoni have described as a 'provocative manner'.[50]

Article 1 of the non-binding, non-governmental Algiers Charter recognises that 'Every people has the right to existence'.[51] Article 4 provides:

> None shall be subjected, because of his national or cultural identity, to massacre, torture, persecution, deportation, expulsion or living conditions such as may compromise the identity or integrity of the people to which [he] belongs.[52]

Grave violations of the obligations contained in the Algiers Charter, 'especially of [the] right to existence', are international crimes attracting individual responsibility under Article 27 of the Algiers Declaration.

When citizens' tribunals address the crime of genocide, they do so in a wider range of situations than official tribunals, with varying degrees of adherence to strict legal norms. Citizens' tribunals have also read genocide alongside other proposed crimes, such as ethnocide[53] and sociocide.[54] Genocide has been considered by PPTs on El Salvador (1981), East Timor (1981) Guatemala (1983), Argentina (1980), the Brazilian Amazon (1990),[55] Sri Lanka (2013)[56] and Myanmar (2017).[57] They have also considered historic acts including genocide against the Armenians in 1915–17 (1984).[58] Furthermore, they have adopted a broader approach than official international criminal tribunals to the identification of genocide. Article 2 of the New Statute of the PPT recognises that genocide may be committed 'with intent to destroy, in whole or in part, a group selected *on a discriminatory criterion*'.[59] For PPTs, 'genocide is considered as expression of

---

[50] S Fraudatario and G Tognoni, 'The Participation of Peoples and the Development of International Law: The Laboratory of the Permanent Peoples' Tribunal' in A Byrnes and G Simm (eds), *Peoples' Tribunals and International Law* (Cambridge University Press, 2018) 133, 144.

[51] Algiers Charter: Universal Declaration of the Rights of Peoples, Algiers, 4 July 1976 at http://permanentpeoplestribunal.org/wp-content/uploads/2016/06/Carta-di-algeri-EN-2.pdf.

[52] ibid.

[53] See further the Declaration of the Fourth Russell Tribunal at www.nzdl.org/gsdlmod?e=d-00000-00---off-0ipc--00-0----0-10-0---0---0direct-10---4-------0-1l--11-en-50---20-about---00-0-1-00-0--4---0-0-11-10-0utfZz-8-00&cl=CL1.4&d=HASH2ad1a2bcf58fc2e5b9d458&x=1.

[54] See further 'New York Session October 2012', Russell Tribunal on Palestine, 6–8 October 2012 at www.russelltribunalonpalestine.com/en/sessions/future-sessions.html.

[55] See further, eg, Fraudatario and Tognoni (n 50) 143.

[56] PPT, *Peoples' Tribunal on Sri Lanka* (n 28).

[57] Fraudatario and Tognoni (n 50) 145.

[58] PPT, 16 April 1984, Verdict of the Tribunal at www.armenian-genocide.org/Affirmation.66/current_category.5/affirmation_detail.html. See further Fraudatario and Tognoni (n 50) 143.

[59] New Statute of the PPT (n 18) (emphasis added).

the institutional intention to destroy peoples' life and future'.[60] It is understood as a process.[61] Understanding genocide as a process means that 'some actions, even if not genocidal in themselves, imply the construction of the conditions which make the genocide viable'.[62] Many PPTs take 'account of social, cultural, political and economic factors as cause of the action of destruction',[63] an approach that Fraudatario and Tognoni argue is 'more faithful' to Lemkin's vision and 'to the real forms of violence against peoples developed since'.[64] For example, the PPT on Myanmar adopted an explicitly sociological approach to identifying intent when it examined what it saw as the different stages of the commission of genocide against Rohingyas and other minorities in Myanmar.[65] A broader approach is also illustrated by the terms of reference of the Myanmar PPT, for example, which include:

> to document and qualify the historical and *structural roots and causes* of the events, to avoid considering them as occasional incidents and strictly internal affairs of a still young and 'fragile democracy', with no political, strategic economic interactions with and impact on regional and global actors and interests.[66]

This emphasis is important, because economic factors are often omitted from international tribunals' accounts of the commission of genocide.[67] Despite the impact of economic policies and the role of external actors on some of the root causes of genocide, Morris observes that judgments contain only fleeting mention of economic conditions and their contribution to genocide, if at all.[68] In contrast, in a statement on genocide, which the Russell Tribunal accepted, Sartre claimed:

> All genocide is a product of history and it always carries the signs of the society from which it springs. The case which we have to judge concerns the largest contemporary capitalist power. It is as such that we must attempt to consider it; in other words,

---

[60] Fraudatario and Tognoni (n 50) 144.

[61] PPT, *Peoples' Tribunal on Sri Lanka* (n 28) 15. See also on genocide as a process, the Canadian Government-established 2019 National Inquiry into Missing and Murdered Indigenous Women and Girls in Canada, referring to a 'slow-moving process' of 'colonial genocide', cited in C Stahn, 'Confronting Colonial Amnesia' (2020) 18 *International Journal of Transitional Justice* 793, 802.

[62] PPT, *Peoples' Tribunal on Sri Lanka* (n 28) 16. Thus, the PPT considered that the 'construction of the Tamil population as alien to a unitary Sri Lankan state was a long process, which included legal and political decisions, as well as countless massacres, processes of discrimination, periods of armed conflict and finally, the implementation of an exterminatory project': ibid.

[63] Fraudatario and Tognoni (n 50) 144.

[64] ibid.

[65] It found that the state of Myanmar 'has the intent to commit genocide against the Kachin people and the other Myanmar Muslims' and is 'guilty of the crime of genocide against the Rohingya': PPT, 'State Crimes Allegedly Committed in Myanmar against the Rohingyas, Kachins and Other Groups' (University of Malaya, Faculty of Law, 18–22 September 2017) 46–48 at http://permanentpeoplestribunal.org/wp-content/uploads/2017/11/PPT-on-Myanmar-Judgment-FINAL.pdf. See further, AM Amin, 'The role of the PPT in securing the rights of Rohingya and other minorities in Myanmar' in RM Paulose (ed), *People's Tribunals, Human Rights and the Law Searching for Justice* (Routledge, 2020) 112.

[66] PPT, 'State Crimes Allegedly Committed in Myanmar' (n 65) 7 (emphasis added).

[67] Morris (n 35).

[68] ibid 24.

inasmuch as it expresses the economic structure, the political aims and the contradictions of that power.[69]

Zunino explains that the 'Vietnam War was presented as one episode in a worldwide struggle of the people against capitalist imperialism', with the tribunal 'foreground[ing] the international economic system's role in the production of violence'.[70] Similarly, the PPT on Myanmar found an account of genocide that emphasised 'a "natural" enmity towards a group' incomplete, 'dangerous' as well as 'highly misleading' to the extent that it might provide a 'justifying explanation' for the perpetrators and possibly observers.[71] Instead it married an explanation of the 'long standing antipathy towards the Rohingya' with broader economic and structural considerations, observing:

> As we have seen in recent decades, when authoritarian states begin to open up their economies and attempt a degree of democratisation, internal conflicts often follow, including attacks on minorities accompanied by an upsurge of extreme nationalism and supremacist ideology. This process seems to have occurred in recent years in Myanmar.

> In times of national economic hardship and political tensions such as exist in contemporary Myanmar, governments have generally found it extremely useful to target the 'Other' as the cause of problems affecting the majority. Given the situation in Myanmar, with an authoritarian government challenged to provide democracy and an effective economic performance failing to meet either challenge, it is not surprising that extreme measures have been put in place by the government to target minorities, thereby diverting attention from its own failures.[72]

Thus, it pointed to the impact of the opening-up of an authoritarian state and the economy on the scapegoating of minorities.[73] One reason this broader frame is possible is because citizens' tribunals focus on state not individual responsibility. As such they can offer an interpretation of genocide and its processes that is not open to official international criminal tribunals.

---

[69] J-P Sartre, 'On Genocide' in Coates, Limqueco and Weiss (eds) (n 16) 350, 350. For Sartre, genocidal intent was 'obvious from the facts'. He claimed (ibid 362) 'we do not have to worry about this psychological hide-and-seek. The truth is to be found *on the field*, in the racialism of the American troops.' See further M Zunino, 'Subversive Justice: The Russell Vietnam War Crimes Tribunal and Transitional Justice' (2016) 10 *International Journal of Transitional Justice* 211, 225; and Z Manfredi, 'Sharpening the Vigilance of the World: Reconsidering the Russell Tribunal as Ritual' (2018) 9(1) *Humanity* 75, 82–83.

[70] Zunino (n 69) 226.

[71] PPT, 'State Crimes Allegedly Committed in Myanmar' (n 65) 40.

[72] ibid 40–41.

[73] ibid 40. For the inclusion of cultural genocide in the context of the Russell Tribunal, see B Duerr, 'Political will and the people's will: The role of People's Tribunals in International Justice' in RM Paulose (ed), *Peoples Tribunals, Human Rights and the Law Searching for Justice* (Routledge, 2020) 22, 33.

IV. Crimes against Humanity

The origins of the concept of crimes against humanity are often traced to the 1915 Russian, British and American condemnation of the 'crimes of Turkey against humanity and civilization' committed against the Armenians.[74] However, it is really Nuremberg (and Tokyo) that gave birth to current understandings of crimes against humanity. As with genocide, the initial framing of crimes against humanity owed a debt to great power concerns. Thus, the definition of crimes against humanity set out in the International Military Tribunal (IMT) (Nuremburg) Charter, which was broadly followed by the International Military Tribunal for the Far East (IMTFE), linked crimes against humanity to crimes committed during war, and General Assembly Resolution 95(1) affirmed this requirement.[75] Article 6(c) of the IMT Charter defined crimes against humanity as

> murder, extermination, enslavement, deportation, and other inhumane acts committed against any civilian population, *before or during the war*, or persecutions on political, racial or religious grounds *in execution of or in connection with any crime within the jurisdiction of the Tribunal*, whether or not in violation of the domestic law of the country where perpetrated. (emphasis added)

At the London Conference (26 June–2 August 1945), Justice Jackson, representing the US, explained:

> We have some regrettable circumstances at times in our country in which minorities are unfairly treated. We think it is justifiable that we interfere or attempt to bring retribution to individuals or states only because the concentration camps and the deportations were in pursuance of a common plan or enterprise of making an unjust or illegal war in which we became involved. We see no other basis on which we are justified in reaching the atrocities which were committed inside Germany, under German law, or even in violation of German law, by authorities of the German state.[76]

The link between crimes against humanity and war may also have gone some way towards meeting criticism that prosecutions of crimes against humanity violated

---

[74] After the First World War, the Allies sought the prosecution of Turkish officials allegedly responsible for the Armenian massacre, having accused members of the Turkish Government of crimes against humanity and civilisation in 1915. The Treaty of Sevres 1920 obliged the Turkish Government to hand suspects over to the Allied Powers for trial before a tribunal to be established by the League of Nations. However, this Treaty was never ratified, and subsequently the Treaty of Lausanne included an amnesty for wartime offences. Some courts martial took place between 1919 and 1921. See further A Kramer, 'The First Wave of International War Crimes Trials? Istanbul and Leipzig' (2006) 14(4) *European Review* 441.

[75] General Assembly, Affirmation of the Principles of International Law Recognised by the Charter of the Nürnberg Tribunal, UNGA Res 95(1) (11 December 1946) UN Doc A/RES/95.

[76] As cited in R Dubler, 'What's in a Name? A Theory of Crimes against Humanity' (2008) 15 *Australian International Law Journal* 85, 89. CC Jalloh, 'What Makes a Crime Against Humanity a Crime Against Humanity?' [2013] *American University International Law Review* 381, 394.

the principle of *nullum crimen sine lege*.[77] The link between crimes against humanity and conflict has since been severed. Even though the ICTY Statute required this connection, it is now widely accepted that crimes against humanity, like genocide, can be committed in peacetime or during armed conflict.[78] There has also been an expansion in the prohibited conduct that constitutes crimes against humanity from Nuremberg and Tokyo to The Hague, including a greater focus on SGBV. However, in line with international criminal law more generally, this has not encompassed structural harm as such. Unlike for genocide, there is no treaty on crimes against humanity, although since 2013 this has been part of the work of the ILC,[79] the body within the UN responsible for the codification and progressive development of international law. The absence of a treaty means that while there are common elements to the definition of crimes against humanity, there are also variations depending on the law of the court or tribunal trying the offence. Along with these differences in practice, there are also several different views about the underpinning rationale of crimes against humanity.[80]

In essence, crimes against humanity are defined as comprising a widespread or systematic attack against a civilian population with knowledge of the attack. As already mentioned, each international criminal tribunal has applied a slightly different definition. Article 7 of the Rome Statute requires that one or more of a series of acts must have been committed (including murder, extermination, enslavement, torture) as part of a 'widespread or systematic attack directed against any civilian population, with knowledge of the attack' (otherwise known as the contextual requirement). A military attack is not required. Unlike genocide, crimes against humanity do not require a specific intent. Perpetrators must, however, know that their conduct is part of a widespread or systematic attack. For the purposes of the Rome Statute, the attack must also be pursuant to a state or organisational policy (Article 7(2)(a)). This requires the Court to consider whether non-state actors allegedly carrying out a crime against humanity are acting according to an organisational policy. The ICC considers that to qualify as an organisation for these purposes,

> the formal nature of the group and the level of its organization should not be the defining criterion. Instead, ... a distinction should be drawn on whether a group has the capability to perform acts which infringe on basic human values.[81]

---

[77] Jalloh (n 76) 394.

[78] *Prosecutor v Tadić*, Opinion and Judgment, 7 May 1997, ICTY IT-94-1-T, para 630.

[79] Draft Articles on Prevention and Punishment of Crimes Against Humanity adopted by the ILC 2019 at https://legal.un.org/ilc/texts/7_7.shtml. See further, eg, SD Murphy, 'The International Law Commission's Proposal for a Convention on the Prevention and Punishment of Crimes Against Humanity' (2018) 50 *Case Western Reserve Journal of International Law* 249.

[80] See further, eg, Jalloh (n 76); C Macleod, 'Towards a Philosophical Account of Crimes Against Humanity' (2010) 21(2) *European Journal of International Law* 28; D Luban, 'A Theory of Crimes Against Humanity' (2004) 29 *Yale Journal of International Law* 85.

[81] Situation in the Republic of Kenya, Decision Pursuant to Article 15 of the Rome Statute on the Authorization of an Investigation into the Situation in the Republic of Kenya, 31 March 2010, ICC-01/09-19-Corr, para 90. For the Chamber this required an analysis case by case. The Chamber

As already emphasised, current definitions of international crimes do not typically expressly include violations of social and economic rights. For the most part, the definition of crimes against humanity under the Rome Statute follows this approach. However, the definition of a crime against humanity is more open-ended than some other crimes. Where violations of social and economic rights, such as a violation of the right to food, are sufficiently severe and fulfil the other requirements of crimes against humanity, they could fall within definitions of crimes against humanity, more specifically within the more open-ended, catch-all provision 'other inhumane acts of similar character intentionally causing great suffering or serious injury to body or to mental or physical health' (Article 7(1)(k)).[82] For example, David Graham has argued that 'acts relating to social security policy which result in ESR's [economic and social rights] violations have the potential to be classified as a CAH [crimes against humanity] under the ICC Statute'.[83] Admittedly, a prosecution on this basis is unlikely, but the argument can seek to disrupt the normalisation of social and economic injustices. Such an argument is more likely when violations of social and economic rights are mobilised as part of political violence, however.

Another step is to deploy crimes against humanity to encompass structural harm. Ioannis Kalpouzos and Itamar Mann have been key proponents of the view that the OTP should and can address 'structural human rights violations rooted in global socio-economic inequality'.[84] In 2017, they were parties to a joint communiqué to the OTP under Article 15 of the Rome Statute (see chapter 7), which urged the OTP to investigate potential crimes against humanity, including unlawful imprisonment, torture, deportation, persecution and other inhumane acts constituting a widespread and systematic attack against refugees (as a civilian population) in off-shore detention facilities in Nauru and Manus Island.[85]

---

listed a number of non-exhaustive factors, which could be taken into account but which were not to be applied rigidly, including '(i) whether the group is under a responsible command, or has an established hierarchy, (ii) whether the group possesses, in fact, the means to carry out a widespread or systematic attack against a civilian population, (iii) whether the group exercises control over part of the territory of a State, (iv) whether the group has criminal activities against the civilian population as a primary purpose, (v) whether the group articulates, explicitly or implicitly, an intention to attack a civilian population, (vi) whether the group is part of a larger group, which fulfils some or all of the abovementioned criteria' (para 93).

[82] SI Skogly, 'Crimes Against Humanity Revisited: Is There a Role for Economic and Social Rights? (2001) 5(1) *International Journal of Human Rights* 58, 70–71. See further L Graham, '"Austerity" Policies as Crimes Against Humanity: An Assessment of UK Social Security Policy Since 2008' (2018) 9(1) *Queen Mary Law Journal* 5.

[83] Graham (n 82) 16.

[84] Kalpouzos and Mann (n 12) 3.

[85] J Cavallaro, D Sharmas and B Van Schaack et al, 'Communiqué to the Office of the Prosecutor of the International Criminal Court under Article 15 of the Rome Statute: The Situation in Nauru and Manus Island: Liability for Crimes Against Humanity (SLS Publications, 14 February 2017) at https://law.stanford.edu/publications/communique-to-the-office-of-the-prosecutor-of-the-international-criminal-court-under-article-15-of-the-rome-statute-the-situation-in-nauru-and-manus-island-liability-for-crimes-against-humanity/.

According to the website of the Global Legal Action Network, this was the 'most comprehensive submission on crimes against humanity perpetrated outside of context of war',[86] and it implicated corporate as well as individual actors.

The submission drew on Kalpouzos and Mann's research on the violation of asylum seekers' rights in Greece. They argue that although international criminal law 'cannot provide a solution' to structural injustice, it can 'be part of a larger necessary reorientation of international law towards such issues',[87] and provide a means to challenge the focus of international criminal legal practice on the global south.[88] They demonstrate that international criminal law could respond to structurally based harm – at least if the will is there. However, on 12 February 2020 the OTP responded by letter to similar concerns raised by Australian MEP, Andrew Wilkie, to the effect that the crimes alleged did not come within the Court's jurisdiction. The letter acknowledged that some of the underlying acts of crimes against humanity (imprisonment or severe deprivation of physical liberty) appeared to have been committed at least for a time, but that other acts (including other inhumane acts, persecution and deportation) had not. In addition, regarding imprisonment or severe deprivation of physical liberty (Article 7(1)(e) of the Rome Statute), the letter observed that

> there is insufficient information at this stage to indicate that the multiple acts of imprisonment or severe deprivation of liberty were committed pursuant to or in furtherance of a State (or organisational) policy to commit an attack against migrants or asylum seekers seeking to enter Australia by sea ... In this context, although Australia's offshore processing and detention programmes were initiated to pursue, among other things, a policy of immigration deterrence, as confirmed by official announcements and statements, the information available at this stage does not support a finding that cruel, inhuman, or degrading treatment was a deliberate, or purposefully designed, aspect of this policy.[89]

The OTP therefore did not consider that the contextual elements for a crime against humanity were present, a decision which Heller has described as 'shocking' because 'The Australian government did not,' he argued, 'simply "fail ... to address" the terrible conditions on Nauru and Manus Island. On the contrary, it *deliberately* created those conditions in order to deter future would-be asylum seekers from trying to reach Australia'.[90]

---

[86] Global Legal Action Network, 'Communication to International Criminal Court requesting investigation of Australia & Corporations' at www.glanlaw.org/single-post/2017/02/13/Communication-made-to-International-Criminal-Court-requesting-investigation-of-Australia-and-corporate-contractors.

[87] Kalpouzos and Mann (n 12) 3–4.

[88] ibid 25.

[89] Letter to Office of Andrew Wilkie MP at https://uploads.guim.co.uk/2020/02/14/200213-Andrew-Wilkie-Response-from-International-Criminal-Court-Australian-Government-treatment-of-asylum-seekers_(1).pdf. See further OTP, *Report on Preliminary Examination Activities 2020* (OTP, 14 December 2020) paras 44–55 at www.icc-cpi.int/itemsDocuments/2020-PE/2020-pe-report-eng.pdf.

[90] KJ Heller, 'The OTP Lets Australia off the Hook' *Opinio Juris* (17 February 2020) at http://opinio-juris.org/2020/02/17/the-otp-lets-australia-off-the-hook/.

The above arguments emphasise the possibility (and value) of including social and economic rights violations and structural harm within the framework of existing crimes against humanity. A further step is to consider accountability for the impact of economic policies themselves. In an essay designed to provoke debate, economist Max-Neef proposed an International Tribunal for Economic Crimes, modelled on the Russell Tribunal, with the aim of developing a concept of economic crimes against humanity. His concern was with harm that has its 'origin in economic processes that, in their turn, comply with economic policies and dominant economic theories'; from this perspective, economics lies at the root of other harms, including environmental harm.[91] He understands economic harms in a similar way to other international crimes. Thus, drawing on the Spanish economist Juan Torres Lopez, he argued that 'we know or can know' that foreseeable mass suffering results from certain ideologically driven economic policies, which simultaneously benefit 'certain minority power groups'.[92] Max-Neef appears to assume that it is possible to think about economic harm within an international criminal law framework. A citizens' tribunal might be particularly useful for this experimental thinking – not (just) because there is no alternative official tribunal but because it allows for experimentation with legal forms and people's engagement with the idea of economic crimes against humanity that Max-Neef hoped his proposal would generate.

V. War Crimes

Serious violations of international humanitarian law, that is the law that regulates the conduct of armed conflict, constitute war crimes. They do not need to form part of a widespread or systematic attack.[93] To understand war crimes, their limitations and potential, it is important to understand the laws of war or, as it came to be known in the second part of the twentieth century, international humanitarian law, the *jus in bello* (in contrast to the *jus ad bellum* or *jus contra bellum* dealing with the legality of the resort to force).

The nineteenth century is usually considered to mark the birth of the modern laws of war.[94] Broadly, two bodies of law constitute international humanitarian law. The Geneva law emerged out of the Red Cross Movement[95] and focuses on the

---

[91] MA Max-Neef, 'The good is the bad that we don't do: economic crimes against humanity: a proposal' (2014) 104 *Ecological Economics* 152. See further ibid 154.

[92] ibid 153.

[93] Although Art 8 of the Rome Statute specifies that the ICC has jurisdiction over war crimes, 'in particular when committed as part of a plan or policy or as part of a large-scale commission of such crimes'.

[94] See, eg, A Alexander, 'A Short History of International Humanitarian Law' (2015) 26(1) *European Journal of International Law* 109; M Howard, GJ Andreopoulos and MR Shulman, *The Laws of War: Constraints on Warfare in the Western World* (Yale University Press, 1994).

[95] For critical perspectives on the history of this movement, see further, eg, J-C Favez, *The Red Cross and the Holocaust* (Cambridge University Press, 1999); JG Hutchinson, *Champions of Charity: War and the Rise of the Red Cross* (Westview Press, 1996).

protection of non-combatants, such as the wounded, prisoners-of-war (POWs) and civilians. The Hague law emerged out of the Hague Peace Conferences from 1899 and deals with the means and methods of warfare. International humanitarian law endeavours to temper some of the immense suffering war causes by protecting those who are not – or no longer – engaged in hostilities, by prohibiting certain weapons and restricting particular methods of warfare. It seeks to balance humanitarian concerns on the one hand against legitimate military interests on the other. The attempt to 'humanise' the waging of war has a strong appeal. However, scholars have pointed out fundamental contradictions that run through the avowed subjection of war to humanitarianism. First, as Mégret has so powerfully shown, the laws of war historically failed to protect non-Europeans and therefore allowed means and methods of warfare against them that would have been condemned had they been directed against Europeans.[96] Second, states have repeatedly been reluctant to limit militarily useful means and methods of warfare,[97] and all too often the law has subordinated humanitarian interests to military necessity.[98] It has been argued that the legal balance between military necessity and humanity has since the nineteenth century swung more toward the side of humanity,[99] but even so – and this is the final point – armed conflict – even carried out according to international humanitarian law – remains inhumane. It is a problem if the cloak of legality interferes with our moral and political judgement about the destruction and devastation that armed conflict causes.[100]

Not all violations of international humanitarian law are war crimes. Article 6 of the IMT Charter described war crimes, the violations of the laws or customs of war, so as to

> include but not be limited to, murder, ill-treatment or deportation to slave labour or for any other purpose of civilian population of or in occupied territory, murder or ill-treatment of prisoners of war or persons on the seas, killing of hostages, plunder of public or private property, wanton destruction of cities, towns or villages, or devastation not justified by military necessity.[101]

---

[96] F Mégret, 'From "Savages" to "Unlawful Combatants": a Postcolonial Look at International Humanitarian Law's "Other"' in A Orford (ed), *International Law and its Others* (Cambridge University Press, 2006) 265, 268, 279 and 285.

[97] C af Jochnick and R Normand, 'The Legitimation of Violence: A Critical History of the Laws of War' (1994) 25 *Harvard International Law Journal* 49, 68–69.

[98] R Normand and C af Jochnick 'The Legitimation of Violence: A Critical Analysis of the Gulf War' (1994) 35(2) *Harvard International Law Journal* 387; Jochnick and Normand (n 97).

[99] R Cryer, D Robinson and S Vasiliev, *An Introduction to International Criminal Law and Procedure* (Cambridge University Press, 2019) 262. Alexander argues that by the end of the 20th century, *jus in bello* 'was a truly international humanitarian law, a law in which considerations of humanity trumped military necessity' (although she recognises the war on terror strains this): Alexander (n 94) 135.

[100] Normand and Jochnick 'Gulf War' (n 98), claiming that 'the laws serve to shield violence from humanitarian scrutiny' (at 399).

[101] Agreement for the prosecution and punishment of the major war criminals of the European Axis, 8 August 1945, 82 UNTS 279.

The indiscriminate bombings of cities on both sides during the Second World War, and the use of nuclear weapons over Hiroshima and Nagasaki, were not prosecuted. The exclusion of the use of nuclear weapons from the post-Second World War trials has been argued to have contributed to the normalising of nuclear weapons.[102] Nuclear weapons states also ensured that these weapons were excluded from the Rome Treaty of the ICC half a century later.

Modern international humanitarian law can be found in the four post-Second World War Geneva Conventions (1949) and two updating protocols (1977). Although each of the 1949 Geneva Conventions has a slightly different scope (individuals wounded and sick in the field, shipwrecked persons, POWs, and civilians in occupied territory), they share common articles and common fundamental principles. These Conventions presume that the dominant mode of conflict is between states, and set out detailed rules of conduct applicable to international armed conflicts between contracting parties, or to conflicts that have been internationalised. As a matter of law, then, it is important to know how an armed conflict is classified. This is not always self-evident. A conflict is internationalised where a third state intervenes directly or indirectly on behalf of an armed group. By providing arms, weapons or training (for example to armed groups fighting in another state), a state might internationalise a conflict, but it will be necessary to show that the state providing such assistance has 'overall control' over the group it is assisting.[103] Also treated as international conflicts under Article 1(4) of Additional Protocol I are 'armed conflicts in which peoples are fighting against colonial domination and alien occupation and against racist regimes in the exercise of their right to self-determination'.

This distinction between international and non-international armed conflicts is significant, because certain war crimes, for example so-called 'grave breaches' of the Geneva Conventions, are recognised only in the context of international armed conflict.[104] Grave breaches are violations of the Conventions carried out against protected persons, who are variously the wounded, sick, shipwrecked, POWs, or civilians in occupied territory.[105] States are required to prosecute or extradite anyone found on their territory whom they suspect of having committed a grave breach. However, conduct that would amount to a grave breach if committed in an international armed conflict will not amount to a grave breach in a non-international armed conflict (although it may constitute a war crime instead). Grave breaches are subject to universal jurisdiction and the obligation to prosecute or

---

[102] R Falk, 'War, War Crimes, Power, and Justice: Toward a Jurisprudence of Conscience' (2013) *Transnational Law and Contemporary Problems* 668, 670–71.

[103] *Prosecutor v Dusko Tadić*, Judgment in Appeal, 15 July 1999, ICTY IT-94-1-A, para 137. This means 'more than the mere provision of financial assistance or military equipment or training', but did not imply 'the issuing of specific orders by the State, or its direction of each individual operation'.

[104] POW status also only applies in an international, not non-international, armed conflict.

[105] Protocol I extended the range of grave breaches, although it is disputed whether all of these represent customary international law.

extradite (*aut dedere, aut judicare*). We shall come back to some of the different crimes applicable to international and non-international armed conflicts when we consider the Rome Statute below.

There is some, but more limited, regulation of non-international armed conflicts. Common Article 3 of the Geneva Conventions sets out minimum humanitarian obligations in a non-international armed conflict. The relatively short Protocol II also covers non-international armed conflicts. Several conditions must be satisfied before the Protocol applies (Article 1(1)), which are not required for the application of Common Article 3. Neither Protocol II nor Common Article 3 specifies criminal consequences for their breach. Until relatively recently, it was widely assumed that war crimes could only be committed – as a matter of law – in an international armed conflict.[106] However, practice since the 1990s has tempered the distinction between international and non-international armed conflicts. In its historic *Tadić* ruling, the ICTY held that 'a number of rules and principles govern-ing international armed conflicts have gradually been extended to apply to internal conflicts'.[107] Many war crimes are now therefore recognised in the context of a non-international armed conflict. The ICTR's jurisdiction included 'serious viola-tions' of Common Article 3 and 'serious' violations of Protocol II. However, the war crimes applicable in a non-international armed conflict do not fully replicate those that are applicable in an international armed conflict, and Article 8 of the Rome Statute maintains the distinction between the two types of conflict.[108]

The definition of war crimes under the Rome Statute is far from radical, the product of a consensus, although noteworthy for its inclusion of SGBV under Article 8(2)(b)(xxii) and Article 8(2)(c)(vi). The opposition of nuclear weapons states to the inclusion of nuclear weapons has already been noted. This exclusion led other states to object to the inclusion of chemical or biological weapons on the grounds that these were the 'poor man's weapons of mass destruction'.[109] The use of these weapons is, however, covered by general principles of international humani-tarian law, including the principles of proportionality and distinction (meaning that it is impermissible to attack directly civilians and civilian objects), as well as more specific provisions on the use of particular weapons, such as 'poison or poisoned weapons' (Article 8(2)(b)(xvii)), 'asphyxiating, poisonous or other gases' (Article 8(2)(b)(xviii)) and expanding bullets (Article 8(2)(b)(xix)).[110] However,

---

[106] Cryer, Robinson and Vasiliev (n 99) 267.

[107] *Prosecutor v Dusko Tadić*, Decision on the Defence Motion for Interlocutory Appeal on Jurisdiction, 2 October 1995, ICTY IT-94-1, para 126. It emphasised further that there had not been a 'full and mechanical transplant of those rules to internal conflicts, rather the general essence of those rules, and not the detailed regulation they contain, has become applicable to internal conflicts'.

[108] Cryer, Robinson and Vasiliev (n 99) 268, note that about 50% of the provisions on international armed conflicts are included in the provisions on non-international armed conflicts in the Rome Statute.

[109] ibid 290.

[110] See further RS Clark, 'Building on Article 8(2)(b)(XX) of the Rome Statute of the International Criminal Court: Weapons and Methods of Warfare' (2009) 12(3) *New Criminal Law Review* 366, 367–68.

these provisions on the use of weapons initially applied to international armed conflicts. It was not until the 2010 Kampala Review Conference that Article 8(2) (e) of the Rome Statute (on serious violations of the laws and customs of war applicable in a non-international armed conflict) was amended. This amendment made the use of 'poison or poisoned weapons', 'asphyxiating, poisonous or other gases' a war crime in a non-international armed conflict.

Specific weapons can also be prohibited and included in an annex to the Rome Statute (Article 8(2)(b)(xx)). Several controversial weapons are not, however, included in a specific ban, although their use could fall under the general principles above. These include the use of depleted uranium weapons and cluster weapons, labelled by their critics as inherently indiscriminate and causing unnecessary suffering or superfluous injury.[111] The citizens' tribunal on Afghanistan (judgment of Professor Bhagwat) referred to 'omnicide' in connection with the use of depleted uranium weapons, called for a cessation of their use, stockpiling and manufacture,[112] and found that international humanitarian law rendered depleted uranium weapons (along with fuel-air explosive devices (daisy cutters) and cluster bombs) illegal.[113]

In line with the distinction between international and non-international armed conflicts, the Rome Statute recognises four categories of war crimes. Applicable in international, including internationalised, armed conflicts are provisions on grave breaches of the Geneva Conventions (Article 8(2)(a)) and 'other serious violations of the laws and customs applicable in international armed conflict, *within the established framework of international law*' (Article 8(2)(b), emphasis added). In non-international armed conflicts, the following are applicable: serious violations of Common Article 3 (Article 8(2)(c)) and 'other serious violations of the laws and customs applicable in armed conflicts not of an international character, *within the established framework of international law*' (Article 8(2)(e), emphasis added). Each category enumerates the relevant crimes that fall within it.

A few examples illustrate the ongoing importance of the distinction between international and non-international armed conflicts. A fundamental principle of international humanitarian law is the principle of distinction, that is, that civilians are not to be made the object of attack. Under the Rome Statute, directing attacks against civilian objects (as opposed to civilian populations) is a war crime in an international, but not a non-international, armed conflict, whereas directing attacks against humanitarian assistance or peacekeeping missions is a war crime in both. Starvation of civilians and launching disproportionate attacks are only

---

[111] See, eg, A Womack, 'The Latest Nuclear War: Does the Use of Depleted Uranium Armaments and Armors Constitute a War Crime?' (2016) 41 *Vermont Law Review* 405, 407, describing the military deployment of depleted uranium 'a cheap, irresponsible, and deadly form of waste removal for the US'.
[112] Describing omnicide as 'the extermination of life, contamination of air, water and food resources; and the irreversible alteration of the genetic code of all living organisms including plant life; as a direct consequence of the use of radioactive munitions in Afghanistan; affecting countries in the entire region': International Criminal Tribunal for Afghanistan at Tokyo, '*The People v George Walker Bush*' Judgment of Professor Ms Niloufer Bhagwat (2004) 8(2) *World Affairs: The Journal of International Issues* 140, 155 and 156.
[113] ibid 150.

war crimes in international armed conflicts under the Rome Statute. For some commentators this conduct would constitute a crime in a non-international armed conflict in customary international law following the criteria set out in the *Tadić* case, even if its commission in a non-international armed conflict could not be prosecuted at The Hague.[114] The definitions of other crimes, for example the provisions on conscripting or enlisting child soldiers, may also vary depending on whether they are committed in a non-international or international armed conflict. Therefore, the finding that the conflict in the Democratic Republic of the Congo (DRC) was non-international at the time the crimes were committed was critical in *Lubanga*, where children had been conscripted into the *Force patriotiques pour la libération du Congo* and not into the national armed forces of the DRC, as would have been required for a war crimes charge had the conflict been considered an international one.[115]

In short, the current legal framework requires a rigorous classification of the relevant conflict (international, internationalised, non-international), because the classification of conflict determines the applicable law. An additional complication is that over time, the nature of the conflict may change, and more than one type of conflict may take place within a territory at the same time. Thus, a non-international armed conflict may at a certain point become internationalised. A non-international armed conflict between the government of a state and rebel groups may take place at the same time as an international armed conflict between the state and a third state. Difficult classification issues are also raised in the context of the asymmetric warfare typified by the so-called 'war on terror'.

Classifying the conflict with ISIS, for example, raises several challenges. On the one hand, the conflict crosses borders. On the other hand, unlike a conventional international armed conflict, it is not a conflict between two or more contracting parties.[116] Some have deployed the term 'a transnational or global non-international armed conflict', leading to the application of at least Common Article 3 of the Geneva Convention. This has the advantage that the basic principles of international humanitarian law apply. However, one disadvantage is that this approach can appear to legitimise a territorially unlimited theatre of operations.[117] The question of the geographical reach of the battlefield has been particularly prominent in the context of the US use of drones for targeted killings or so-called signature strikes.[118] The US has argued that drone strikes in Yemen, Somalia and Pakistan

---

[114] Cryer, Robinson and Vasiliev (n 99) 268.

[115] *Prosecutor v Lubanga*, Judgment, 5 April 2012, ICC-01/04-01/06-2842, paras 523–67.

[116] See further, eg, L Hajjar, 'The Counter Terrorism War Paradigm versus International Humanitarian Law: The Legal Contradictions and Global Consequences of the US "War on Terror"' (2019) 4 *Law and Social Inquiry* 922.

[117] See further, eg, International Committee of the Red Cross, 'International Humanitarian Law and the Challenges of Contemporary Armed Conflicts' EN 321C/15/11 (ICRC October 2015) 15. See further Hajjir (n 116) 949; Stahn (n 4) 79.

[118] See further, eg, N Lubell and N Derejko, 'A Global Battlefield? Drones and the Geographical Space of Armed Conflict' (2013) 11 *Journal of International Criminal Justice* 65.

are legal if they adhere to international humanitarian law.[119] Others have argued that, outside the immediate theatre of operations, human rights law (and not international humanitarian law) applies, because international humanitarian law only applies in cases of armed conflict, whereas human rights law applies during peace (and in armed conflict). While these bodies of law have some similarities, human rights law would prohibit such drone strikes in most cases.[120] Extending the application of international humanitarian law, then, may not necessarily restrict the use of force.[121] Against that, however, international humanitarian law could only legitimate the use of force if drone strikes satisfy the international humanitarian law principles of proportionality and distinction, a matter about which there is doubt, particularly in the context of 'signature strikes'.[122]

Finally, even when international humanitarian law is applied, it may still allow for considerable carnage.[123] Take the requirement of proportionality, one of the fundamental principles of international humanitarian law, alongside the principles of distinction, necessity and humanity. Article 8(2)(b)(iv) of the Rome Statute deals with proportionality – at least in the context of an international armed conflict – in the following way (emphasis added):

> *Intentionally* launching an attack *in the knowledge* that such attack will cause incidental loss of life or injury to civilians or damage to civilian objects or widespread, long-term and severe damage to the natural environment which would be *clearly excessive* in relation to the concrete and direct *overall* military advantage anticipated.

Thus, collateral damage even to civilians and civilian objects is permissible, but it must be proportionate. Assessing proportionality will inevitably involve difficult judgements, the outcomes of which are likely to depend on the viewer's standpoint, because military advantage and civilian loss are ultimately incommensurable. As was noted in the 'Final Report to the Prosecutor by the Committee Established to Review the NATO Bombing Campaign against the Federal Republic of Yugoslavia', 'It is unlikely that a human rights lawyer and an experienced combat commander would assign the same relative values to military advantage and to injury to non-combatants.'[124] However, this balancing act is tilted in favour of the military. Lawrence and Heller argue that Article 8(2)(b)(iv) of the Rome Statute seems to protect 'the zealous commander who routinely overestimates the military

---

[119] CA Jones, 'Lawfare and the Juridification of Late Modern War' (2016) 40(2) *Progress in Human Geography* 221, 226.

[120] ibid.

[121] See also Stahn (n 4) 75.

[122] See further, K Benson, '"Kill' Em and Sort It out Later:" Signature Drone Strikes and International Humanitarian Law' (2014) *Global Business and Development Law Journal* 17.

[123] See further, Normand and Jochnick 'Gulf War (n 98).

[124] International Criminal Tribunal for the former Yugoslavia, 'Final Report to the Prosecutor by the Committee Established to Review the NATO Bombing Campaign against the Federal Republic of Yugoslavia' (United Nations International Criminal Tribunal for the Former Yugoslavia nd) para 50 at www.icty.org/en/press/final-report-prosecutor-committee-established-review-nato-bombing-campaign-against-federal. See further Stahn (n 4) 88.

utility of his attacks' more 'than his more sober and conservative counterpart', and there is no requirement that his judgement about anticipated military advantage be reasonable.[125]

From a humanitarian perspective, armed conflict without legal restraint is unthinkable. However, as the above scholars have shown, international humanitarian law is problematic to the extent that it legitimises practice that still causes significant destruction. The judgements international humanitarian law requires are often incommensurable. Once again, international criminal lawyers can be faced with a conundrum. On the one hand they might not want to overemphasise the importance of questions about legality, given these limitations. On the other hand, it is important to emphasise the adherence to legal standards, if only as a bare minimum, given the devastation of unrestrained conflict.[126]

Here, as elsewhere, how international lawyers (and others) respond to the above dilemma is likely to depend on what they think law can achieve, in general and in this specific context. Some might encourage further reform of the law, for example by advocating limiting the distinction between international and non-international armed conflict; by expanding the range of prohibited weapons (as some citizens' tribunals seek to do); or by closely interrogating the adherence to the fundamental principles of international humanitarian law of the deployment of weapons not expressly prohibited. Others might instead focus on the effective enforcement of existing law, including by encouraging enhanced international humanitarian law training amongst military and civilian populations during peacetime. Some might do all the above while remaining sceptical of law's power to restrain, because the above at least is a contribution that law can make to mitigate the horrors of armed conflict. On the other hand, different preoccupations might dominate. For example, others might explore the legacies of the relationship between the laws of war and colonialism.[127] Others might seek to reimagine international humanitarian law in a way that addresses more firmly the underlying structures, causes and beneficiaries of conflict. It is particularly in thinking about how war crimes law might be re-thought that the work of citizens' tribunals provides a useful provocation.

Arundhati Roy claimed, in her opening speech at the World Tribunal on Iraq (WTI), that 'This tribunal is an attempt to correct the record. To document the history of the war not from the point of view of the victors but of

---

[125] JC Lawrence and KJ Heller, 'The First Ecocentric Environmental War Crime: The Limits of Article 8(2)(b)(iv) of the Rome Statute' (2007-08) 20 *Georgetown International Environmental Law Review* 61, 81.

[126] For a rich discussion of similar concerns in a related context (the question of the legality of the use of force against Iraq and the authors' public responses to it), see M Craven et al, '"We Are Teachers of International Law' (2004) 17 *Leiden Journal of International Law* 363.

[127] See further, eg, Mégret (n 96) 265; and for a feminist critique of the laws of war, see F Mégret, 'The Laws of War and the Structure of Masculine Power' (2018) 19(1) *Melbourne Journal of International Law* 200.

the temporarily … vanquished.'[128] What might war crimes law look like from the perspective of the 'vanquished' or subaltern subject? Interestingly, the New Statute of the PPT defines war crimes as 'the crimes referred to in Art 8' of the Rome Statute.[129] Given the issues with Article 8 of the Rome Statute noted above, this approach might be considered surprising. However, in practice, citizens' tribunals often inject a more radical perspective into their consideration of war crimes, both through their interpretations of specific crimes and through their more general framing of responsibility (chapter 6) and their tribunal practice. For example, in the WTI, several features were apparent. First, allegations of international crime were contextualised broadly, set within a history of the role of the west in the region, including its prior support for the Ba'ath regime,[130] and a longer-term history of British imperialism.[131] The abuses, Falk claimed in his opening statement on behalf of the Panel of Advocates, could not be separated from a US 'project of world empire' that 'hides its true colors beneath the banner of anti-terrorism'.[132] Second, as explored in the next chapter, because the focus of citizens' tribunals is typically not on individual criminal responsibility, the narratives they produce deal with systemic rather than individualised causes of harm. Alongside detailed accounts alleging abuses during the occupation, testimony was also given about the origins of wrongdoing by members of the military, which encompassed, it was claimed, features of soldiers' recruitment and military training.[133] Third, the WTI paid attention to the economic drivers and beneficiaries of conflict.[134] In her testimony, Bhagwat extended her analysis of pillage to take account of post-war reconstruction and the transformation of the economy and the legal system.[135] Furthermore, the WTI Jury of Conscience charged private corporations winning contracts for reconstruction with 'profiting from the war with complicity'.[136] Finally, following the approach of citizens' tribunals

---

[128] A Roy, 'Opening Speech of the Spokesperson of the Jury of Conscience' in MG Sökmen (ed), *World Tribunal on Iraq: Making the Case against War* (Olive Branch Press, 2008) 1, 2.

[129] Art 4, New Statute of the PPT (n 18).

[130] Roy (n 128) 3.

[131] L Everest, 'The History of US and UK Interventions in Iraq' in Sökmen (ed) (n 128) 35 ff.

[132] R Falk, 'Opening Speech on Behalf of the Panel of Advocates' in Sökmen (ed) (n 128) 5, 8.

[133] T Goodrich, 'The Conduct of the US Army' in Sökmen (ed) (n 128) 228, 228–33.

[134] See eg S Amin, 'The Militarization of Economy and the Economy of Militarization' in Sökmen (ed) (n 128) 404; Jury of Conscience, 'Declaration of the Jury of Conscience of World Tribunal on Iraq – Istanbul, 23–27 June 2005' in Sökmen (ed) (n 128) 492, 494, 496, 498. See further, albeit in another context, Sartre (n 69) 357.

[135] N Bhagwat, 'The Privatization of War' in Sökmen (ed) (n 128) 280 ff. Scholars have increasingly also sought to develop the law of pillage (Arts 8(2)(b)(xvi) and 8(2)(c)(v), Rome Statute), but international criminal prosecutors have typically focused on what Keenan describes as an 'episodic theory of pillage', that is 'relatively small-scale episodes of theft'. See, eg, PJ Keenan, 'Conflict Minerals and the Law of Pillage' (2014) 14(2) *Chicago Journal of International Law* 524, 527; Stahn (n 4) 86–87. Noteworthy is that Art 28L *bis* of the Malabo Protocol criminalises 'the illegal exploitation of natural resources'. See further, SC Wisner, 'Criminalizing Corporate Actors for Exploitation of Natural Resources in Armed Conflict' (2018) 16 *Journal of International Criminal Justice* 963.

[136] Jury of Conscience (n 134) 492, 498.

more generally (see chapter 6), the WTI aimed to generate resistance, including conscientious objection, explored in more detail in section VI.[137]

It would be overly simplistic to claim that citizens' tribunals inevitably promulgate a vision of international humanitarian law or war crimes law from the perspective of the victims of armed conflict, even if they do provoke the critically important question of what war crimes law might look like from the perspective of those who have become caught up in conflict unwillingly. However, as the above illustrates, citizens' tribunals can provide a counter-point to dominant narratives about conflict, in particular when powerful states are involved, and they can suggest alternative interpretations of law that address broader causes and consequences of violence, for example by highlighting international humanitarian law's myopia in relation to the economic facets of conflict and post-conflict situations. It is not just the *jus in bello* that citizens' tribunals challenge. An alternative and more people-centred approach can also be seen in the WTI's approach to the question of aggression, the final and perhaps most controversial of the core crimes included within the Rome Statute.

VI. Aggression

Although at the end of the First World War the majority view was that aggression was not an international crime, by the end of the Second World War, the US was strongly advocating for its prosecution.[138] Article 6(a) of the IMT Charter provided for the prosecution of crimes against peace, that is the

> planning, preparation, initiation or waging of a war of aggression, or a war in violation of international treaties, agreements or assurances, or participation in a common plan or conspiracy for the accomplishment of any of the foregoing.

Although these novel charges were controversial, the IMT considered that aggression (albeit without defining it) was 'the supreme international crime differing only from other war crimes in that it contains within itself the *accumulated evil* of the whole'.[139] Despite this, the post-Second World War period was marked by states' failure to agree a definition of aggression, which in turn stymied efforts to formulate a comprehensive code against the peace and security of mankind and a permanent international criminal court. However, in 1974, General Assembly Resolution 3314 set out a non-binding definition of aggression. This distinguished

---

[137] ibid 501. See further, in relation to the Russell Tribunal, AJ Klinghoffer and JA Klinghoffer, *International Citizens' Tribunals* (Palgrave, 2002) 109–10, 134.

[138] C Kress, 'On the Activation of ICC Jurisdiction over the Crime of Aggression' (2018) 16(1) *Journal of International Criminal Justice* 1, 8. But see Art 231 of the Treaty of Versailles, the so-called 'war guilt clause'. See further, K Sellars, 'Delegitimizing Aggression: First Steps and False Starts after the First World War' (2012) 10 *Journal of International Criminal Justice* 7, 14. C Kress, 'The Iraqi Special Tribunal and the Crime of Aggression' (2004) 2 *Journal of International Criminal Justice* 347.

[139] Judgment IMT (1947) 41 *AJIL* 172, 218 (emphasis added).

between an undefined 'war of aggression', which was a 'crime against international peace' giving rise to individual criminal responsibility, and 'an act of aggression', giving rise to international responsibility (Article 5(2)).[140] The ILC Draft Code of Crimes against the Peace and Security of Mankind 1996 also failed to define aggression (Article 16).[141] The ad hoc tribunals and hybrid bodies established in the 1990s excluded it. The Iraqi Special Tribunal Statute incorporated aggression, but likely because of concerns about *tu quoque* arguments,[142] it was a limited definition and only included as a crime under domestic, and not international, law.[143] Bosco observes that intervention by NATO against the Former Republic of Yugoslavia exacerbated the unwillingness amongst many western states to include aggression in the Rome Statute.[144] At Rome, the five permanent member states were concerned to safeguard the role of the Security Council as the body with primary responsibility for international peace and security, but finally the conference was able to agree to the inclusion of aggression as a core crime, subject to its subsequent definition and subject to an agreement on the conditions under which the ICC could exercise jurisdiction (Article 5(1)(d) of the Rome Statute).

The Preparatory Commission's Working Group on the Crime of Aggression and, from 2002, the Special Working Group on the Crime of Aggression became responsible for developing proposals on aggression.[145] Eventually, in February 2009, the Assembly of States Parties (ASP) adopted the Working Group's proposal on aggression, which was presented to the Kampala Review Conference. At Kampala, it was agreed to amend the Rome Statute to enable the ICC to exercise jurisdiction over aggression. These amendments required ratification. A two-stage process was agreed. This required 30 states to ratify the amendments and, after a year, the ASP to decide by a two-thirds majority to activate the amendments after 1 January 2017.[146] On 15 December 2017, the ICC's jurisdiction over aggression was activated.

The circumstances in which aggression may be prosecuted at the ICC are more restrictive than for other crimes, although not as restrictive as they might have been. States may opt-out of the ICC's jurisdiction for aggression under Article 15*bis*(4) of the Rome Statute. Additionally, the United Kingdom (UK) and France insisted that, in situations not referred by the SC, the territorial and nationality

---

[140] UNGA Res 3314 (XXIX) (14 December 1974) UN Doc A/RES/3314, Arts 1–5.

[141] International Law Commission, Draft Code of Crimes against the Peace and Security of Mankind 1996, *Yearbook of the International Law Commission 1996*, vol II (Part Two) at https://legal.un.org/ilc/texts/instruments/english/draft_articles/7_4_1996.pdf.

[142] JE Alvarez, 'Trying Hussein: Between Hubris and Hegemony' (2004) 2 *Journal of International Criminal Justice* 319, 327.

[143] Defined under Art 14(c) as 'the abuse of position and the pursuit of policies that may lead to the threat of war or the use of the armed forces of Iraq against an Arab country'. Kress, 'The Iraqi Special Tribunal' (n 138) 348; Alvarez, 'Trying Hussein' (n 142) 327.

[144] D Bosco, *Rough Justice: The International Criminal Court in a World of Power Politics* (Oxford University Press, 2014) 67.

[145] Resolution F of the Final Act of the Rome Conference on the Establishment of an International Criminal Court, 17 July 1998, UN DOC A/Conf.183/10*.

[146] Art 15*bis*(2) and (3) and 15*ter*(2) and (3).

states must first have consented to the amendments, in line with Article 121(5) of the Rome Statute. In cases where a Prosecutor is acting *proprio moto* (see chapter 7) or based on a state referral, Article 15*bis* does not require Security Council consent for an investigation to proceed. However, the Prosecutor must consider whether the Security Council has determined, under Article 39 of the UN Charter, that an act of aggression has taken place, and if not, must wait six months before seeking Pre-Trial Division authorisation to proceed. The effect of these restrictions can be seen in the response to the situation in Ukraine. The ICC is unable to consider the crime of aggression in the situation in Ukraine because Russia and Ukraine are not parties to the Kampala amendments (or to the Rome Statute). The Security Council is unable to refer the situation because Russia is a veto-holding permanent member state. This had led several leading figures to call for the establishment of a special tribunal for the punishment of the crime of aggression against Ukraine.[147] A model criminal indictment has been drafted by the Open Society Justice Initiative against Putin and others, which could be drawn on in national or international proceedings.[148] Others have responded to this jurisdictional challenge by suggesting the prosecution of aggression as a crime against humanity, specifically as an 'other inhumane act'.[149]

Article 8*bis*(1) of the Rome Statute defines the 'crime of aggression' as the

> planning, preparation, initiation or execution by a person in a position effectively to exercise control over or to direct the political or military action of a State, of an act of aggression which, by its character, gravity and scale, constitutes a manifest violation of the Charter of the United Nations.

An 'act of aggression' is defined in Article 8*bis*(2) as

> the use of armed force by a State against the sovereignty, territorial integrity or political independence of another State, or in any other manner inconsistent with the Charter of the United Nations.

The article then lists exhaustively acts that constitute aggression following General Assembly Resolution 3314.[150]

Mark Drumbl has criticised the definition of aggression for several reasons. One major concern is its state-centrism. The fact that states are constructed as

---

[147] See, eg, G Brown et al, 'Statement Calling for the Creation of a Special Tribunal for the Punishment of the Crime of Aggression Against Ukraine' (6 January 2023) at https://gordonandsarahbrown.com/wp-content/uploads/2022/03/Combined-Statement-and-Declaration.pdf.

[148] R Goodman and R Hamilton, 'Model Indictment for Crime of Aggression Against Ukraine Prosecutor v President Vladimir Putin' *Just Security* (14 March 2022) at www.justsecurity.org/80669/model-indictment-of-the-crime-of-aggression-against-ukraine-vladimir-putin/2022; www.justsecurity.org/81411/osji-model-indictment-for-the-crime-of-aggression-committed-against-ukraine/.

[149] G Pinzauti and A Pizzuti, 'Prosecuting Aggression against Ukraine as an "Other Inhumane Act" before the ICC' (2022) 20 *Journal of International Criminal Justice* 1061.

[150] See further, K Ambos, 'The Crime of Aggression after Kampala' (2010) 53 *German Yearbook of International Law* 463, 487.

both the victims and perpetrators of aggression excludes threats to international peace and security that emanate from non-state actors, which, for example, limits the utility of the crime in the context of asymmetric warfare amongst others.[151] Drumbl also suggests that this state centrism fails to encompass the full range and nature of the threats to peace that confront 'the global community, in particular ... developing nations'.[152] In contrast, Article 28A of the Malabo Protocol recognises that 'a state or organization, whether connected to the state or not' can commit aggression. Another concern, which has been raised elsewhere, is the threshold requirement. As Article 8*bis*(1) of the Rome Statute states (emphasis added), to be a crime, an act of aggression by its 'character, gravity *and* scale' must constitute 'a manifest violation of the Charter of the United Nations'. For example, legally uncertain deployments of the use of force are unlikely to constitute aggression because they are unlikely to be a 'manifest violation'.[153] As a result, it is anticipated that, at least for now, the ICC would exclude humanitarian intervention from the definition of aggression. Scholars have also highlighted problems stemming from the designation of aggression as a leadership crime. Drumbl has argued that the effective exculpation of those below the leader fails to encourage resistance.[154] Typically, courts have been unsympathetic to military personnel making such claims. For example, in April 2006, Flight Lieutenant Kendall-Smith was found guilty in court martial of disobeying a lawful command relating to training and deployment to Iraq.[155] He had argued that he did not want to be complicit in aggression. The court martial emphasised that

> responsibility for [aggression] does not trickle down to those at lower levels of the chain of command. The order for you to go to Basra cannot therefore have made you complicit to such a crime given your junior rank and position as a doctor.[156]

In contrast, citizens' tribunals, which have concerned themselves with aggression since their inception, have sought to mobilise resistance to aggression and support conscientious objection, alongside a more explicitly human-centred

---

[151] MA Drumbl, 'The Push to Criminalize Aggression: Something Lost Amid the Gains?' (2009) 41 *Case Western Reserve Journal of International Law* 291, 305–06; see also, on quasi-states, SD Bachmann and Y Abdelkader, 'Reconciling Quasi-States with the Crime of Aggression under the ICC Statute' (2018) 33 *Emory International Law Review* 91.

[152] Drumbl (n 151) 308.

[153] See further, T Ruys, 'Criminalizing Aggression: How the Future of the Law on the Use of Force Rests in the Hand of the ICC' (2018) 29(3) *European Journal of International Law* 887, 893.

[154] Drumbl (n 151) 316–17.

[155] H Gulam and M O'Connor, 'Selective Conscientious Objection: The Court-Martial of Flight Lieutenant Malcolm Kendall-Smith, RAF' (2006) 7 *ADF Health* 68.

[156] Cited in SD Bachmann and G Kemp, 'The International Crime of Aggression in the Context of the Global "War On Terror": Some Legal and Ethical Perspectives' (2010) 2 *Journal for South African Law* 309, 326. See further, on the right to disobey, T Dannenbaum, 'Why Have We Criminalized Aggressive War?' (2017) 126 *Yale Law Journal* 1242, 1309–12. This decision contrasted with the decision of the German *Bundesverwaltungsgericht* which overturned the conviction of Major Pfaff; Bachmann and Kemp (above) 327–28. The court considered the war to be 'substantially unlawful', with the resulting moral dilemma entitling the defendant to disobey.

approach to security.[157] The WTI illustrates this juridical understanding of a people's approach to aggression.

The WTI found that the invasion and occupation of Iraq was illegal, and charged the UK and US Governments with having planned, prepared and waged a war of aggression in violation of the UN Charter and the Nuremberg principles. It recommended the withdrawal of the coalition forces and an 'exhaustive investigation of those responsible'.[158] It found that international legal and political institutions had failed to prevent the war and ensure accountability,[159] and it therefore charged the SC, amongst others, for 'failing to protect the Iraqi *people* against the crime of aggression'.[160]

Resistance to the war was central to the WTI's approach. According to the opening statement of the Declaration of the Jury of Conscience:

> In February 2003, weeks before an illegal war was initiated against Iraq, millions of people protested in the streets of the world. That call went unheeded. No international institution had the courage or conscience to stand up to the threat of aggression of the US and UK governments.[161]

The Declaration charged the US and UK with having committed a crime against peace 'by violating the will of the global anti-war movement'.[162] The WTI emphasised the legitimacy of resistance to the occupation[163] and urged that people 'launch nonviolent actions against US and UK corporations' profiting directly from the war, including 12 listed corporations.[164] Moreover, it urged states to provide political asylum to conscientious objectors.[165] Indeed, the session was framed to provide a basis for a record that could be deployed 'as legitimate grounds for conscientious objection'.[166]

The WTI documented wide-ranging social, economic and security consequences of the occupation.[167] Far from positioning aggression as an abstract crime against the state, it emphasised its human consequences for the Iraqi people, highlighting people as victims of aggression.[168] In that sense, it arguably came closer

---

[157] eg, the recommendations of the WTI were explicitly directed at, inter alia, laying 'the groundwork for a world in which ... human security will prevail over state security and corporate profits'. Jury of Conscience (n 134) 501.

[158] ibid 500.

[159] ibid 493.

[160] ibid 497 (emphasis added). By sanctioning the occupation, the WTI argued, the Security Council became 'a collaborator in an illegal occupation': ibid 498.

[161] Jury of Conscience (n 134) 492.

[162] ibid 497. See further A Çubukçu, *For the Love of Humanity The World Tribunal on Iraq* (University of Pennsylvania Press, 2019) 68.

[163] Jury of Conscience (n 134) 494.

[164] ibid 500.

[165] ibid 501. See further on resistance, Çubukçu (n 162) 82–83.

[166] MG Sökmen, 'Preface' in Sökmen (ed) (n 128) x. See also Dannenbaum (n 156) 1308–10.

[167] Jury of Conscience (n 134) 493–94.

[168] ibid 497.

to the understanding of crimes against peace at Nuremberg and Tokyo.[169] Its approach challenges the claims of those who argue that aggression is a different kind of crime from the other core crimes because it is inherently a political crime against the state.[170] The emphasis on the political nature of the crime of aggression also risks underplaying the inherently political nature of international criminal law more generally.

VII. Conclusion

This chapter has introduced the core crimes in international criminal law and the alternative approaches adopted towards them by citizens' tribunals. Since there is no clearly accepted underpinning rationale for international crimes, their definitions are susceptible to the political and historical contingencies existing at the time of their creation. At the same time, as citizens' tribunals have shown, the lack of a clear rationale for international crimes renders those definitions inherently contestable.

Critical voices have raised concern about the failure of international criminal law to deal with structural violence. Citizens' tribunals provide a powerful provocation for thinking about international crime more broadly, including by addressing structural and systemic harms.

To some extent – with political will – some forms of structural violence could be incorporated within existing international criminal law. How far it is desirable to extend definitions of international criminality in this way depends on what international criminal law can achieve, about which views differ. On the one hand, it might be considered that the achievements of international criminal law depend on positioning international crimes as exceptional, and that expanding categories of crime raises important doctrinal questions about legality and concerns about overreach. On the other hand, it might be thought that expanding the definition of international crimes challenges a western bias in international criminal law, and makes a powerful statement about human agency and responsibility for forms of suffering that are all too often normalised. However, even with a broader definition of international crime, an international criminal legal response – and one

---

[169] See further, eg, US Prosecutor Jackson at Nuremberg, '[w]ar necessarily is a calculated series of killings, of destructions of property, of oppressions', cited in Dannenbaum (n 156) 1283. The IMTFE considered that aggression was the most serious crime precisely because 'death and suffering will be inflicted on countless human beings', cited ibid 1284.

[170] See, eg, E Creegan, 'Justified Uses of Force and the Crime of Aggression' (2012) 10 *Journal of International Criminal Justice* 59. For a contrary view, see Dannenbaum (n 156) 1245, who argues that at the 'normative core' of the crime of aggression is the fact that individuals, including soldiers, are 'wronged gravely'. As a result, international law should 'take seriously the human rights and refugee claims of soldiers who refuse to fight in aggressive war' (ibid 1248). The crime of aggression, he argues, fills a 'crucial gap, providing otherwise missing criminal law protection to the right to life of combatants and collateral civilians' (ibid 1274–75).

that focuses on the formal institutions in particular – is only ever incomplete, or part of a broader strategy. There might therefore be a certain ambivalence – for both pragmatic and normative reasons – in seeking the expansion of crimes under international law. Without it, however, the causes and consequences of atrocity will remain only partially addressed. It is here, then, that deploying international criminal law to generate resistance can be so productive, as evidenced in the practice of citizens' tribunals. The following chapter explores resistance further in relation to responsibility.

Further Reading

RC DeFalco, *Invisible Atrocities: The Aesthetic Biases of International Criminal Justice* (Cambridge University Press, 2022).

I Kalpouzos and I Mann, 'Banal Crimes Against Humanity: the Case of Asylum Seekers in Greece' (2015) 16 *Melbourne Journal of International Law* 1.

C Lingaas, *The Concept of Race in International Criminal Law* (Routledge, 2020).

MG Sökmen (ed), *World Tribunal on Iraq: Making the Case Against War* (Olive Branch Press, 2008).

6

Responsibility and Resistance

I. Introduction

This chapter provides an introduction to how responsibility is – and how else it might be – conceptualised in international criminal law. International criminal law is commonly criticised for taking a narrow approach to responsibility because it provides only for the prosecution of individuals. As Nuremberg famously pronounced:

> Crimes against international law are committed by men, not by abstract entities, and only by punishing individuals who commit such crimes can the provisions of international law be enforced.[1]

It is widely observed that the focus on individual criminal responsibility does not provide a complete response to international criminal offending because international crimes are inherently collective.[2] Courts and tribunals have sought to account for the collective element in the commission of international crime through interpretations of modes of liability. However, notwithstanding broad interpretations of modes of liability, individual criminal responsibility is still criticised for not addressing the wider social, economic and political processes and structures that underpin the commission of international crime. Relatedly, the mechanism of individual criminal responsibility does not reflect the range of actors who may be implicated in the commission of international crime or in the failure of efforts to prevent it. These actors may include corporations,[3]

---

[1] International Military Tribunal (Nuremberg), Judgment and Sentence, 1 October 1946, (1947) 41 *AJIL* 172, 221.

[2] A Nollkaemper, 'Introduction' in A Nollkaemper and H Van der Wilt (eds), *System Criminality in International Law* (Cambridge University Press, 2009) 1, 4. On system criminality, see ibid 1, where the author described it as 'the phenomenon that international crimes ... are often caused by collective entities in which the individual authors of these acts are embedded'. For a discussion of the Bosnian Women's Court's approach to system criminality, see K Campbell, *The Justice of Humans Subject, Society and Sexual Violence in International Criminal Law* (Cambridge University Press, 2022) 228.

[3] See further, eg, JG Stewart, 'Overdetermined Atrocities' (2012) 10 *Journal of International Criminal Justice* 1189; J Kyriakakis, 'Corporations before International Criminal Courts: Implications for the International Criminal Justice Project' (2017) 30(1) *Leiden Journal of International Criminal Law* 221, 232; A Reggio, 'Aiding and Abetting in International Criminal Law: The Responsibility of Corporate Agents and Businessmen for "Trading with the Enemy" of Mankind' (2005) 5 *International Criminal Law Review* 623.

states[4] and even a rather amorphous international community.[5] The key questions then are what are, and what should be, the responsibilities of actors other than individuals in international criminal law (or in other fields of law), and to what extent would holding them accountable address the structures and processes that underpin international crime?

For alternative visions of responsibility, here as elsewhere, we can turn to civil society actors, inside and outside the courtroom. As already made clear in chapter 4, citizens' tribunals enjoy no formal enforcement power. At first sight a disadvantage, this frees them to adopt forms of responsibility that are not open to official international criminal institutions (rightly) constrained by principles of legality and the strictures of the sources of international law. In this way, citizens' tribunals can offer a measure of justice and accountability that is not open to official international criminal institutions, and inspire alternative thinking about responsibility.

II. The Responsibilities of International Criminal Law

The ascription of individual criminal responsibility is one of the hallmarks of international criminal law. The focus on individual criminal responsibility is said to reflect a liberal sensibility, resting as it does on an assumption that the defendant is a rational, autonomous individual who is responsible for his or her actions.[6] It also reflects a political commitment to the avoidance of collective guilt, and the position that individual accountability better enables groups to reconcile.[7] However, individual criminal responsibility struggles to capture the complexity of international criminal offending. This in turn limits international criminal law's potential to achieve the aims ascribed to it (see chapter 3). A key feature of international criminal offending, as already noted, is its collective nature. International criminal offending is, as Simpson observes, '*both* collective and individual.'[8]

---

[4] See further, eg, PNS Rumney, 'Getting away with Murder: Genocide and Western State Power' (1997) 60 *Modern Law Review* 594; H Cameron, 'British State Complicity in Genocide: Rwanda 1994' (2012) 1(1) *State Crime Journal* 70, 72.

[5] See further, eg, R Dallaire, *Shake Hands with the Devil* (Arrow, 2005); R Dallaire, K Manocha and N Degnarin, 'The Major Powers on Trial' (2005) 3 *Journal of International Criminal Justice* 861. For an exhaustive discussion of bystanders in international criminal law, see LE Fletcher, 'From Indifference to Engagement: Bystanders and International Criminal Justice' (2005) 26 *Michigan Journal of International Law* 1013.

[6] P McAuliffe and C Schwöbel-Patel, 'Disciplinary Matchmaking Critics of International Criminal Law Meet Critics of Liberal Peacebuilding' (2018) 16(5) *Journal of International Criminal Justice* 985, 988. For further discussion on liberal legalism, see, eg, MA Drumbl, *Atrocity, Punishment and International Law* (Cambridge University Press, 2007) 5.

[7] See, eg, Fletcher (n 5) 1015, 1021. For an exhaustive discussion on ascribing collective guilt, GP Fletcher, 'The Storrs Lectures: Liberals and Romantics at War: The Problem of Collective Guilt' (2002) 111 *Yale Law Journal* 1499.

[8] G Simpson, 'Men and Abstract Entities: Individual Responsibility and Collective Guilt in International Criminal Law' in Nollkaemper and Van der Wilt (eds) (n 2) 69, 71.

For one thing, the commission of international crimes may, as already noted, implicate collective actors, such as corporations and states, either as direct perpetrators or as complicit in the crimes of others. More than that, as the ICTY Appeals Chamber recognised in *Tadić*, typically, international crimes 'do not result from the criminal propensity of single individuals but constitute manifestations of collective criminality'.[9] Thus, it has been estimated that upwards of 100,000 individuals participated in the Holocaust and 200,000 people in the genocide in Rwanda in 1994.[10] Within this collective context, individuals' participation varies. For example, Drumbl classifies perpetrators of international crime as 'conflict entrepreneurs', 'leaders' and 'actual killers', with another group bystanders, many of whom he describes as 'beneficiaries' who 'bear responsibility for atrocity even though its members are not, strictly speaking, perpetrators'.[11] In a similar vein, Guilfoyle contrasts the 'high leader who plans a campaign of extermination' with 'the politician or broadcaster who ... contributes to the moral climate that makes such acts acceptable', 'the mid-ranking bureaucrat ... who enables a part of the plan to run smoothly' and 'the foot soldier'.[12] Overall, then, the question is how appropriately international criminal law ascribes responsibility given the different contributions that individuals (and other actors) make to the commission of international crime?

One consequence of the collective nature of international criminal offending is that the commission of international crime may be less contingent on a particular individual than individual criminal responsibility suggests. Stewart describes international crimes as 'overdetermined', in the sense that 'very few atrocities are so dependent on the acts of any one individual that we can say with confidence that they would certainly *not* have transpired absent any one accused's individual agency'.[13] It follows that it is necessary to 'address the social structures and group solidarity' that enables international criminal offending.[14] For example, perpetrators may act in the belief that they are 'part of a common project', with victims being identified because perpetrators consider them to belong to a particular group.[15] For crimes such as genocide, the intention on the part of the perpetrator to destroy a particular group 'in whole or in part' is a key part of the crime.[16] Another aspect of this collective context is that international criminal offending often takes place within the context of a 'climate of hate'.[17] In such a context,

---

[9] *Prosecutor v Duško Tadić*, 15 July 1999, ICTY IT-94-1-A, para 191.
[10] RJ Hamilton, 'State-Enabled Crimes' (2016) 41 *Yale Journal of International Law* 301, 318.
[11] Drumbl (n 6) 25.
[12] DJA Guilfoyle, 'Responsibility for Collective Atrocities: Fair Labelling and Approaches to Commission in International Criminal Law' (2001) 64 *Current Legal Problems* 255, 257–58.
[13] Stewart (n 3) 1190.
[14] N Jain, 'Individual Responsibility for Mass Atrocity: In Search of a Concept of Perpetration' (2013) 61(4) *American Journal of Comparative Law* 831, 836.
[15] ibid 835. See further Fletcher, 'The Storrs Lectures' (n 7) 1514; Drumbl (n 6) 42.
[16] Simpson (n 8) 71.
[17] Fletcher, 'The Storrs Lectures' (n 7) 1542.

Mark Drumbl explains that 'the extraordinary acts of individual criminality that collectively lead to mass atrocity are not so deviant in the times and places where they are committed'.[18] Fletcher observes:

> The potential criminal in a normally diverse society has an opportunity for self-correction, to revise his criminal impulse in light of generally prevailing moral norms of the society. Now what happens in a society in which all the external signals point in favour of the criminal action? This is the moral condition that generates 'the banality of evil'.[19]

All this raises considerable questions about the ascription of individual criminal responsibility. In this context, scholars typically point to the famous Milgram and Zimbardo experiments to illustrate how limited people's capacity to resist orders can be – even when those orders are to harm others.[20] Immi Tallgren observes that 'criminal law that could be obeyed only by exceptional individuals is hard to justify'.[21] Yet at Nuremberg, superior orders were only allowed to mitigate punishment.[22] Article 33 of the Rome Statute provides that superior orders can relieve an individual of responsibility only in limited circumstances, including where the order was not 'manifestly unlawful', with orders to commit genocide and crimes against humanity always considered to be manifestly unlawful. However, as Leebaw observes, the manifest illegality test may be problematic in a context in which military training necessarily desensitises soldiers to violence and conditions them to obedience.[23]

It may be thought that too much focus on societal processes exculpates the individual and deprives him or her of agency.[24] From this perspective, these situational factors might be considered irrelevant, because the role of law is to set out expected standards of behaviour for us all. Alternatively, it might be thought that an international criminal law that fails to account for context is likely to have limited preventive force. It might also be considered that individual international criminal prosecutions run the risk of scapegoating and/or bestowing 'collective innocence' on others.[25]

Whichever of the above positions is adopted, it is clear that individual criminal responsibility throws up many dilemmas. How might international criminal law

---

[18] Drumbl (n 6) 8. See further, I Tallgren, 'The Sensibility and Sense of International Criminal Law' (2002) 13(3) *European Journal of International Law* 561, 575; Jain (n 14) 836.

[19] Fletcher, 'The Storrs Lectures' (n 7) 1541.

[20] See, eg, Drumbl (n 6) 31; B Leebaw, 'Justice and the Faithless: The Demand for Disobedience in International Criminal Law' (2018) 24(2) *European Journal of International Relations* 344, 345.

[21] Tallgren (n 18) 573. See further Leebaw (n 20) 358.

[22] Art 8, Charter of the International Military Tribunal (adopted 8 August 1945) 251 UNTS 279. See further, Leebaw (n 20) 352.

[23] Leebaw (n 20) 352–53. See further, A Smeulers, 'Why Serious International Crimes Might Not Seem "Manifestly Unlawful" to Low-Level Perpetrators: A Social-Psychological Approach to Superior Orders' (2019) 17(1) *Journal of International Criminal Justice* 105.

[24] See further, on discussion of structure/agency, Simpson (n 8) 90 ff.

[25] Fletcher (n 5) 1038 (referring to Drumbl). See further, M Koskenniemi, 'Between Impunity and Show Trials' (2002) 6 *Max Planck Yearbook of United Nations Law* 1, 14–15. See further LG Minkova, 'Expressing What? The Stigmatization of the Defendant and the ICC's Institutional Interests in the Ongwen Case' (2021) 34(1) *Leiden Journal of International Law* 223.

address them? Courts could be more explicit about their role. Fletcher, for example, suggests that judgments could make it clear that they 'should not be considered to exonerate those who are not before the Court'.[26] Alternatively, the collective could be incorporated into international criminal proceedings, or a balance between individual and collective responsibility could be sought. There have been several suggestions as to how this might be done. For example, Hamilton has proposed integrating state responsibility into ICC proceedings 'where state policies and practice have played an essential role'.[27] George Fletcher advocates a 'humanistic approach to collective guilt' that requires thinking 'about the distribution of guilt between the individual perpetrator and the nation in whose name he or she acts'.[28] For Laurel Fletcher, even though international criminal law does not – and should not – criminalise bystanders,[29] 'tribunal judges should draft their opinions in a manner that explicitly leaves open the question of bystander contribution to atrocities'.[30] Another approach would be to reflect on the potential of international criminal law – and specifically international criminal responsibility – to generate resistance to international crime, the conditions that enable it, and the actors that support or benefit from it.[31] The generation of resistance is key to the way that some civil society actors have approached responsibility through their radical interpretations of Nuremberg's individual responsibility paradigm.

A. Responsibility and Resistance: A Return to Nuremberg

Civil society actors engaged in international criminal law do not all share the same vision of international criminal responsibility. However, one theme in civil society activism has been the use of international criminal law to generate legal and political contestation. One way in which civil society actors have done this is by trying to bring this law into the courtroom indirectly where it could not be brought directly. A long history of civil disobedience against war, and its conduct, draws on international legal arguments.[32] However, some civil society actors go

---

[26] Fletcher (n 5) 1082.

[27] Hamilton (n 10) 304.

[28] Fletcher, 'The Storrs Lectures' (n 7) 1537–38.

[29] Fletcher (n 5) 1016.

[30] ibid 1018.

[31] See, further, Leebaw (n 20) 345, who argues that 'Prominent approaches to strengthening international criminal law through measures aimed at securing compliance downplay the importance of resistance as a response to organized atrocity.'

[32] See, eg, F Mégret, 'Civil Disobedience and International Law: Sketch for a Theoretical Argument' (2008) 46 *Canadian Yearbook of International Law* 143, 149; A Zelter, 'Civil Society and Global Responsibility: The Arms Trade and East Timor' (2004) 18(1) *International Relations* 125; M Lippman, 'Liberating the Law: The Jurisprudence of Civil Disobedience and Resistance' (1994) 16(2) *San Diego Justice Journal* 299; JF Bannan and RS Bannan, *Law, Morality and Vietnam: The Peace Militants and the Courts* (Indiana University Press, 1974); N Grief, 'Legal Challenges to the United Kingdom's Nuclear Defence Policy' [1989] *Public Law* 541; SC Neff, 'International Law and Nuclear Weapons in Scottish Courts' (2002) 51 *International and Comparative Law Quarterly* 171.

beyond civil disobedience, because they do not just disobey law that they consider unjust; rather, they seek to enforce the law themselves. For example, Anghie Zelter was one of four women acquitted of criminal damage to a Hawk aircraft, one of a number sold to Indonesia, which they believed would be used to commit human rights violations and international crimes in East Timor. She observed:

> It is every citizen's right and duty to try and uphold international law by trying to prevent such horrendous crimes from being committed ... We thus had a duty to take affirmative action under international law, the reasonable exercise of which made our Ploughshares action lawful.[33]

Thus, such individuals claim to enforce the law based on the Nuremberg precedent, which they argue vests individuals with the right – or even a duty – to enforce international law where the state fails to do so or is in breach itself.[34] By bringing international criminal law into a national criminal trial, litigants also challenge international criminal law's 'exceptional' nature. They endeavour to overcome some of the barriers to the accountability of actors from powerful states. They also challenge the monopoly of the state to enforce international law,[35] and seek to broaden the reach of the law to bystanders. Zelter explained in court:

> The longer and more complex the chain of events, the more moral responsibility gets dispersed and reduced. Then the point comes when the system may be guilty of an appalling crime against humanity but no individual feels obliged to own the consequences of their actions ... Therefore we were obliged to take responsibility.[36]

Individuals who take such action risk being tried and convicted. Yet authorities also risk potentially damaging publicity when pursuing such cases. While acquittals are unusual, winning the *legal* case may not be the only desirable outcome for those involved. For example, 20 peace protestors who had engaged in various antiwar activities during the Iraq war brought three separate but related appeals before the English House of Lords in *R v Jones*.[37] They failed to persuade the court that aggression was a crime in English law.[38] Therefore they could not seek to justify the conduct charged (including criminal damage and aggravated trespass) on the basis that they were acting to prevent aggression in Iraq. However, this did not prevent

---

[33] Zelter (n 32) 134.

[34] Usually, from a legal perspective at least, unsuccessfully, see further M Lippman, 'Nuremberg: Forty Five Years Later'(1991) 7 *Connecticut Journal of International Law* 1, 52–57.

[35] 'We stood in the dock, but we knew that the real criminals were the Indonesian military, security and police forces, the British and other western governments who traded with and provided the support and means for the ongoing repression and the powerful corporations who actually made and sold the equipment. We used every opportunity during our defence to put these real criminals on trial': Zelter (n 32) 133.

[36] ibid 135.

[37] *R v Jones, Milling et al* [2006] UKHL16.

[38] See further *R (on the application of General Abdul Waheed Shannan Al Rabbat) v Westminster Magistrates' Court and Others* [2017] EWHC 1969; and A Orakhelashvili, 'The High Court and the Crime of Aggression' (2018) 5(1) *Journal on the Use of Force and International Law* 3.

activists from claiming they were attempting to prevent the commission of war crimes, and to bring in evidence to this effect in criminal trials.

How might this approach to the Nuremberg legacy be interpreted? Mégret, who is generally supportive of the legacy and potential of civil disobedience in international law,[39] claims that, strictly speaking, the Nuremberg precedent applies only to those who 'are in a position where they are the recipients of orders directly and if, in obeying these orders, they will actively participate, or be complicit in crimes'.[40] The question of doctrine is of course important. Another important consideration is what these interpretations reveal about international criminal law's appeal and reach. Another approach would be to consider strategically whether it might be more productive in the context of any one situation to seek accountability through this form of citizen intervention or other legal and/or political routes. These approaches are of course not mutually exclusive. The questions are (i) what role international criminal law can play – and where and across which sites – to prevent international crimes and their causes and/or to provide accountability after atrocity, (ii) and which actors it needs to speak to and/or implicate in order to do so. Reading civil society activism alongside 'official' international criminal law not only provides alternative thinking about responsibility: it does more than that. It demonstrates how responsibility as mediated through international criminal law is arguably already wider than official doctrine suggests. The rest of this chapter reflects in more depth on different approaches to responsibility, beginning with modes of liability in international criminal law.

III. Modes of Liability

Modes of liability are the legal mechanisms that link the defendant to the commission of a crime. Essentially, they are the legal tools by which responsibility is allocated. As already stated, the individual criminal responsibility paradigm does not easily fit the commission of international crime. At the same time, the collective nature of international offending has had a profound – and sometimes controversial – influence on modes of liability. It is to this that we now turn.

One key challenge, given the nature of international criminal offending, is, as Guilfoyle observes, for international criminal law to account for the contributions to international crime of individuals who do not directly carry out atrocity but who participate in it by organising or masterminding it.[41] Doctrines have been developed that have expanded the notion of principal liability in such circumstances. These doctrines are a creative response to the challenge of finding individuals

---

[39] See, eg, Mégret (n 32) 165.
[40] ibid 175.
[41] Guilfoyle (n 12) 285.

culpable in the context of collective crime, but they have arguably strained the principle of individual criminal responsibility.

In international criminal law, individuals may be held responsible as principals not only for international crimes they have directly perpetrated but also for crimes they have not actually physically carried out. Indeed, they may even be physically distant from the commission of the crime. Drawing in particular on English law, the ICTY, ICTR and the SCSL applied and developed a doctrine of joint criminal enterprise for the commission of collective crimes. At the ICC, German law has been the inspiration for the development of a 'control of crime' model of indirect and co-perpetration. These modes of liability, drawn from western legal concepts, can hardly be universal, and these doctrines are very complex. Only a brief overview is given here, but there is plenty of literature to follow in order to understand these doctrinal debates further.[42]

The expansion of principal liability does not affect just leaders. However, although no more consequences – in sentencing terms – attach to finding someone liable as a principal rather than as an accessory,[43] there has been an assumption that holding the leaders and masterminds of international crime responsible as principals more fairly reflects their moral blameworthiness for crime and does justice to the historical record.[44] However, early on, the chambers in *Lubanga* and *Katanga* diverged on the extent of principal liability and the importance of holding someone guilty as a principal rather than as an accessory.[45] Scholars have also challenged the assumption that principal liability expresses a more serious form of offending. For example, Guilfoyle suggests that accessories can be 'more culpable than principals, because they are aggregators of responsibility'.[46] Gil and Maculan argue that such judgments 'should label defendants as "masterminds" or "intellectual perpetrators" in the reasoning, although considering them as accessories from a technical point of view'.[47] Moreover, the expansion of principal liability has also

---

[42] See further, R Cryer, D Robinson and S Vasiliev, *An Introduction to International Criminal Law and Procedure* (Cambridge University Press, 2019) 344–55; H Van der Wilt, 'Joint Criminal Enterprise and Functional Perpetration' in Nollkaemper and Van der Wilt (eds) (n 2) 158; LD Yanev, 'Joint Criminal Enterprise' in J de Hemptinne, R Roth and E Van Sliedregt (eds), *Modes of Liability in International Criminal Law* (Cambridge University Press, 2019) 121.

[43] eg, as Guilfoyle notes, 'an aider and abettor of genocide is convicted of genocide': Guilfoyle (n 12) 261.

[44] For discussion of these assumptions, see Jain (n 14) 833; AG Gil and E Maculan, 'Current Trends in the Definition of "Perpetrator" by the International Criminal Court: From the Decision on the Confirmation of Charges in the *Lubanga* Case to the *Katanga* Judgment' (2015) 28 *Leiden Journal of International Law* 349, 369; Guilfoyle (n 12) 260.

[45] Gil and Maculan (n 44) 363–66; *Prosecutor v Thomas Lubanga Dyilo*, Judgment, 14 March 2012, ICC-01/04-01/06-2842; *Prosecutor v German Katanga*, Judgment, 7 March 2014, ICC-01/04-07-3436-tENG. In the end, Katanga was not convicted as a principal but for having contributed to the commission of a crime under Art 25(3)(d), Rome Statute, because the Trial Chamber controversially re-characterised the charges against him after the parties had made their closing arguments. This decision has been criticised because this was a mode of liability on which neither the Prosecutor nor the defendant had addressed the court.

[46] Guilfoyle (n 12) 255.

[47] Gil and Maculan (n 44) 366.

given rise to concerns that the prosecutorial net has been spread too widely at the risk of violating the principle of legality.[48] This concern is particularly evident in the development of joint criminal enterprise by the ad hoc tribunals. International criminal law also provides for accessorial liability, which, it has been argued, can overcome some of the challenges inherent in an expanded doctrine of principal liability.[49] Accessorial liability is explored in section IV.

The doctrine of joint criminal enterprise (JCE), developed first in the *Tadić* case at the ICTY and then applied more widely, essentially renders individuals who are part of a common plan liable for crimes committed in pursuit of it, even if they did not perpetrate them directly. On appeal, Tadić was therefore found guilty of the grave breach of wilful killing and murder as a war crime and crime against humanity, for participating in the killing of five men, although there was no evidence that he had personally killed them. The ICTY Appeals Chamber explained:

> [T]o hold criminally liable as a perpetrator only the person who materially performs the criminal act would disregard the role as co-perpetrators of all those who in some way made it possible for the perpetrator physically to carry out that criminal act. At the same time, ... to hold the latter liable only as aiders and abettors might understate the degree of their criminal responsibility.[50]

To establish joint criminal responsibility, the Prosecutor must show the existence of a group that agrees a common plan encompassing the commission of a crime within the jurisdiction of the court.[51] An individual must contribute 'significantly' to the plan, although his or her own contribution need not involve the commission of a crime or its elements; 'the contribution need not be necessary or substantial',[52] and it may be by omission. It is not necessary for direct perpetrators to be parties to the common plan if 'the crime in question forms part of the common purpose'.[53]

The doctrine of JCE enables the prosecution of individuals for acts that come within a criminal plan or policy but which are physically perpetrated by others. The *Tadić* appeal decision explained the three types of JCE.[54] In the first (basic) category (JCE I), all the accused share the same mens rea to commit a particular crime. The second category, the systemic JCE II form, applies in a context where an accused participates in a system of repression, such as a concentration camp.[55] The third and final type of JCE (JCE III) is the one that has attracted the most criticism. In this extended form, an accused who intended to participate in the common plan and its crimes can be held liable for foreseeable crimes resulting from the

---

[48] See, eg, ibid.

[49] See, eg, Guilfoyle (n 12).

[50] *Tadić* (n 9) para 192.

[51] ibid para 227.

[52] *Prosecutor v Brđanin*, 3 April 2007, ICTY IT-99-36-A, para 430.

[53] ibid para 410.

[54] *Tadić* (n 9) para 228.

[55] Here it is necessary to show that the accused had 'personal knowledge of the system of ill-treatment' and 'the intent to further this common concerted system of ill-treatment': ibid.

plan, where that person 'willingly' risked that the crimes might be perpetrated, as was the case in *Tadić*. The Appeals Chamber held:

> [T]he only possible inference to be drawn is that the Appellant had the intention to further the criminal purpose to rid the Prijedor region of the non-Serb population, by committing inhumane acts against them. That non-Serbs might be killed in the effecting of this common aim was, in the circumstances of the present case, foreseeable. The Appellant was aware that the actions of the group of which he was a member were likely to lead to such killings, but he nevertheless willingly took that risk.[56]

The doctrine of JCE, sometimes rather disparagingly referred to as 'just convict everyone',[57] has been criticised. Amongst the criticisms is one that, essentially, a judge-made doctrine, JCE III (and according to some, JCE in its entirety) lacks customary international law status.[58] The threshold 'for determining who can be considered part of the "enterprise"' has been argued to be low, thereby risking 'catching big and little fish in the one net and labelling them all principals'.[59] This extended form also allows for conviction of a specific-intent crime such as genocide, where the mens rea requirement of genocide would not otherwise be met. Whether someone should be convicted of genocide (or crimes against humanity) based on foresight is controversial. The Extraordinary Chambers in the Courts of Cambodia (ECCC) has rejected this extended form of JCE on the basis that it was not customary international law when crimes within its jurisdiction were committed.[60] The Rome Statute incorporates a limited kind of joint enterprise liability in Article 25(3)(d) that does not encompass JCE III.[61] Liability at the ICC thus takes a slightly different form from liability at the ICTY and ICTR.

Principal liability under the Rome Statute is provided for in Article 25(3)(a), which states that an individual

> Commits such a crime, whether as an individual, jointly with another or through another person, regardless of whether that other person is criminally responsible ...

Under Article 25(3)(a), therefore, an individual can have sole and direct responsibility for an international crime (direct perpetration). That person may also have joint liability for the crime (direct co-perpetration). In addition, an accused may commit the crime through another person, whether that person is guilty or not (indirect perpetration). The ICC has also amalgamated the second (co-perpetration) and third (indirect perpetration) bases of liability to form a doctrine of

---

[56] ibid para 232.

[57] E Van Sliedregt, 'System Criminality at the ICTY' in Nollkaemper and Van der Wilt (eds) (n 2) 183, 195.

[58] Yanev (n 42) 122.

[59] Guilfoyle (n 12) 264–65.

[60] *ECCC Prosecutor v Samphan, Chea*, Appeal Judgment, 23 November 2016, 002/19-09-2007-ECCC/SC. See also *ECCC Prosecutor v Chea, Sary, Thirith, and Samphan*, Decision on the Appeals Against the Co-Investigative Judges Order on Joint Criminal Enterprise, 20 May 2010, 002/19-09-2007-ECCC-OCIJ, paras 79–82.

[61] Cryer, Robinson and Vasiliev (n 42) 349.

indirect co-perpetration. Each of these types of perpetration is outlined briefly below. As befits an evolving body of jurisprudence, the ICC's approach has not been entirely consistent.[62] In essence, however, the main distinction the Court has drawn between principal liability and accessory liability is that the principal is someone who has control over the crime.[63]

To establish joint liability or direct co-perpetration, several conditions must be satisfied. There must be a common plan, which must ordinarily lead to the perpetration of an international crime. An individual must have made an 'essential contribution' to the crime, and the defendant must have either intended to have committed the crime or been aware that the carrying out of the plan will ordinarily result in the commission of a crime. The defendant must also have been aware that he or she had 'provided an essential contribution to the implementation of the common plan'.[64]

The doctrine of indirect perpetration or perpetration by means of the control of an organisation derives from German law, in particular the work of Claus Roxin.[65] This covers the situation where a perpetrator acts through another person, whose will he or she controls. Here it is necessary to show that the person who directly carried out the crime was effectively an instrument of the mastermind behind it. If a crime is carried out through an organisation, the defendant must control the organisation. The character of the organisation must also be such that its members automatically conform to orders given, so that the individuals within its structure are for all intents and purposes interchangeable.[66] The defendant must also have the requisite mens rea for the crime and be aware that obedience to his or her commands would be 'near automatic'.[67] Perpetration by means, or indirect perpetration, has been criticised for assuming that those below leaders are simply instruments, denuding them of 'individual moral responsibility'.[68]

Finally, ICC jurisprudence has developed a doctrine of indirect co-perpetration by combining co-perpetration with indirect perpetration. As a result, an individual may be charged with crimes committed by people under the control of a co-perpetrator, an approach that has similarities to the JCE doctrine.[69]

The doctrines of JCE and indirect perpetration are attempts to deal with the collective context of the international offending. The mens rea and actus reus under each diverge.[70] These doctrines therefore differ in the way they represent

---

[62] For criticism of this lack of consistency, see Gil and Maculan (n 44) 366 and 369.

[63] M Aksenova, *Complicity in International Criminal Law* (Hart Publishing, 2019) 142.

[64] *Lubanga* (n 45) para 1018.

[65] E Van Sliedregt and LD Yanev, 'Co-Perpetration Based on Joint Control over the Crime' in de Hemptinne, Roth and Van Sliedregt (eds) (n 42) 85, 87.

[66] *Prosecutor v Germain Katanga and Mathieu Ngudjolo Chui*, Decision on Confirmation of Charges, 30 September 2008, ICC-01/04-01/07-717, paras 515–17.

[67] ibid para 534.

[68] Guilfoyle (n 12) 266.

[69] C Stahn, *A Critical Introduction to International Criminal Law* (Cambridge University Press, 2019) 138.

[70] See further, Van Sliedregt and Yanev (n 65) 91.

the context of international crime and individuals' relationship to it, as Guilfoyle explains. They are therefore likely to channel different understandings of how crime unfolds in the historical record. Unlike JCE, which does not presume a hierarchical formal structure,[71] the control of crime through an organisation, which is not customary international law,[72] presumes that organisations operate in vertical hierarchical power structures.[73] However, not all organisations involved in the commission of international crime are organised hierarchically. For Van Sliedregt, then, '[o]ne cannot escape the impression that scholars pushing for this theory and judges applying it lost sight of the specific African context'.[74]

From a law and policy perspective, it might thus be asked whether one approach is more or less likely to raise questions about fairness to the accused, more or less likely to facilitate prosecution, adhere to the principle of legality and/or to contribute to the prevention of international crime. Common to both these approaches is the ascription of responsibility for international crime to the individual. They therefore do little to acknowledge the role of collective actors, such as corporations or the state, to which we now turn.

IV.   International Criminal Responsibility and Collective Actors

One of the central criticisms of individual criminal responsibility is its failure to address the broad range of actors who contribute to or benefit from international crime. This in turn limits its ability to address the underlying causes of international crime. This criticism is directed in particular at international criminal law's failure to ensure corporate and state international criminal responsibility. In contrast, citizens' tribunals broaden international criminal law's gaze by locating international criminal wrongdoing within a wider context and implicating a broader range of actors. In so doing, as already mentioned, they emphasise the responsibility to resist international crime and its causes.

A.   The Responsibilities of Corporate Actors

Armed conflict and international crime may often be driven by economic motivations and/or influenced by economic conditions.[75] Economic actors may also play

---

[71] Guilfoyle (n 12) 264.

[72] Van Sliedregt and Yanev (n 65) 116.

[73] Guilfoyle (n 12) 265.

[74] E Van Sliedregt, 'International Criminal Law: Over-Studied and Underachieving?' (2016) 29 *Leiden Journal of International Law* 1, 7.

[75] On the economic underpinnings of international conflict and international crime, see, eg, Panel of Experts on the Illegal Exploitation of Natural Resources and other Forms of Wealth of the Democratic

a role in international crime. For example, although not a criminal body, the South African Truth and Reconciliation Commission concluded that '[c]ertain businesses were involved in helping to design and implement apartheid policies. Other businesses benefited from cooperating with the security structures of the former state.'[76] The Liberian Truth and Reconciliation Commission included a chapter on the role of economic actors, including foreign corporations.[77] The economic bases of and motivations for international crimes are not reflected in current definitions of international crime (see chapter 5), nor in current understandings of responsibility. International criminal law does not currently have a doctrine of corporate criminal responsibility.[78]

In the absence of international corporate criminal responsibility, attention focuses on the criminal responsibility of individual corporate actors. For example, Van Anraat was convicted of complicity in war crimes, namely inhuman treatment and causing death or severe bodily harm through the use of chemical weapons, because he supplied thiodiglycol (a mustard gas precursor) to the regime of Saddam Hussein.[79] However, such prosecutions have been criticised for focusing on 'individual businessmen who traded arms in violation of arms embargoes' rather than 'executives of multinational corporations that receive licences for their arms exports and supply the largest portion of arms worldwide, even when their exports have contributed to violation of international criminal law'.[80] Another challenge is that individuals' actions may not constitute a crime in circumstances where the actions of corporations may 'cumulatively' be at fault.[81] Moreover, international criminal courts have been criticised for the limited commitment they

Republic of the Congo, *Final Report*, 16 October 2002, S/2002/1146, para 12, referring to a 'self-financing war economy centred on mineral exploitation'; Reggio (n 3) 623–25.

[76] Cited in Stewart (n 3) 1191. See further, Reggio (n 3).

[77] Kyriakakis (n 3) 232.

[78] See further on debates on corporate responsibility in international criminal law, eg, A Garcia, 'Corporate Liability for International Crimes: A Matter of Legal Policy Since Nuremberg' (2015) 24 *Tulane Journal of International and Comparative Law* 98; International Commission of Jurists Expert Legal Panel on Corporate Complicity in International Crimes, *Corporate Complicity and Legal Accountability*, vol 2: *Criminal Law and International Crimes* (International Commission of Jurists, 2008) 5; C Plomp, 'Aiding and Abetting: The Responsibility of Business Leaders under the Rome Statute of the International Criminal Court' (2014) 4 *Utrecht Journal of International and European Law* 4; Kyriakakis (n 3); N Farrell, 'Attributing Criminal Liability to Corporate Actors' (2010) 8 *Journal of International Criminal Justice* 873; JG Stewart, 'The Turn to Corporate Criminal Liability for International crimes: Transcending the Alien Tort Statute' (2014) 47(1) *New York University Journey International Law and Politics* 121.

[79] *Public Prosecutor v van Anraat*, LJN AX6406, The Hague District Court, 23 December 2005, cited in International Commission of Jurists (n 78) 9–10; Court of Appeal, 9 May 2007, LJN: BA4676 ILDC 753 (NL 2007).

[80] L Bryke and M Saage-Maas, 'Individual Criminal Liability for Arms Exports under the ICC Statute' (2019) 17(5) *Journal of International Criminal Justice* 1117, 1121.

[81] CH Wheeler, 'Re-Examining Corporate Liability at the International Criminal Court through the Lens of Article 15 Communication against Chiquita Brands International' (2018) 19 *Melbourne Journal of International Law* 369, 375.

have shown to prosecuting corporate actors and recognising the economic contributions they might make to international crime.[82]

After the Second World War, some business leaders were prosecuted under Control Council Law No 10.[83] For Van der Wilt, these trials evidenced 'a symbiotic relationship between big business and a criminal regime which could not have survived without the former's unfaltering support'.[84] However, the perceived threat from communism tempered the political commitment to prosecuting industrialists more expansively.[85] The ICC Prosecutor has pledged to take the financial drivers of international crime seriously.[86] As regards crimes allegedly committed in the Democratic Republic of the Congo, former Prosecutor Moreno-Ocampo noted the 'general concern' that alleged crimes 'may be fuelled by the exploitation of natural resources there and the arms trade, which are enabled through the international banking system', with the result that

> [i]nvestigation of the financial aspects of the alleged atrocities will be crucial to prevent future crimes and for the prosecution of crimes already committed. If the alleged business practices continue to fuel atrocities, these would not be stopped even if current perpetrators were arrested and prosecuted.[87]

Civil society actors have also sought to persuade the OTP to investigate corporate actors. For example, there was an attempt by a non-governmental organisation (NGO) to persuade the OTP to include corporate officials in its preliminary investigation relating to Columbia.[88] However, the ICC has to date focused its attention on governmental and military personnel. Even if it had focused on

---

[82] See further Plomp (n 78) 4; Kyriakakis (n 3); A Sehmi, 'Judicializing Economic Violence as Means of Dismantling the Structural Causes of Atrocity in the Democratic Republic of Congo' (2020) 14(3) *International Journal of Transitional Justice* 423. For discussion in the context of the transition process in Colombia, see P Wesche, 'Business Actors, Paramilitaries and Transitional Criminal Justice in Columbia' (2019) 13(3) *International Journal of Transitional Justice* 478.

[83] See, eg, UN War Crimes Commission, *Law Reports of Trials of the War Criminals*, vol X: *The IG Farben and Krupp Trials* (HMSO, 1949); UN War Crimes Commission, *Law Reports of Trials of the War Criminals*, vol I: *Trial of Tesch and Two Others* (HMSO, 1947) 93.

[84] H Van der Wilt, 'Corporate Criminal Responsibility for International Crimes: Exploring the Possibilities' (2013) 12 *Chinese Journal of International Law* 43, 52.

[85] See further, eg, G Baars, 'Capitalism's Victor's Justice? The Hidden Stories behind the Prosecution of Industrialists Post-WWII' in K Heller and G Simpson (eds), *The Hidden Histories of War Crimes Trials* (Oxford University Press, 2013) 163, 179; JA Bush, 'The Prehistory of Corporations and Conspiracy in International Criminal Law: What Nuremberg Really Said' (2009) 109 *Columbia Law Review* 1094, 1237; F Jessberger, 'On the Origins of Individual Criminal Responsibility under International Law for Business Activity' (2010) 8 *Journal of International Criminal Justice* 783, esp 800 ff, noting that the 'IG managers had a soft fall, so to say, from a place not far behind the ranks of the *Wehrmacht* into the warm bosom of the western powers' (ibid 801–02). Koskenniemi (n 25) 9.

[86] Office of the Prosecutor, Policy Paper on Case Selection and Prioritisation (OTP, 15 September 2016) para 41. See further J Graff, 'Corporate War Criminals and the International Criminal Court: Blood and Profits in the Democratic Republic of Congo' (2004) 2 *Human Rights Brief* 23.

[87] Office of the Prosecutor, Communications Received by the Office of the Prosecutor of the ICC (OTP, 16 July 2003) at www.icc-cpi.int/NR/rdonlyres/B080A3DD-7C69-4BC9-AE25-0D2C271A9A63/277502/16_july__english.pdf.

[88] Discussed in Wheeler (n 81).

individual corporate actors, it is by no means clear that this would have addressed the economic dimension to international criminal offending, because such prosecutions would be subject to the same limitations that mark individual criminal responsibility more generally. At best, prosecutions of individual corporate actors are necessary but insufficient. At worst, as explored further below, they present international criminal lawyers with a troubling double bind, which does not reduce the need for other approaches, such as those evident in the practice of citizens' tribunals.

At Rome there was discussion of corporate criminal responsibility. A French proposal in favour of a limited form of corporate criminal responsibility was rejected. One reason was that national jurisdictions adopted different approaches to corporate criminal responsibility, therefore making problematic the application of the principle of complementarity. Some commentators argue that this objection no longer holds good because states have increasingly incorporated corporate criminal responsibility into their national legal systems.[89] However, significant differences remain as to the circumstances in which national jurisdictions hold corporations criminally responsible.[90] Consequently, even if international corporate criminal responsibility could be agreed upon, work remains to be done regarding the definition of its elements and parameters. When the issue came up at the Review Conference of the Rome Statute in Kampala in 2010, the Conference was preoccupied with the question of aggression.[91] In contrast, Article 46C of the Malabo Protocol provides for corporate criminal responsibility; and increasingly, international legal instruments recognise the possibility of corporate criminal responsibility at the national level.[92] For example, Article 6(8) of the Draft Articles on Prevention and Punishment of Crimes Against Humanity 2019 provides for the criminal, civil or administrative liability of legal persons subject to the provisions of national law.[93]

Individual corporate actors could be prosecuted in international (and national) law as direct perpetrators (including through the extended forms of liability discussed in section III). They might also be prosecuted as accessories. While the following discussion of corporate responsibility focuses on accessorial modes of responsibility, these modes of liability are not only applicable to corporate

---

[89] See, eg, C Kaeb, 'The Shifting Sands of Corporate Liability under International Criminal Law' (2016) 49 *George Washington International Law Review* 351, 353. See, however, Andrew Clapham, who describes the restriction of international criminal tribunals to individual criminal responsibility as 'a "rule of procedure"': A Clapham, 'Extending International Criminal Law beyond the Individual to Corporations and Armed Opposition Groups' (2008) 6 *Journal of International Criminal Justice* 899, 902.

[90] Wheeler (n 81) 377.

[91] Van der Wilt (n 84) 45.

[92] eg, Art 10(1), UN Convention against Transnational Organized Crime 2000, UNGA Res 55/25 (15 November 2000).

[93] Draft Articles on Prevention and Punishment of Crimes against Humanity 2019 A/74/10 (2019) *Yearbook of the International Law Commission 2019*, vol II.

actors. Analysing corporate responsibility through the lens of accessorial liability, however, provides an introduction to accessorial liability.

i. *Complicity*

At the ICC, complicity or accessory liability is set out in Article 25(3)(b)–(e) of the Rome Statute. Unlike the situation with co-perpetrators explained in section III, which relates to principal liability, complicitly refers to secondary liability. Accordingly, an individual will be liable if he or she orders, solicits or induces the commission of a crime (Article 25(3)(b)); aids, abets or otherwise assists in the commission or attempted commission of a crime, including by 'providing the means for its commission' (Article 25(3)(c); or contributes to the commission or attempted commission of a crime 'by a group of persons acting with a common purpose' (Article 25(3)(d)). Article 25(3)(e) also provides for responsibility for incitement to commit genocide. Of particular relevance for corporate actors is aiding and abetting under Article 25(3)(c) and contributing to the commission or attempted commission of a crime under Article 25(3)(d)).

At the ad hoc tribunals, an individual could be held liable for aiding and abetting when providing 'practical assistance, encouragement, or moral support which has a substantial effect on the perpetration of the crime', with knowledge 'that his actions assist the perpetrator in the commission of the crime'.[94] The Rome Statute, in contrast, does not specify that the assistance must make a substantial contribution, and current practice at the ICC varies.[95] At the ICTR and ICTY, the mens rea requirement focused on knowledge, not purpose. Much of course depends on how the requirement of knowledge is interpreted. The International Commission of Jurists has suggested:

> Demanding a low price from suppliers (especially when the supplier is in a weak bargaining position and therefore more likely to be compelled to accept the price), while knowing from the economics of the deal that the supplier will have to use criminal employment practices, such as slavery, to satisfy the demand, may also be enough to show knowing encouragement.[96]

In contrast, the Rome Statute imposes a higher threshold, requiring the accused to act 'for the purpose of facilitating the commission of such a crime'. Thus, individuals who are only aware their actions will assist a crime would not be held liable under Article 25(3)(c). This mens rea standard under the Rome Statute is likely to operate as a significant restriction on the potential responsibility of corporate actors. It will therefore be difficult to satisfy these conditions, particularly where

---

[94] *Prosecutor v Anto Furundzija*, 10 December 1998, ICTY IT-95-17/1-T, paras 235, 245, although the extent to which the accused must have knowledge of the specific crime intended is also debated.

[95] See further, Aksenova (n 63) 155.

[96] International Commission of Jurists (n 78) 41, although it would also have to be shown 'that the company knew it was encouraging the criminal activity through purchasing goods'.

objects or personnel supplied by corporate officials (whether to governmental or paramilitary groups) could be used for both lawful and unlawful purposes.[97] There is, however, an intriguing suggestion by the International Commission of Jurists that it is an 'open question whether this notionally higher subjective standard will have a practical effect' in so far as it may be established by indirect and circumstantial evidence.[98]

Under Article 25(3)(d), accessorial liability also extends to individuals who contribute 'to the commission or attempted commission' of an international crime 'by a group of persons, acting with a common purpose'. The contribution must be 'intentional' and either:

(i)   Be made with the aim of furthering the criminal activity or criminal purpose of the group, where such activity or purpose involves the commission of a crime within the jurisdiction of the Court; or

(ii) Be made in the knowledge of the intention of the group to commit the crime …

The accused must also act with the aim of furthering that purpose or knowing that the group intends to commit the crime.[99] The contribution must be 'significant' – in other words, it must have 'a bearing on the occurrence of the crime and/or the manner of its commission'.[100] The Pre-Trial Chamber in *Mbarushimana* observed that in terms of Article 25(3)(d):

> [M]any members of a community may provide contributions to a criminal organisation in the knowledge of the group's criminality, especially where such criminality is public knowledge. Without some threshold level of assistance, every landlord, every grocer, every utility provider, every secretary, every janitor or even every taxpayer who does anything which contributes to a group committing international crimes could satisfy the elements of 25(3)(d) liability for their infinitesimal contribution to the crimes committed.[101]

It is thoroughly reasonable not to ascribe individual criminal responsibility in such circumstances. However, the problem is that international crimes may be collectively enabled by 'infinitesimal' contributions. On an even larger scale, Stewart has observed, in 'a globalized society where markets enable atrocities, we all make utterly banal contributions to international crimes', with the result that 'we are left with the unsettling sense that participating in atrocity is terrifyingly normal'.[102] Faced with these difficulties, international criminal law might be drawn upon not

---

[97] See further, eg, KR Jacobson, 'Doing Business with the Devil: The Challenges of Prosecuting Corporate Officials Whose Business Transactions Facilitate War Crimes and Crimes Against Humanity' (2005) 56 *Air Force Law Review* 167, 169. Cryer, Robinson and Vasiliev (n 42) 359.

[98] International Commission of Jurists (n 78) 23.

[99] *Prosecutor v Germain Katanga*, Judgment Pursuant to Article 74 of the Statute, 7 March 2014, ICC-01/04-01/07-3436-tENG, para 1640.

[100] ibid paras 1632–33.

[101] *Prosecutor v Callixte Mbarushimana*, Decision on the Confirmation of Charges, 16 December 2011, ICC-01/04-01/10-465-Red, para 277.

[102] Stewart (n 3) 1218.

just for its ability to ascribe responsibility but also for its potential to generate resistance to international crime, which, as already observed, is one of the hallmarks of citizens' tribunals, to which we return below.

An alternative approach towards corporate liability is to rely on superior responsibility under Article 28 of the Rome Statute. There is some dispute about the precise rationale for this ground of liability. Whether it is a form of complicity is disputed.[103] Essentially, it provides for the responsibility of a superior in certain circumstances, depending on whether there is a military or non-military relationship.[104] The NGO, the International Commission of Jurists, has argued that

> [a]ny company operating in countries in conflict, or where gross human rights violations or abuses are widespread or systematic, should be especially vigilant to exercise due diligence and put into place policies and procedures of management oversight to ensure that superiors take necessary and reasonable measures to prevent or punish acts committed by subordinates that could amount to crimes.[105]

In a controversial decision, the ICTR convicted Musema, the director of a tea factory, of genocide and crimes against humanity on the basis of superior responsibility because he had '*de jure* power and *de facto* control' over employees who participated in genocide and crimes against humanity.[106] However, to return to the Rome Statute, the more complex a supply chain, and where companies operate

---

[103] See further Cryer, Robinson and Vasiliev (n 42) 377–78.

[104] Art 28(a), Rome Statute provides for the responsibility of a military commander or a 'person effectively acting as a military commander' for international crimes 'committed by forces under his or her effective command and control, or effective authority and control'. Liability arises when a commander has failed to 'exercise control property' over those forces in circumstances where: '(i) That military commander or person either knew or, owing to the circumstances at the time, should have known that the forces were committing or about to commit such crimes; and (ii) That military commander or person failed to take all necessary and reasonable measures within his or her power to prevent or repress their commission or to submit the matter to the competent authorities for investigation and prosecution.' In cases of non-military 'superior and subordinate relationships', responsibility arises where crimes have been committed by subordinates as a result of a 'failure to exercise control properly' where, under Art 28(b): '(i) The superior either knew, or consciously disregarded information which clearly indicated, that the subordinates were committing or about to commit such crimes; (ii) The crimes concerned activities that were within the effective responsibility and control of the superior; and (iii) The superior failed to take all necessary and reasonable measures within his or her power to prevent or repress their commission or to submit the matter to the competent authorities for investigation and prosecution.' See further, Art 27 of the non-binding Montreux Document on Pertinent International Legal Obligations and Good Practices for State Related to Operations of Private Military and Security Companies during Armed Conflict (ICRC, 2008) at www.icrc.org/en/doc/assets/files/other/icrc_002_0996.pdf, which provides that 'Superiors of PMSC personnel, such as: a) governmental officials, whether they are military commanders or civilian superiors, or b) directors or managers of PMSCs, may be liable for crimes under international law committed by PMSC personnel under their effective authority and control, as a result of their failure to properly exercise control over them, in accordance with the rules of international law. Superior responsibility is not engaged solely by virtue of a contract.'

[105] International Commission of Jurists (n 78) 35.

[106] *Prosecutor v Alfred Musema*, Judgment, 27 January 2000, ICTR-96-13-T, para 880. See further, eg, A Zahar, 'Command Responsibility of Civilian Superiors for Genocide' (2001) 14 *Leiden Journal of International Law* 591, 602–03.

through subsidiaries, the more difficult it will be to establish that the precondi-
tions of Article 28 are satisfied in the context of civilian leaders, in particular the
requirements for 'effective responsibility and control'.[107]

Holding individuals accountable, and moreover extending corporate criminal
responsibility, promises – much like individual criminal prosecution does –
to contribute to justice, to deter and to establish a historical record. It has been
argued that the deterrent justification of international criminal law may be more
persuasive in the context of corporations than individuals.[108] It is hoped that
emphasising the actual *and potential* criminal responsibility of corporate actors
will incentivise better business culture[109] and will go some way towards addressing
some aspects of the economic underpinnings of international crime. It may also
meet some of the criticisms of a north–south divide in the practice of international
criminal law. For example, Kyriakakis has suggested that '[t]hrough engaging with
the relationship between commerce and atrocity, in the context of a contemporary
global economy dominated by transnational corporations, international criminal
institutions may invite a re-investment of faith in the international criminal justice
project'.[110] However, whether these objectives are satisfied will depend upon *how*
corporate actors are incorporated into international criminal law. Baars's work,
discussed earlier (chapter 4), shines a cautionary light on optimism that corporate
actors will be incorporated into international criminal law in a way that addresses
the economic underpinnings of international crime, given the law's ideological
functions.[111]

Thus, whilst the need to address corporate responsibility and the economic
drivers of international crime are clearly related, it is important to consider whether
the current thresholds of international criminal law are suitable for addressing
the economic drivers of violence, in so far as the thresholds for determining
mens rea and actus reus as applied to corporate actors are likely to cover only the
most 'spectacular' corporate contributions to international crime.[112] As already
mentioned, the application of these thresholds raises challenges when the support
corporations lend to the commission of international crime covers legitimate and
illegitimate business activities. It may be considered that existing international
law draws the international criminal legal line in the most appropriate legal place,
given the seriousness of international crimes. However, the thresholds for establishing liability are set high and could, therefore, give a green light to corporate
practices that may contribute to the conditions that facilitate international crime if

---

[107] E Mankowski, 'Conflict Minerals and Crimes against Humanity in the DRC: How to Hold
Individual Corporate Officers Criminally Liable' (2019) 94 *Notre Dame Law Review* 1453, 1473–74.

[108] See, eg, Kyriakakis (n 3) 236; Stewart (n 78) 73.

[109] International Commission of Jurists (n 78) 59.

[110] See further, eg, Kyriakakis (n 3) 240.

[111] Baars (n 85) 192.

[112] On the spectacular, see I Kalpouzos and I Mann, 'Banal Crimes against Humanity: The Case of
Asylum Seekers in Greece' (2015) 16(1) *Melbourne Journal of International Law* 1.

not to international crime itself. Moreover, these thresholds do little to encourage resistance to the economic underpinnings of international crime.

Despite the – perhaps rather optimistic – claim that international criminal law will become increasingly relevant to corporate actors,[113] international criminal lawyers are faced with a double bind. On the one hand, for international criminal law to ignore the economic aspects of international crime is myopic. On the other, to push for the prosecution of corporate actors within the current system risks exculpating conduct that may contribute to international crime. This risk of exculpation may be outweighed by the fact that litigation might generate contestation that contributes to longer-term societal or legal change. Whether it is considered to do so is a factual, political and strategic judgement.

Taken together, all these challenges to responsibility in 'official' international criminal law render the work of citizens' tribunals so valuable precisely because they adopt a broader approach to responsibility, including that of corporations, thereby shifting the gaze from more conventional objects of international criminal law.

Citizens' tribunals are not homogeneous, but common themes stand out. Typically, they address the alleged responsibility and complicity of a wide range of actors, including states, transnational corporations and (occasionally) also individuals.[114] Some focus on human rights violations, others on (international) criminal law violations, and yet others address both. Citizens tribunals focus on the processes underpinning the commission of (international) crime and human rights, including by paying attention to the economic bases of violations. Verdicts typically aim at generating change, including, for example, in the case of the World Tribunal on Iraq (WTI), through draft resistance and consumer boycotts. The WTI called on people to begin 'nonviolent actions against US and UK corporations that directly profit' from the war, including boycotts and divestment campaigns,[115] seeking to energise elite and non-elite bystanders. The idea of elite bystanders here derives from the work of Cameron, who acknowledges the diversity of bystanders and provides a productive way of thinking through different bystanders to

---

[113] International Commission of Jurists (n 78) 5.

[114] See further, eg, Permanent Peoples' Tribunal, *Sessions on Transnational Corporations in Southern African* (PPT 2016–2018) at http://permanentpeoplestribunal.org/wp-content/uploads/2016/09/PPT_VERDICT_JHB_August-2017-Final-Version.pdf; Permanent Peoples' Tribunal, *Session on Agrochemical Transnational Corporations* (PPT 2011) at http://permanentpeoplestribunal.org/wp-content/uploads/2011/12/TPP_Bangalore3Dec2011.pdf; Permanent Peoples' Tribunal, *The EU and Transnational Corporations in Latin America* (PPY 2010) at http://permanentpeoplestribunal.org/wp-content/uploads/2010/05/TPP-MADRID-2010-EN.pdf.

[115] Jury of Conscience, 'Declaration of the Jury of Conscience of World Tribunal on Iraq – Istanbul, 23–27 June 2005' in MG Sökmen (ed), *World Tribunal on Iraq: Making the Case against War* (Olive Branch Press, 2008) 492, 500–01. Byrnes and Simm explain that PPT hearings are not without effect on corporations. For example, they claim that 'the "ethical-moral pressure" of the PPT hearings on transnational corporations in Latin America helped create a more conducive climate for negotiations with corporations': A Byrnes and G Simm, 'Reflections on the Past and Future of International People's Tribunals' in A Byrnes and G Simm (eds), *People's Tribunals and International Law* (Cambridge University Press, 2018) 259, 268.

international crime. She explains that bystanders are far from homogeneous: they may be individuals or collectives; they may be near the site of the crime, or far away from it; they may be ordinary or 'elite'. Thus, she refers to 'global elite bystanders' to describe 'the global ruling elites and states with enforceable and non-enforceable legal obligations to society as a whole, … who are … physically distanced from the loci of atrocity'.[116]

A focus on citizens' tribunals is particularly apt in the context of structurally based harm. As Dianne Otto explains, 'The means of challenging structural injustice lie largely outside the law, in the politics of the everyday, for which we all share some responsibility'.[117] In focusing on economic processes and actors, and seeking to generate resistance to them, citizens' tribunals raise fundamental questions about the conditions that might enable and/or limit the commission of international crimes and human rights violations. These include but are not limited to the role of corporate actors. Citizens' tribunals are not the only actors that raise these questions, or that encourage boycotts and divestment campaigns. What is unique about citizens' tribunals is their attempt to do so specifically through an albeit informal (quasi) legal process. That is not to downplay other campaigning strategies. However, citizens' tribunals can bestow some quasi-legal authority on such campaigns, whilst simultaneously casting a light on the limitations and alternative possibilities of international criminal law.

B. State Responsibility

The focus on individual criminal responsibility also risks glossing over the way states commit or support – or fail to prevent – the commission of international crime.[118] As Simpson explains, it can also 'exonerate the state system'.[119] International criminal law does not provide for state criminal responsibility.[120] Some crimes, for example, perhaps most obviously but by no means only, aggression, are inherently state-centric and/or committed through the state and its organs. Those who would like international criminal law to include state criminal responsibility will likely consider the removal of state criminal responsibility from the Draft Articles on State Responsibility a loss (chapter 4). However, to some

---

[116] Cameron (n 4) 72.

[117] D Otto, 'Beyond Legal Justice: Some Personal Reflection on People's Tribunals, Listening And Responsibility' (2017) 5(2) *London Review of International Law* 225, 229.

[118] See further, eg, Rumney (n 4) 595, claiming that 'there is an abundance of evidence concerning Anglo-American involvement in genocide within the public domain'; Dallaire (n 5); Cameron (n 4) 72.

[119] Simpson (n 8) 83.

[120] For the argument that the 'criminalization of states' or the so-called 'Versailles Model' exists alongside the 'punishment of individuals (the Nuremberg Model)', see Simpson (n 8) 77; and, arguing that the 'outlawry of whole states' has become 'a favoured technique of international administration in Serbia, in Afghanistan and in relation to Iraq', ibid 85. See further, on state responsibility, I Scobbie, 'Assumptions and Presuppositions: State Responsibility for System Crimes' in Nollkaemper and van der Wilt (eds) (n 2) 270; A Zimmermann and M Teichmann, 'State Responsibility for International Crimes' in Nollkaemper and van der Wilt (eds) (n 2) 298.

extent this exclusion is symbolic, in so far as state criminal responsibility was understood by its supporters as 'an aggravated regime of state responsibility',[121] which the current ILC articles on state responsibility retain.[122]

Although states cannot be found criminally responsible, they can be held responsible in other ways, for example at the International Court of Justice (ICJ) (which does not exercise criminal jurisdiction) for committing or facilitating the commission of international crime. States, then, are responsible for internationally wrongful acts committed against other states. Injured states may act on their own behalf or on behalf of their injured nationals. The increasing recognition of the potential importance of state responsibility can be seen in the Draft Articles on Prevention and Punishment of Crimes Against Humanity 2019, which require reparation to victims of crimes against humanity 'committed through acts attributable to the State under international law' (Article 12).[123] However, there are numerous occasions on which states, including powerful western states, have for strategic, economic and/or political reasons supported states that are alleged to have committed international crimes.[124] The assistance that states have lent to extraordinary rendition by the US in the context of the War on Terror has been described as the 'single most extensive example of complicity in recent history'.[125] Addressing state responsibility for international crime may therefore offer a potential avenue to address some of the underlying actors and factors in the commission of international crime.[126]

States are obliged in certain circumstances not to aid and assist in the commission of international crime. For example, Article 6(3) of the Arms Trade Treaty 2013 provides:

> A State Party shall not authorize any transfer of conventional arms covered under Article 2(1) or of items covered under Article 3 or Article 4, if it has knowledge at the time of authorization that the arms or items would be used in the commission of

---

[121] G Abi-Saab, 'The Uses of Article 19' (1990) 10(2) *European Journal of International Law* 339, 351. There is an extensive literature on Art 19: see further, eg, G Gilbert, 'The Criminal Responsibility of States' (1990) 39 *International and Comparative Law Quarterly* 345; S Rosenne, 'State Responsibility and International Crimes: Further Reflection on Article 19 of the Draft Articles on State Responsibility' (1997) 30 *New York University Journal of International Law and Politics* 145.

[122] See further, Arts 40, 42, 42 and 48, ILC Articles on the Responsibility of States for Internationally Wrongful Acts 2001, GAR 56/83.

[123] Draft Articles on Prevention and Punishment of Crimes against Humanity (n 93).

[124] For a discussion in the context of support to Khmer Rouge, see Rumney (n 4) 599–600; Cameron (n 4) 70–87. See further, eg, JS Bachman, 'A "Synchronised Attack" on Life: The Saudi-Led Coalition's "Hidden and Holistic" Genocide in Yemen and the shared Responsibility of the US and UK' (2019) 40(2) *Third World Quarterly* 298.

[125] A Nollkaemper, 'Complicity in International Law – Some Lessons from the US Rendition Program' (2015) 109 *American Society of International Law Proceedings* 177, 178. See further NHB Jørgensen, 'Complicity in Torture in a Time of Terror: Interpreting the European Court of Human Rights Extraordinary Rendition Cases' (2017) 16 *Chinese Journal of International Law* 11.

[126] See, eg, the discussion in the context of the arms trade, S Kendall and C da Silva, 'Beyond the ICC: State Responsibility for the Arms Trade in Africa' in KM Clarke, AS Knottnerus and de Volder (eds), *Africa and the ICC: Perceptions of Justice* (Cambridge University Press, 2016) 407.

genocide, crimes against humanity, grave breaches of the Geneva Conventions of 1949, attacks directed against civilian objects or civilians protected as such, or other war crimes as defined by international agreements to which it is a Party.[127]

In the absence of a specific similar primary obligation, the secondary rules of state responsibility also bestow – albeit in some cases – less stringent obligations on states not to aid international crimes.[128] Article 16 of the ILC Articles on the Responsibility of States for Internationally Wrongful Acts 2011 provides:

A State which aids or assists another State in the commission of an internationally wrongful act by the latter is internationally responsible for doing so if:

(a)   that State does so *with knowledge* of the circumstances of the internationally wrongful act; and

(b)   the act would be internationally wrongful if committed by that State.[129]

Although not in the text of Article 16, the ILC commentary suggests that 'the aid or assistance must be given with a view to facilitating the commission of' the act. In other words, the state should have 'intended' to facilitate it.[130] Much depends on how the requirements of knowledge and intention are interpreted. This knowledge requirement could encourage states to turn a 'blind eye' to the internationally wrongful acts of the state receiving assistance.[131] As a result, the intention requirement could exculpate states that lend support for primarily political, strategic or economic reasons.[132]

---

[127] See further, eg, Common Art 1 of the Geneva Conventions; see further, Bryk and Saage-Maas (n 80); Kendall and da Silva (n 126) 407.

[128] Art 41(1), Responsibility of States for Internationally Wrongful Acts 2001, provides that 'states shall cooperate to bring to an end through lawful means any serious breach within the meaning of Article 40' and shall not 'recognise as lawful a situation created by a serious breach within the meaning of Article 40, nor render aid or assistance in maintaining that situation' (Art 41(2)).

[129] Emphasis added. For extensive discussion, see H Moynihan, *Aiding and Assisting: Challenges in Armed Conflict and Counterterrorism* (Chatham House, Royal Institute of International Affairs, 2016). See further J Howard, 'Invoking State Responsibility for Aiding the Commission of International Crimes – Australia, the United States and the Question of East Timor' [2001] *Melbourne Journal of International Law* 2; G Nolte and HP Aust, 'Equivocal Helpers: Complicit States, Mixed Messages and International Law' (2009) 58 *International and Comparative Law Quarterly* 1. See also Art 14, ILC Draft Articles on the Responsibility of International Organizations 2011, which states that 'An international organization which aids or assists a State or another international organization in the commission of an internationally wrongful act by the State or the latter organization is internationally responsible for doing so if: (a) the former organization does so with knowledge of the circumstances of the internationally wrongful act; and (b) the act would be internationally wrongful if committed by that organization.'

[130] *Case Concerning Application of the Convention on the Prevention and Punishment of the Crime of Genocide (Bosnia and Herzegovina v Serbia and Montenegro)* [2007] ICJ Rep 43, para 417 (hereinafter 'Bosnian Genocide').

[131] For a discussion of European Court of Human Rights (ECtHR) cases and the softening of the knowledge requirement, see Nollkaemper (n 125) 180; and Jørgensen (n 125) 33. For the argument that the knowledge requirement will be satisfied 'where an assisting state has actual or near-certain knowledge that the assistance will be used for unlawful purposes by the recipient state, or where the state is wilfully blind to such knowledge', see Moynihan (n 129) 15.

[132] For the counter argument that the intention requirement will be satisfied if the supporting state has 'knowledge or virtual certainty that the recipient state will use the assistance unlawfully', see Moynihan (n 129) 20.

In the *Bosnian Genocide* case, the ICJ held that for a state to be found complicit in genocide, it was necessary to show that the state was aware of the principal's specific intent to commit genocide.[133] In contrast, the knowledge requirement necessary to substantiate a finding that a state has failed in its obligation to prevent genocide is lower. Whereas for complicity, the alleged accomplice must have '*full* knowledge of the facts' (emphasis added), for a state to be responsible for its failure to prevent genocide, it was 'enough that the State was aware, or should normally have been aware, of the serious danger that acts of genocide would be committed'.[134] Thus, the ICJ held that Serbia had breached the obligation to prevent genocide. Because the standard was one of due diligence, a state's capacity to influence the recipient state was critical, and this depended on several factors, including geographical distance and political and other links.[135] It seems reasonable to conclude that states that supply military aid may have capacity to influence the receiving state. Critically:

> [A] State's obligation to prevent, and the corresponding duty to act, arise at the instance that the State *learns of, or should normally have learned of, the existence of a serious risk that genocide will be committed.* From that moment onwards, if the State has available to it means likely to have a deterrent effect … it is under a duty to make such use of these means as the circumstances permit.[136]

In that case, it can be argued that the obligation to prevent requires a state to cease providing aid, even if providing aid might not amount to complicity under the stricter intention requirement of Article 16. In this context, the work of citizens' tribunals can contribute to the knowledge that a state has, or should have, of potential abuse,[137] demonstrating another way in which the work of citizens' tribunals can be used to pressure governments. Noteworthily, the ILC Draft Articles on

---

[133] *Bosnian Genocide* (n 130). Although Art 16, ILC Articles was not applicable, the Court considered the applicable provision, that is Art III(e) of the Genocide Convention, through the prism of Art 16, even though the assistance was not provided to a state as such.

[134] *Bosnian Genocide* (n 130) para 432.

[135] ibid. See also, albeit in a different context, Human Rights Council, '"They Came to Destroy": ISIS Crimes against the Yazidis', 15 June 2016, A/HRC/32/CRP.2, para 194: 'In order to determine whether States have violated their obligations under the Genocide Convention, further investigation is required as to whether States – and notably Syria and Iraq, being the territories in which ISIS is committing genocide – are taking all measures to prevent genocide which are within their power.'

[136] *Bosnian Genocide* (n 130) para 431 (emphasis added).

[137] See, eg, the parliamentary question Lord Alton of Liverpool posed on the British Government response to the Uyghur Tribunal: 'Given that the Uyghur Tribunal, led by Sir Geoffrey Nice QC, who prosecuted Slobodan Milošević, has conducted easily the most comprehensive examination of the Uighur crisis, having reviewed hundreds of thousands of pages of evidence and declared in a very tightly drawn judgment there to be a genocide, will the Minister … tell us whether the Government have performed the required assessment under the genocide convention of whether the Uighurs are at serious risk of genocide and, if not, whether they will now do so?' Cited in J Curtis and T Robinson, 'The Uyghur Tribunal' (House of Commons Library, 18 January 2022) 19 at https://researchbriefings.files.parliament.uk/documents/CDP-2022-0009/CDP-2022-0009.pdf. See further, UK Tribunal to Investigate China's Alleged Genocide and Crimes Against Humanity against Uyghur, Kazakh and Other Turkic Muslim populations at https://uyghurtribunal.com/.

Prevention and Punishment of Crimes Against Humanity also establish obligations of prevention.[138]

State responsibility, then, may offer a means to challenge support that states
lend to other states that are accused of committing international crimes. At least
one commentator has argued that 'states increasingly take into account Article 16
in their assessments of the risks of cooperation'.[139] However, in the absence of a
breach of a specific primary rule, the threshold for holding a state complicit in
wrongfulness is high, and its application to specific circumstances is likely to be
challenging.[140] Even if a state could be found that was willing to raise this alleged
breach against another state, it would likely face numerous jurisdictional hurdles
if it were to seek to bring a challenge before the ICJ, since that Court's jurisdiction
is limited in so far as it is based on the consent of states. In practice, then, legal
action regarding state complicity might more easily be brought – and in fact has
been – before domestic or regional human rights courts.[141] Faced with these challenges, another or parallel approach would be to consider the role that complicity
doctrines could play in mobilising resistance on the part of civil society to international crime and the conditions underpinning it. Here again, we might turn to the
work of citizens' tribunals, which adopt a broader approach to the question of state
responsibility for international crime.

While state responsibility is not the primary focus of international criminal
law, citizens' tribunals typically focus on state rather than individual responsibility.
Some do, however, consider state and individual criminal responsibility alongside
each other, as the WIWCT did. The focus on the state reflects the more general
concern of citizens' tribunals with systemic processes and structures behind the
commission of atrocity, rather than individual 'bad apples'. Unsurprisingly, then,
citizens' tribunals also emphasise the complicity of official institutions – both
international and domestic – in the perpetration of, or failure to prevent, international crime and/or the so-called 'crime of silence' (chapter 5). For example,
the WIWCT criticised the Tokyo Tribunal's failure to deal with crimes against
'comfort women', observing '[t]hat a court, especially an internationally constituted
court, could ignore a systematic atrocity of this dimension is unconscionable'.[142]

---

[138] These are understood as 'effective legislative, administrative, judicial or other appropriate preventive measures in any territory under [the State's] jurisdiction' and 'cooperation with other States,
relevant intergovernmental organizations, and, as appropriate, other organizations': Art 4, Draft
Articles on Prevention and Punishment of Crimes Against Humanity (n 93).

[139] Moynihan (n 129) 4.

[140] See further, eg, Nolte and Aust (n 129) 16.

[141] On cases at the ECtHR, including *Al Nashiri v Poland*, Judgment (ECtHR, 24 July 2014) and
Husayn v Poland, Judgment (ECtHR, 24 July 2014), see Jørgensen (n 125).

[142] Quoted in S Jayasimha, 'Victor's Justice, Crime of Silence and the Burden of Listening: Judgement
of the Tokyo Tribunal 1948, Women's International War Crimes Tribunal 2000 and Beyond' (2001) 1
Law, Social Justice and Global Development Journal 35 at http://elj.warwick.ac.uk/global/issue/2001-/
jayashimha.html. See further, on the Cambodian tribunal as a response to the lack of recognition
by regional transitional justice mechanisms of gender violence, D Otto, 'Beyond Legal Justice: Some
Personal Reflections on People's Tribunals, Listening and Responsibility' (2017) 5 *London Review of
International Law* 225, 231–32.

A further example can be seen in the WTI's criticism of what it considered to be the complicity and responsibility of the Security Council for 'loss of civilian life and destruction of Iraqi infrastructure'.[143] When responsibility is considered to lie not just in individuals but also in the state or international institutions, a longer historical view of the causes and responsibility for international crime is enabled, and indeed required. Thus, citizens' tribunals can address a broader colonial legacy more directly and explicitly than can a court process that focuses on individual responsibility. For example, amongst its findings, the PPT on Sri Lanka considered that the 'events of 2009 [were] the logical manifestation of the structural genocide that had been put in place during the colonial period and in the construction of the newly independent unitary Sri Lankan state'.[144] Though their focus on state responsibility, citizens' tribunals address a broader range of actors within the state than 'official' international criminal law does. Thus, responsibility is positioned not just as a (bilateral) matter between states on the international plane. For example, for the Guatemalan PPT, it was 'essential that citizens of the United States be informed about the human consequences of 30 years of US interventionism in Guatemala'.[145] In this way, citizens' tribunals seek to encourage resistance to international crimes/human rights violations and the conditions that underpin them amongst a broader constituency, typically shifting the didactic gaze from communities of the global south to (powerful) actors in states, typically in the global north. While citizens' tribunals focus on state responsibility, then, their approach to state responsibility does not just mimic conventional international law's approach to state responsibility; rather, here as elsewhere, they use responsibility in a broader provocative manner.

V. Conclusion

Individual criminal responsibility is a key feature of international criminal law. However, a widespread concern is that this paradigm meshes uneasily with the collective context of international criminality. As such, it arguably contributes to the inability of international criminal law to deal with some of the fundamental causes of international criminal offending. Civil society actors have sought to fill some of the accountability gaps left by official international criminal law. They have gone beyond just acting as a supplementary site of accountability. They have put forward alternative narratives about responsibility, based on encouraging resistance to international crime, especially amongst bystanders of

---

[143] Jury of Conscience (n 115) 497.

[144] PPT, *Peoples' Tribunal on Sri Lanka*, 7–10 December 2013 (PPT 2014) 32 at www.ptsrilanka.org/wp-content/uploads/2017/04/ppt_final_report_web_en.pdf.

[145] S Jonas, E McCaughan and ES Martinez, *Guatemala Tyranny on Trial Testimony of the Permanent Peoples' Tribunal* (Synthesis Publications, 1984) v.

different kinds,[146] and emphasise that international crime (although not international criminal responsibility per se) is the responsibility of a much broader audience. Here as elsewhere, then, the chapter has emphasised that there is not a single vision of international criminal law, its scope and potential, but multiple visions deployed by, and amongst, different actors. In that sense, the subjects and subjectivity of international criminal law are mutually re-enforcing.

Given the widespread commission of international crime, there is still much work to be done in thinking about responsibility. Most immediately, from a doctrinal perspective, modes of liability, their fit on the ground and their fairness to the accused can be considered. Thinking about the law from a critical perspective, it is important to pay continuous attention to what or whom individual criminal responsibility inculpates/exculpates, and the underpinning relations of power that are supported by the vision of the world that it expresses.[147] Still from within the existing law, the work of those who develop creative legal strategies to address accountability gaps inside the courtroom might be emphasised. Alternatively, the work of those who imagine a transformed vision of responsibility, such as citizens' tribunals, might be accentuated. There may be potential for official and unofficial international criminal law together to address international crime collectively or in a complementary fashion. Finally, the responsibilities of international criminal law and international criminal courts might also be considered.[148] As we have seen, international criminal law can also be a source of injustice, for example by glossing over certain harms (chapter 5) and, as will become apparent (chapter 8), through its tendency to instrumentalise victims of international crime.[149] International law may also have contributed to the conditions that enabled international crime.[150] While there is not space to pursue this here, these factors provoke consideration whether it is possible and desirable for international criminal courts to be held accountable for practices, including omissions, that have negative consequences for identifiable individuals or groups of individuals beyond the accused. If so, should such accountability be through legal or political processes, within the existing international criminal court structure or beyond, and to which actors? Here as elsewhere, citizens' tribunals may provide some means of holding official institutions to account.

---

[146] For a further argument (albeit not in the context of citizens' tribunals) that 'exemplary accounts of disobedience might usefully inform the legal pedagogy of war crimes tribunals', see Leebaw (n 20) 356.

[147] eg, for discussion of gendered nature of modes of liability, S SáCouto, LN Sadat and PV Sellers, 'Collective Criminality and Sexual Violence: Fixing a Failed Approach' (2020) 33(1) *Leiden Journal of International Law* 207.

[148] I am grateful to Christine Schwöbel-Patel for this provocation. For discussion of compensation on acquittal, see JD Michels, 'Compensating Acquitted Defendants for Detention before International Criminal Courts' (2010) 8(2) *Journal of International Criminal Justice* 407. See further Art 85(3), Rome Statute; *Prosecutor v Jean-Pierre Bemba Gombo*, Decision on Mr Bemba's claim for compensation and damages, 18 May 2020, ICC-01/05-01/08-3694.

[149] See further E Haslam, *The Slave Trade, Abolition and the Long History of International Criminal Law The Recaptive and the Victim* (Routledge 2020) 130.

[150] ibid 129.

There is plenty of work still to do in thinking about responsibility, but running through each of these approaches is the question: How far should international (criminal) responsibility extend and in what form? The answer to this is not just a matter of international criminal legal responsibility, even though it is mediated through international criminal law. Ultimately, as citizens' tribunals' and acts of civil disobedience make clear, this is a question that implicates, but goes beyond, international criminal law strictly understood. It is a question to be asked of us all.[151]

Further Reading

G Baars, 'Capitalism's Victor's Justice? The Hidden Stories behind the Prosecution of Industrialists Post-WWII' in K Heller and G Simpson (eds), *The Hidden Histories of War Crimes Trials* (Oxford University Press, 2013) 179.

MA Drumbl, *Atrocity, Punishment and International Law* (Cambridge University Press, 2007).

B Leebaw, 'Justice and the Faithless: The Demand for Disobedience in International Criminal Law' (2018) 24(2) *European Journal of International Relations* 344.

A Nollkaemper and H Van der Wilt, *System Criminality in International Law* (Cambridge University Press, 2009).

[151] See further, D Otto, 'Impunity in a Different Register: People's Tribunals and Questions of Judgment, Law and Responsibility' in E Engle, Z Miller and DM Davis (eds), *Anti-Impunity and the Human Rights Agenda* (Cambridge University Press, 2016) 291, 308.

7

International Criminal Law and the Conditions of Possibility: Jurisdiction

I. Introduction

International criminal law has considerable attraction. It promises to speak to injustice, including that allegedly perpetrated by powerful actors. Speaking to injustice in the authoritative language of the law has material and expressive effects. Jurisdiction determines not just who comes before courts – and for what – but also the narratives or historical record that courts produce about atrocity. Principles of jurisdiction therefore play a key role in determining the extent to which international criminal law can fulfil its multiple promises, many of which were outlined in chapter 3. International criminal jurisdiction is, unsurprisingly, therefore, often fiercely contested.

This chapter offers an introduction to international criminal jurisdiction across a range of different sites. A central criticism of international criminal jurisdiction is that its exercise has tended to track geo-political realities. It is vital, then, to appreciate the criss-crossing relations of power that underpin jurisdiction's exercise. At the same time, it is important to consider the conditions under which international criminal law might speak to power. Thus, the chapter encourages an alertness to the factors that shape, constrain and enable international criminal jurisdiction, in order to understand the possibilities and limitations of international criminal law in its different forms.

II. Jurisdiction

It is easy to become preoccupied with the, albeit important, jurisdiction of international criminal courts, especially the ICC. After all, we tend to associate international criminal law with international courts and tribunals. Much international criminal law takes place at the domestic level, however.[1] The ICC's

---

[1] Langer and Eason wrote in 2019 that the last 10 years saw 'substantially more completed universal jurisdiction trials than completed trials at the ICC': M Langer and M Eason, 'The Quiet Expansion of Universal Jurisdiction' (2019) 30(3) *EJIL* 779, 782.

jurisdiction can also only be properly understood alongside that of national courts. At best, national prosecution can contribute to avoiding impunity, offer a potentially more pluralistic response to international crime, a more direct engagement with victims and affected communities, and a basis for the further development of international criminal law, particularly where it touches on matters where international criminal institutions currently do not tread. However, geo-political realities are such that individuals from less powerful states are more likely to be the object of prosecution than those from powerful states.[2]

Discussion about national prosecution of international crimes often centres on the scope and exercise of universal jurisdiction, including so-called universal jurisdiction *in absentia* (see below). However, universal jurisdiction is not the only basis on which courts exercise jurisdiction over international crimes. Generally, international law permits, but – with some exceptions – does not require, jurisdiction over people on the several grounds explored below. Jurisdiction may refer to prescriptive (or legislative) jurisdiction and enforcement jurisdiction, which includes adjudicative jurisdiction. The focus in this chapter is on adjudicative jurisdiction: that is, the power of courts to exercise jurisdiction over individuals, including in respect of their conduct abroad.

States have territorial jurisdiction. In other words, states exercise jurisdiction over offences that take place within their territorial boundaries. This is a concomitant of sovereignty. It is also where most witnesses and evidence are likely to be located. This is one of the grounds of jurisdiction that the ICC exercises. To be effective, international crime control requires the exercise of extra-territorial jurisdiction. In other words, states may need to exercise jurisdiction in respect of conduct that has taken place outside their territorial jurisdiction. There are several grounds on which courts may exercise jurisdiction over individuals in these circumstances. They may exercise jurisdiction on grounds of active nationality, that is, the state of the defendant's nationality may exercise jurisdiction over the conduct of an individual abroad. This is also a ground of jurisdiction the ICC exercises. Passive personality is a more controversial ground of jurisdiction. It is exercised by the state of the victims' nationality. This basis of jurisdiction was accepted by the Supreme Court of Israel in the prosecution and conviction of Adolf Eichmann, who was responsible for implementing the so-called 'Final Solution' to the Jewish Question. Eichmann was convicted for crimes against the Jewish people, crimes against humanity and war crimes under the Nazis and Nazi Collaborators (Punishment) Law 1950, and was sentenced to death.[3]

---

[2] As Cowell notes, 'any utopian project to dilute sovereignty is invariably going to affect some states more than others'. F Cowell, 'Inherent Imperialism: Understanding the Legal Roots of Anti-Imperialist Criticism of the International Criminal Court' (2017) 15 *Journal of International Criminal Justice* 667, 681.

[3] *Attorney-General of the Government of Israel v Eichmann Supreme Court of Jerusalem* (1969) 36 ILR 277.

The *Eichmann* case is important for understanding another controversial issue connected to jurisdiction, and a slight digression is in order here to explore it. This concerns the impact of abduction/kidnapping on courts' jurisdiction. Israeli security services had abducted Eichmann from Argentina to Israel. As a result, Argentina complained that its territorial sovereignty had been violated, and in 1960 the UN Security Council passed Resolution 4349 criticising Israel.[4] Eventually, Argentina and Israel agreed to consider the incident settled. Even so, the abduction raised a jurisdictional question, namely, whether the Israeli courts should still exercise jurisdiction despite Eichmann's having been brought to the court's jurisdiction unlawfully. The Israeli District Court that observed that Israel and Argentina had considered the matter settled between them, noted:

> [T]here can be no escaping the conclusion that the violation of international law through the mode of bringing of the accused into the territory of the country pertains to the international level, namely the relations between the two countries concerned only, and must find its solution at such level.[5]

Thus, the remedy for the abduction and associated violation of sovereignty was a question for the two states concerned.[6] Whether international courts should refuse to exercise jurisdiction where an individual has been illegally arrested and detained has also been an issue. The ICTY was confronted with this issue in the *Nikolić* case. Nikolić had been abducted in Serbia, taken to Bosnia and Herzegovina and handed over to the Stabilisation Force, which then passed him to the ICTY.[7] The ICTY noted that

> [t]he Appeals Chamber does not consider that in cases of universally condemned offences, jurisdiction should be set aside on the ground that there was a violation of the sovereignty of a State, when the violation is brought about by the apprehension of fugitives from international justice, whatever the consequences for the international responsibility of the State or organisation involved.[8]

However, it also held that 'certain human rights violations are of such a serious nature that they required that the exercise of jurisdiction be declined', although 'apart from such exceptional cases ... the remedy of setting aside jurisdiction will ... usually be disproportionate.'[9]

The issue of abductions raises two conflicting interests. In *Nikolić*, the court referred to the need for a 'correct balance ... between the fundamental rights of the accused and the essential interests of the international community in the

---

[4] UNSC Res S/4349 (24 June 1960).

[5] *Attorney-General Israel v Eichmann (District Court)* Ciminal Case No 40/61 at para 50; (1968) 26 ILR 5, (1962) 56 *AJIL* 805, 839.

[6] Compare, eg, *US V Alvarez-Machain* (1992) 31 *ILM* 900 and *State v Ebrahim* (1992) 31 *ILM* 888.

[7] *Prosecutor v Nikolić*, Decision on Interlocutory Appeal Concerning Legality of Arrest, 5 June 2003, IT-94-3-AR73.

[8] ibid para 26.

[9] ibid paras 30–31.

prosecution of persons charged with serious violations of international humanitarian law'.[10] On the one hand, allowing a trial to go ahead even when someone has been brought to the court unlawfully avoids impunity. On the other, it can encourage illegal abductions, individual human rights violations and violations of state sovereignty. A variant of state-sponsored abduction, known as extraordinary rendition, has been of particular concern in the context of the so-called War on Terror. Those who are extraordinarily rendered are rarely accorded the opportunity to face trial before a regularly constituted court as Eichmann and Nikolić were.

To return to jurisdiction, states may also exercise protective jurisdiction, also accepted by the Supreme Court of Israel in *Eichmann*. This arises where states' essential interests are threatened, such as their national security. In *Eichmann*, the Supreme Court of Israel affirmed the District Court's decision, which based its jurisdiction on the protective principle (along with passive personality and universal jurisdiction), considering that his crime 'very deeply concerns the vital interests of the State of Israel'.[11]

Finally, the ground of jurisdiction most associated with international law is universal jurisdiction, although it is important to be aware that this is not a ground of jurisdiction the ICC exercises. Universal jurisdiction, unlike the other grounds, does not require a link between the state exercising jurisdiction and the crime allegedly committed. Rather, it allows states to prosecute an individual by virtue of his or her presence on a state's territory alone, irrespective of where the crimes took place or the nationality of the victim or alleged perpetrator. This was also a ground of jurisdiction in the *Eichmann* case. International crimes are often said to shock the conscience of humankind, thereby justifying universal jurisdiction. Historically, however, scholars have shown how universal jurisdiction for piracy, which is often claimed to be the first international crime, was in fact based on self-defence rather than heinousness.[12]

International crimes are often identified by virtue of their attracting universal jurisdiction, and it is the basis of jurisdiction most closely associated with international criminal law. Although not all international courts are empowered to apply it, the ICTR and ICTY, creations of Security Council resolutions, did have that power. They also had supremacy over national proceedings in so far as they could request such proceedings to defer to them, under Article 9 of the ICTY Statute and Article 8 of the ICTR Statute, respectively.[13] The ICC, as we shall see, is a different matter. It does not exercise universal jurisdiction. Since the crimes prosecuted at the ICC typically attract universal jurisdiction in customary international law,

---

[10] ibid para 31.

[11] *Eichmann* (n 5) para 35.

[12] E Kontorovich, 'The Piracy Analogy: Modern Universal Jurisdiction's Hollow Foundation' (2004) 45(1) *Harvard International Law Journal* 183, 186.

[13] Statute of the International Tribunal for the former Yugoslavia, adopted by S/RES/827 (25 May 1993); Statute of the International Criminal Tribunal for Rwanda, adopted by S/RES/955 (8 November 1994).

and in some cases under treaty law, the jurisdiction of the ICC over international crimes is more limited than that of other international and national courts.

Universal jurisdiction by its very name holds out the promise of inescapable justice. However, criticisms that states of the global north have overused universal jurisdiction have formed a key part of the concerns expressed by some African states about the exercise of international criminal law. This is the case even though the African Union Model Law on Universal Jurisdiction approaches universal jurisdiction broadly, to include not just crimes against humanity, genocide, war crimes and piracy but also narcotics trafficking and terrorism.[14] Trial International's *Universal Jurisdiction Annual Review* shows that the exercise of universal jurisdiction still predominates in the global north, with cases against individuals from the global north in states of the global south being exceptional.[15] However, noteworthy is that Argentinian authorities have investigated allegations of crimes against humanity committed under the Franco regime in Spain between 1936 and 1978.[16]

The exercise of universal jurisdiction *in absentia* has attracted controversy. Universal jurisdiction *in absentia* goes further than simple universal jurisdiction because it does not require (at least for the purpose of investigation, if not for prosecution) the presence of the accused on the territory of the state undertaking proceedings. The legality of universal jurisdiction *in absentia* was raised but not finally determined by the ICJ in the *Arrest Warrant* case.[17] This was an interstate dispute at the ICJ, a court that does not exercise criminal jurisdiction and does not have jurisdiction over individuals. However, it is relevant to international criminal law because it dealt with the legality of a Belgian arrest warrant issued against the then Foreign Minister of the Democratic Republic of the Congo (DRC) *in absentia*. In fact, the case was decided on the grounds of the individual's immunity, but some judges expressed views about universal jurisdiction more generally. A range of views were put forward. Amongst the critical views was that of Judge Guillaume, who observed in his Separate Opinion that

> at no time has it been envisaged that jurisdiction should be conferred upon the courts of every State in the world to prosecute such crimes, whoever their authors and victims and irrespective of the place where the offender is found. To do this would, moreover, risk creating total judicial chaos. It would also be to encourage the arbitrary for the

---

[14] African Union Model National Law on Universal Jurisdiction Over International Crimes 2012, EX CL/731 (XXI).

[15] Trial International, *Universal Jurisdiction Annual Review 2020: Terrorism and International Crimes: Prosecuting Atrocities for What They Are* (Trial International, 2020) at https://trialinternational.org/wp-content/uploads/2020/03/TRIAL-International_UJAR-2020_DIGITAL.pdf. For further discussion, see L Arimatsu, 'Universal Jurisdiction for International Crimes: Africa's Hope for Justice?' (Chatham House Briefing Paper, April 2010).

[16] Langer and Eason (n 1) 800–02.

[17] *Case Concerning the Arrest Warrant of 11 April 2000* [2002] ICJ Rep 1, 3. See further, eg, N Boister, 'The ICJ in the Belgian Arrest Warrant Case: Arresting the Development of International Criminal Law' (2002) 7 *Journal of Conflict and Security Law* 293.

benefit of the powerful, purportedly acting as agent for an ill-defined 'international community'.[18]

States have more recently adopted a narrower approach to universal jurisdiction. For example, Belgium had enacted legislation in 1993, as amended in 1999, to permit universal jurisdiction, including universal jurisdiction *in absentia*. This led to controversial (and unsuccessful) attempts to ensure proceedings against several military and civilian leading figures from the US and elsewhere. Amidst significant backlash, including the US suggestion that NATO headquarters be withdrawn from Brussels, Belgium amended the legislation in 2003 to restrict the exercise of universal jurisdiction so that its implementation required a link between the offence and Belgium.[19] Spanish legislation has followed a similar trajectory. It was amended after a complaint was made against the so-called 'Bush Six'.[20] These proceedings were closed in July 2015, after the Spanish national court decided it lacked jurisdiction because 2014 reforms required suspects to be either Spanish citizens or living in Spain.[21] Similarly, the European Center for Constitutional and Human Rights had filed criminal complaints in Germany against individuals, including Donald Rumsfeld, based on universal jurisdiction. However, in 2005 and 2006 respectively, the German Federal Prosecutor declined to act on the basis that a prosecution could only go ahead if the territorial state, or victims' or perpetrators' home state, was unwilling or unable to investigate and (in the case of the second complaint) the suspects resided in Germany.[22]

Thus, states have moved to a narrower vision of universal jurisdiction. Langer and Eason are two scholars who have explored the implementation of universal jurisdiction empirically. They suggest that there has been a 'quiet expansion of universal jurisdiction' exercised against 'low-level' or 'low cost defendants', not the sort of defendants considered above.[23] They argue this represents a shift 'from the interventionist "global enforcer" model' of universal jurisdiction, which is

---

[18] *Case Concerning the Arrest Warrant of 11 April 2000* (n 15) para 35. Ad hoc judge Bula-Bula (ibid para 81) questioned whether a state can 'pose as prosecutor for all mankind, in other words, to claim the right to redeem human suffering across national borders and over generations'.

[19] See further, L Vervaet, 'The Guantánamo-isation of Belgium' (2015) 56(4) *Race and Class* 26, 29; and, for a contrasting perspective, L Reydams, 'The Rise and Fall of Universal Jurisdiction' Leuven Centre for Global Governance Studies, Working Paper 37/2010, 24, 27 ('As an almost exclusively European affair [universal jurisdiction] represented a curious mixture of *mission civilisatrice and resistance against United States Hegemony and Israeli exceptionalism*.') cited in R Ben-Ari, 'Universal Jurisdiction: Chronicle of a Death Foretold?' (2015) 43(2) *Denver Journal of International Law and Policy* 165, 192.

[20] See further on Spanish proceedings, J Borger and D Fuchs, 'Spanish Judge to Hear Torture Case Against Six Bush Officials' *The Guardian* (19 March 2009).

[21] A later complaint to the Spanish Constitutional Court was also denied: see 'Torture in Guantánamo: Spain Closes Investigations into "Bush Six"' (European Center for Constitutional and Human Rights, nd) at www.ecchr.eu/en/case/torture-in-guantanamo-spain-closes-investigations-into-bush-six/. See further, on Spanish legislation, C Peters, 'The Impasse of Tibetan Justice: Spain's Exercise of Universal Jurisdiction in Prosecuting Chinese Genocide' (2015) 39 *Seattle University Law Review* 165.

[22] 'The Rumsfeld Torture Cases' (European Center for Constitutional and Human Rights, nd) at www.ecchr.eu/en/case/rumsfeld-torture-cases/.

[23] Langer and Eason (n 1) 809.

typical of attempts, for example, to bring individuals such as Pinochet to justice, to a model based on 'a "no safe haven"' approach, 'in which resources were almost exclusively devoted to prosecutions involving defendants who were residents, asylum seekers or people otherwise present in their territories'.[24] Since such trials involve defendants resident in the prosecuting state, trials have, they argue, tended to track migration patterns.[25] As a result, they may 'not reflect the distribution and gravity of crimes committed by different groups even within a given situation'.[26] Trial International has also noted an 'unprecedented willingness' on the part of states to prosecute based on universal jurisdiction. However, it has observed that prosecutions are increasingly directed at terrorist offences, rather than at international crimes such as war crimes, crimes against humanity and aggression.[27] Its concern is that prosecutions of terrorist-type offences are unlikely to cover the full range of crimes committed and are less likely to encompass state actors.[28] Such research provides an important reminder of the need, when examining law and its practice, to think beyond the number of cases brought before national courts and – as with any law – to consider the nature of the cases brought and the political dynamics they reflect, buttress and/or challenge. It shows how important it is, when considering the politics of international criminal law, to go beyond the polarised and broad-brush statements of principle through which debates about universal jurisdiction can sometimes be presented.

In other words, universal jurisdiction, like international criminal law more generally, has many faces. It is a potentially powerful legal and rhetorical tool that promises to deliver justice and to contribute to avoiding impunity. At the same time, its exercise is the outcome of criss-crossing power relations at any one moment, coupled with a fair dose of historical and political contingency. The more recent shifts that Langer and Eason and Trial International observe might be considered to reflect an increasing normalisation and practical utilisation of universal jurisdiction, or a regrettable 'taming' of a more radical vision. Whichever view is adopted, their research demonstrates the importance of exploring the practices that constitute universal jurisdiction, an importanace that is also evident at the ICC.

III. Jurisdiction and the ICC: Constraints and Possibilities

Two of the central concerns that have dominated criticism of the ICC are jurisdictional: its focus in its early years on situations in Africa; and its limited ability to address actors from western states and their allies. It is important, therefore, to

---

[24] ibid 807.
[25] ibid 813.
[26] ibid 815.
[27] Trial International (n 15) 12.
[28] ibid 11.

understand the legal and political factors that enable and constrain the exercise of
the ICC's jurisdiction, as well as the possibilities for these to be challenged.

A. Jurisdiction

The ICC is a treaty-based body. As such, its jurisdiction depends on the consent
of states in most cases. Without the consent of states, it enjoys limited legal and
factual power, especially over non-party states. Moreover, the ICC is 'at the mercy
of the good will of States, through the cooperation and the funding it receives
from them'.[29] Under Article 12(2) of the Rome Statute, the ICC exercises jurisdiction over individuals for crimes committed in the territory of a state party or by
the nationals of a state party but, under Article 11, only in respect of crimes that
occurred after the Rome Statute entered into force for the state concerned.[30] It
does not exercise universal jurisdiction. Thus in 2020, the ICC Chief Prosecutor
announced that she was unable to investigate the complaint of two Uyghur exile
groups, for lack of jurisdiction against Chinese nationals allegedly committing
crimes solely within the territory of China, a non-party state.[31]

However, under Article 12(3) of the Rome Statute, non-party states may also
accept the jurisdiction of the Court with respect to specific crime. For example,
non-party state Ukraine accepted the jurisdiction of the Court in 2014 with respect
to crimes committed between 21 November 2013 and 22 February 2014, and then
again in 2015 with respect to crimes committed since 20 February 2014. The 2009
attempt by the Palestinian authority to do this was unsuccessful because, as an
observer entity at the UN, it was not considered to be a state with capacity to sign
the Rome Statute. However, after the UN General Assembly recognised Palestine
as a non-member observer state in November 2012, Palestine successfully applied
to join the ICC. On 22 May 2018, Palestine referred the situation in Palestine to
the Prosecutor. On 5 February 2021, a majority of the Pre-Trial Chamber held that
the Court's territorial jurisdiction in the situation (for at least the relevant stage
reached in the proceedings) included Gaza and the West Bank and East Jerusalem,
although it emphasised it was not deciding the question of Palestinian statehood,
or its borders, under international law more generally.[32] As a result, on 3 March

---

[29] See, eg, Concurring and Separate Opinion of Judge Antoine Kesia-Mbe Mindua, Decision
Pursuant to Article 15 of the Rome Statute on the Authorisation of an Investigation into the Situation in
the Islamic Republic of Afghanistan, 12 April 2019, 31 May 2019, ICC-02/17-33-Anx-Corr07-06-2019,
para 42.

[30] Special jurisdictional provisions apply in the context of aggression (see ch 5). Defendants must also
be 18 or over at the time the alleged crime took place.

[31] J Curtis and T Robinson, 'The Uyghur Tribunal' (House of Commons Library, 18 January 2022) 5
at https://researchbriefings.files.parliament.uk/documents/CDP-2022-0009/CDP-2022-0009.pdf.

[32] Decision on the 'Prosecution request pursuant to article 19(3) for a ruling on the Court's territorial jurisdiction in Palestine', 5 February 2021, ICC-01/18-143. See further, D Bosco, 'Palestine in the
Hague: Justice, Geopolitics, and the International Criminal Court' (2016) 22 *Global Governance* 155.

2021, the then ICC Prosecutor Fatou Bensouda announced an investigation by the ICC into crimes allegedly committed in Palestine since 13 June 2014.[33]

When a state withdraws from the jurisdiction of the Court, the Court continues to claim jurisdiction over crimes committed while the state was still a party. For example, although the Philippines withdrew from the Rome Statute in March 2018, with effect from March 2019, the ICC's investigation into allegations of crimes committed pursuant to the so-called 'war on drugs' continues.[34]

The ICC has interpreted its territorial jurisdiction broadly. This has enabled it to consider situations involving nationals of non-party states in certain circumstances. For example, in the situation of the Rohingya, deported from non-party state Myanmar to party state Bangladesh, the Pre-Trial Chamber decided that the Court could exercise jurisdiction according to Article 12(2)(a) if 'at least one legal element of a crime within the jurisdiction of the Court or part of such a crime' was carried out on a state party's territory.[35] While deportation was by its nature 'inherently transboundary',[36] the Chamber accepted that its reasoning could also apply to other crimes, such as persecution in connection with deportation or preventing the return of Rohingya individuals as an inhumane act under Article 7(1)(k) of the Rome Statute.[37] A broad application of the Court's jurisdiction also opened the door to an investigation of alleged crimes committed by the Central Intelligence Agency (CIA), nationals of a non-party permanent Security Council member state, in so-called 'black sites' in Lithuania, Poland and Romania.[38] Thus, on 5 March 2020, the Appeals Chamber authorised an investigation into alleged crimes committed in Afghanistan and into other crimes allegedly committed since 1 July 2002 in other state parties, as long as they had 'a nexus to the armed conflict in

---

[33] 'Statement of ICC Prosecutor, Fatou Bensouuda, respecting an investigation of the Situation in Palestine'(ICC, 3 March 2021) at www.icc-cpi.int/news/statement-icc-prosecutor-fatou-bensouda-respecting-investigation-situation-palestine.

[34] ICC, 'Situation in the Republic of the Philippines' at www.icc-cpi.int/philippines.

[35] ICC Decision on the 'Prosecution's Request for a Ruling on Jurisdiction under Article 19(3) of the Statute', 6 September 2018, ICC-RoC46(3)-01/18, para 64. For criticism of this decision, see DJA Guilfoyle, 'The ICC Pre-Trial Chamber Decision on Jurisdiction over the Situation in Myanmar' (2019) 73 *Australian Journal of International Affairs* 2. For analysis of this decision, see KJ Fisher, 'The Problems with the Crime of Forced Migration as a Loophole to ICC jurisdiction' (2020) 11(2) *Journal of International Humanitarian Legal Studies* 385.

[36] ICC Decision on the 'Prosecution's Request for a Ruling' (n 32) para 71.

[37] ibid paras 74–77. However, an analogous argument failed on the facts at the preliminary examination stage in the context of allegations of international crimes committed against the Uyghurs. Office of the Prosecutor, Report on Preliminary Examination Activities 2020 (OTP, 14 December 2020) paras 70 et seq at www.icc-cpi.int/itemsDocuments/2020-PE/2020-pe-report-eng.pdf.

[38] Detainees were extraordinarily rendered to such CIA-led sites, where they were unable to challenge their detention and did not benefit from international oversight. Significant abuses that have taken place at such sites have been well documented. See further L Tayler and E Epstein, 'Legacy of the "Dark Side": The Costs of Unlawful US Detentions and Interrogations Post-9/11' (Watson Institute & Brown, Brown University, January 2022) at https://watson.brown.edu/costsofwar/files/cow/imce/papers/2022/Costs%20of%20War%20-%20Legacy%20of%20the%20%27Dark%20Side%27%20-%20Tayler%20and%20Epstein%20-%20FINAL%20Jan%209%202022.pdf.

Afghanistan and [were] sufficiently linked to the situation.'[39] This decision opened a door for the ICC to speak to the extra-territorial practices that have marked the War on Terror that was initiated after the attacks of 11 September 2001, and puts individuals in third states on notice of potential complicity.

In practice, without state consent and cooperation, such cases are unlikely to progress. However, even if they do not proceed to trial and/or conviction, framing a situation in the language of international criminal law is not without consequences, which may go some way towards meeting some of the objectives of international criminal justice discussed in chapter 3. Such framing may have expressive potential, may have some deterrent effect, may contribute to the historical record and may provide some space for acknowledging the experiences of survivors, although the lack of progress of a case may also risk disappointing them. Whether these effects are sufficient to outweigh the failure of a case to progress is ultimately a judgement call about which there is likely to be disagreement. Beyond this normative question, though, it is also important to understand the conditions that contributed to the Court's adoption of these interpretations in the first place.

One such condition is input from victims. The ICC accords victims a much greater role than other international criminal courts (chapter 8). Thus, victims may 'submit observations to the Court' in jurisdiction or admissibility proceedings under Article 19(3) of the Rome Statute. At least one commentator credits victims' representatives with pushing 'the envelope on the legal issues' around jurisdiction in the Rohingya situation.[40] Victims' representatives were also active in the Afghanistan appeal on jurisdiction, discussed further below. Victims' representations have also been credited with playing a key role in persuading pre-trial judges in the Georgia situation to authorise, and widen, the parameters of the ICC's investigation.[41]

Another way in which the Court receives broader input from a range of voices is through *amici curiae*, which are permitted by rule 103 of the Rules of Procedure and Evidence. This rule allows a chamber, 'if it considers it desirable for the proper determination of the case', to 'invite or grant leave to a State, organization, or person to submit, in writing or orally, any observation on any issue that the chamber deems appropriate'. Through *amici curiae*, a court can hear from a broad range of voices,[42] including experts and other stakeholders who may have a

---

[39] Situation in the Islamic Republic of Afghanistan, Judgment on the appeal against the decision on the authorisation of an investigation into the situation in the Islamic Republic of Afghanistan, 5 March 2020, ICC-02/17 OA4 (hereinafter 'Afghanistan Article 15 appeal') para 79.

[40] W Jordash and UY Aysev, 'Victim Participation in the Pre-Situation Phase: Insights from the Pre-Trial Chamber's Rohingya decision' in FIDH (International Federation for Human Rights), *Victims at the Centre of Justice: From 1998 to 2018: Reflections on the Promises and the Reality of Victim Participation at the ICC* (FIDH, 2018) 13, 14 at www.fidh.org/IMG/pdf/droitsdesvictimes730a_final.pdf.

[41] N Tsagareishvili, 'The ICC Investigation into the Situation of Georgia: Lack of Victims' Involvement and Related Challenges' in FIDH (n 40) 63, 65.

[42] See further, eg, D Shelton, 'The Participation of Nongovernmental Organisations in International Judicial Proceedings' (1994) 88 *American Journal of International Law* 611; J Razzaque, 'Changing Role

direct or indirect interest in the proceedings.[43] The ICC has issued 'open calls' in several cases for such observations.[44] In the Afghanistan appeals decision, numerous *amici curiae* made written and oral submissions, with the majority seeking to persuade the Appeals Chamber to overturn the decision of the Pre-Trial Chamber, which had refused to authorise an investigation into the situation in Afghanistan. However, it is not just victims or civil society organisations that play an important role in establishing the parameters of jurisdiction. Critical, as already mentioned, is the role of the state. This is perhaps most obviously seen in the role states play in referring situations to the ICC.

B. Referrals

Under Article 13 of the Rome Statute, for the Court to exercise its jurisdiction, it must receive a referral. Either a state party (Article 14) or the UN Security Council (as explored in section IV) (Article 13) can refer a situation to the ICC, or the ICC's independent Prosecutor can act *proprio motu*, that is of his or her own accord, 'on the basis of information on crimes within the jurisdiction of the Court' (Article 15). While a referral from one state party is sufficient, it is possible for referrals to come from multiple states; for example, between March and April 2022, 43 state parties referred the situation in Ukraine to the ICC. Situations, not specific individuals or cases, are referred to the Court.

Early in the life of the ICC, the Prosecutor encouraged voluntary referrals from states in which crimes were alleged to have taken place; as a result, the first situations to be referred to the Court (Uganda in January 2004 and the DRC in April 2004) resulted from the territorial state's referral (self-referral).[45] For the Prosecutor, 'voluntary referral has increased the likelihood of important cooperation and on-the-ground support'.[46] However, in practice, a referring state's options, that is whether to refer or not, can often be limited, not least because the encouragement to self-refer exists alongside the Prosecutor's power to initiate an investigation independently of a state referral (the *proprio motu* power explored in more detail below).[47] For example, when Kenya refused to self-refer, the OTP deployed its *proprio motu* power.[48] Scholars have also argued that

of Friends of the Court in the International Courts and Tribunals' (2001) 1(3) *Non-State Actors and International Law* 169.

[43] See S Williams and H Woolaver, 'The Role of State *Amici Curiae* in the Article 18(3) ICC Statute Proceedings: Friends or Distraction' (2020) 18(4) *Journal of International Criminal Justice* 891, 894–95.

[44] See further ibid 892–93.

[45] OTP, *Report on the Activities Performed during the First Three Years: June 2003–June 2006* (OTP, 12 September 2006) 7.

[46] ibid.

[47] Cowell (n 2) 677. See further A Kiyani, 'Group-Based Differentiation and Local Repression: The Custom and Curse of Selectivity' (2016) 14 *Journal of International Criminal Justice* 939, 949.

[48] Kiyani (n 47) 949.

governments have self-referred to the ICC as a way of exerting pressure on their opponents.[49] For example, indictments in the situation in Uganda that, as already mentioned, stemmed from Uganda's self-referral, have focused on members of the Lord Resistance Army but have not included allegations of crimes committed by Ugandan national armed forces, a pattern of apparently one-sided prosecutions that has been repeated in other situations before the Court.[50] Thus, it has been argued that self-referrals have 'instrumentalised' the ICC.[51] This is a regrettable situation, but one that may be difficult to avoid in the light of the state consent-based nature of the ICC.

Here, as elsewhere, then, it is important to drill down into the specific practices of the ICC and their effects to understand the multiple ways in which ICC jurisdiction can channel and resist power. On the one hand, as scholars have shown, while self-referrals may suggest a state's willingness to engage with the court, the examples above demonstrate that the question of consent is more complex. On the other hand, while the ICC has been criticised for its focus on Africa, it has been demonstrated that African governments have not just been the object of international criminal jurisdiction; they have also been able to deploy it to their own ends.

As mentioned, the ICC Prosecutor can also act *proprio motu*. In other words, the Prosecutor can begin a preliminary examination on his or her own initiative. This *proprio motu* power owes a huge debt to the activism of civil society at the Rome Conference.[52] However, unlike the case where a state or the Security Council has referred a situation, under Article 15(3) of the Rome Statute, the authorisation of the Pre-Trial Chamber is needed for a formal investigation to proceed when the Prosecutor is acting *proprio motu*. When the Court initially refused to authorise the prosecution's request to open an investigation into the Afghanistan situation for reasons that it would not serve the interests of justice (see section III.E), it took a narrower view of the extent of its authorisation than it had done previously. Seeking to avoid giving the Prosecutor a 'blank cheque', it held that an authorisation covers 'only those events or categories of events that have been identified by the Prosecution' and those 'closely related'.[53] However, this approach was overturned on appeal, with the Chamber noting that 'restricting the authorised investigation

---

[49] See further, eg, P Clark, *Distant Justice: The Impact of the International Criminal Court on African Politics* (Cambridge University Press, 2018); MW Mutua, 'Africans and the ICC: Hypocrisy, Impunity, and Perversion' in KM Clarke, AS Knottnerus and E de Volder (eds), *Africa and the ICC Perceptions of Justice* (Cambridge University Press, 2016) 47, 56.

[50] Kiyani (n 47) 950–51.

[51] Clark (n 49) 86. See further, SMH Nouwen and WG Werner, 'Doing Justice to the Political: The International Criminal Court in Uganda and Sudan' (2011) 21(4) *European Journal of International Law* 941.

[52] See further, eg, M Glasius, 'Expertise in the Cause of Justice: Global Civil Society Influence on the Statute for an International Criminal Court' in M Glasius, M Kaldor and HK Anheier (eds), *Global Civil Society Yearbook 2002* (Oxford University Press, 2002) 137, 153–55.

[53] Decision Pursuant to Article 15 of the Rome Statute on the Authorisation of an Invesitgation into the Situation in the Islamic Republic of Afghanistan, 12 April 2019, ICC-02/17-33 (hereinafter 'Afghanistan Article 15 decision') para 42.

to the factual information obtained during the preliminary examination would erroneously inhibit the Prosecutor's truth-seeking function.[54] In so holding, the Chamber affirmed the independence of the Prosecutor.

Even when the Prosecutor acts on his or her own initiative, there can be advantages in a state referral. For example, in February 2022 the ICC Prosecutor, having announced his decision to request the Pre-Trial Chamber to authorise an investigation into Ukraine, encouraged state parties to refer the situation to the Court. In the end, 43 state parties referred the situation in Ukraine to the ICC (in line with the acceptance by Ukraine of the Court's jurisdiction previously mentioned) and requested the Prosecutor to investigate allegations of war crimes, crimes against humanity and genocide.[55] The referrals enabled the Prosecutor to proceed with a formal investigation right away, thereby avoiding the need for Pre-Trial Chamber authorisation.

Civil society actors have no power to refer a situation to the ICC. However, individuals and organisations can provide information to the Prosecutor on alleged crimes within the Court's jurisdiction, and this could have the effect of generating a preliminary examination. Early on, the OTP stated its intention 'to encourage States and civil society to take ownership of the Court'.[56] The Prosecutor has received communications on a wide range of issues, 813 such communications being submitted between 1 November 2019 and 31 October 2020. Of these, the OTP determined that '612 were manifestly outside the Court's jurisdiction; 104 were linked to a situation already under preliminary examination; 71 were linked to an investigation or prosecution; and 26 warranted further analysis'.[57] It is difficult to assess the impact of such Article 15 communications, because the ICC does not always formally or publicly respond to them. Preliminary examinations in Iraq/UK were re-opened in 2014 following an Article 15 communication from the European Centre for Constitutional and Human Rights and Public Interest Lawyers. Writing in 2016, Megan Fairlie observes that none of the 11,500 communications to the Prosecutor resulted in a formal investigation.[58] However, even when formally unsuccessful in persuading the Prosecutor to take further action, such as the 2014 communication from the Global Legal Action Network (GLAN) and the Stanford International Human Rights Clinic regarding Australia's offshore

---

[54] Afghanistan Article 15 appeal (n 39) para 61.

[55] Statement of ICC Prosecutor, on the Situation in Ukraine, 28 February 2022 at www.icc-cpi.int/news/statement-icc-prosecutor-karim-aa-khan-qc-situation-ukraine-i-have-decided-proceed-opening. The referral by 38 states can be found at State Party Referral under Article 14 of the Rome Statute at www.icc-cpi.int/sites/default/files/2022-04/State-Party-Referral.pdf.

[56] ICC-OTP, 'Paper on Some Policy Issues before the Office of the Prosecutor' (2003) 2 at www.icc-cpi.int/sites/default/files/NR/rdonlyres/1FA7C4C6-DE5F-42B7-8B25-60AA962ED8B6/143594/030905_Policy_Paper.pdf.

[57] OTP Report (n 37) para 30.

[58] MA Fairlie, 'The Hidden Costs of Strategic Communications for the International Criminal Court' (2016) 51(3) *Texas International Law Journal* 281, 283.

detention of refugees and asylum seekers (chapter 5),[59] communications offer the potential to contribute to a shift in the way in which situations are framed in political and public discourse.[60] They are usually part of broader activism in relation to a particular issue or situation.[61] They may develop innovative legal argument and make (more) public evidence and information available to a broader audience.[62] Hodgson explains how information contained in the GLAN communication was included in the Australian Parliament's Legal and Constitutional Affairs References Committee.[63] The Prosecutor's response also involved some significant criticism of the practice of detention, which was used in ongoing civil society campaigns.[64] Here, as elsewhere, it is useful to think back to the aims and objectives of international criminal law (chapter 3) and reflect on the extent to which some of these may be achieved through certain aspects of the legal process, even without an indictment and trial.

C. Security Council

A key concern about the ICC's jurisdiction has been the role played by the UN Security Council. As explained below, the Security Council has the power to refer situations to the ICC and to request deferrals of prosecutions and investigations. This inevitably risks politicising the exercise of the ICC's jurisdiction.

In order to refer a situation to the ICC, the Security Council must act according to its powers under Chapter VII of the UN Charter. These are triggered by its finding of a threat to or breach of international peace and security. A Security Council referral enables the ICC to exercise jurisdiction without the consent to ICC jurisdiction of the territorial state or the state of the nationality of the defendant, in other words over nationals of non-party states. Concerns about Security Council referrals are exacerbated because currently, of the permanent member states of the Security Council (the so-called P5), only France and the UK are parties to the Rome Statute. So far, the Security Council has referred two situations to the ICC, Darfur (Security Council Resolution 1593) in 2005 and Libya (Security Council Resolution 1970) in 2011. However, the Security Council has failed to

---

[59] Communiqué to the Office of the Prosecutor of the International Criminal Court under Article 15 of the Rome Statute: The Situation in Nauru and Manus Island: Liability for Crimes against Humanity in the Detention of Refugees and Asylum Seekers at https://docs.wixstatic.com/ugd/b743d9_ e4413cb72e1646d8bd3e8a8c9a466950.pdf. This was one of a number of such communications. See further N Hodgson, 'International Criminal Law and Civil Society Resistance to Offshore Detention' (2020) 26(3) *Australian Journal of Human Rights* 449, 455.

[60] See further Hodgson (n 59) 453.

[61] See further, on this and other initiatives in connection with the policy, ibid 450–51.

[62] See, eg, ibid 456.

[63] ibid 457.

[64] ibid 460–61.

refer the situation in Syria because of Russian and Chinese opposition.[65] For some, the power to refer situations in non-party states violates the principles underpinning the law of treaties, which is that treaties bind by state consent. The impact of Security Council referrals on the immunity of a head of state or state official of a non-party state has caused friction between the African Union and the ICC.[66]

As already noted, the Malabo Protocol controversially affirms the immunity of heads of state, a stance that reflects the position of the African Union that heads of state enjoy immunity in international law. Two provisions of the Rome Statute are relevant when considering immunity. Article 27 provides that immunities that would otherwise apply at the national or international level to an official do not prevent the Court from exercising its jurisdiction. At the same time Article 98 prohibits the Court from proceeding

> with a request for surrender or assistance which would require the requested State to act inconsistently with its obligations under international law with respect to the State or diplomatic immunity of a person or property of a third State, unless the Court can first obtain the cooperation of that third State for the waiver of immunity.

The question of head-of-state immunity has been particularly controversial in the context of the referral to the ICC by Security Council Resolution 1593 of the situation in non-party state Sudan. Whether Sudan, as a non-party state, was bound by Article 27 of the Rome Statute as a result of Resolution 1593, or whether party states were bound by Article 98 not to transfer the then President Al-Bashir of Sudan to the Court has been a major point of contestation. In March 2017, host state Jordan failed to arrest and surrender Al-Bashir at the Summit of the Arab League. As a result, the Pre-Trial Chamber and then the Appeals Chamber found that Jordan had failed to comply with its obligations under the Rome Statute. Security Council Resolution 1593 required Sudan to cooperate with the court. Therefore, Sudan was unable to rely successfully on a claim of head-of-state immunity, and states were not bound by Article 98 of the Rome Statute to respect immunity that they would otherwise have been obliged to.[67]

The Security Council is also empowered to request the ICC to defer an investigation or prosecution for a year under Article 16 of the Rome Statute, in the exercise of its powers under Chapter VII of the UN Charter. Controversially, this provision has only been used so far to protect – in effect – US service members

---

[65] On 21 December 2016, UN General Assembly Resolution 71/248 established the International, Impartial and Independent Mechanism to Assist in the Investigation and Prosecution of Those Responsible for the Most Serious Crimes under International Law Committed in the Syrian Arab Republic since March 2011, available at https://iiim.un.org/who-we-are/mandate/. See further, on the establishment of the Independent International Commission of Inquiry on Ukraine, A/HRC/RES/491, 7 March 2022.

[66] See further, eg, D Tladi, 'The Immunity Provision in the AU Amendment Protocol' (2015) 13 *Journal of International Criminal Justice* 3.

[67] *Prosecutor v Omar Hassan Ahmad Al-Bashir*, Judgment in the Jordan Referral re Al-Bashir Appeal, 6 May 2019, ICC-02/05-01/09-397-Corr.

from ICC jurisdiction in a series of resolutions. For example, in 2002, in a highly criticised resolution,[68] the US persuaded the Security Council to pass Resolution 1422 under Chapter VII. The Resolution requested,

> consistent with the provisions of Article 16 of the Rome Statute, that the ICC, if a case arises involving current or former officials or personnel from a contributing State not a Party to the Rome Statute over acts or omissions relating to a United Nations established or authorized operation, shall for a twelve-month period starting 1 July 2002 not commence or proceed with an investigation or prosecution of any such case, unless the Security Council decides otherwise.

This Resolution protected members of UN peacekeeping operations from states that were not party to the Rome Statute from the ICC's jurisdiction for 12 months. The Resolution was renewed the following year (Security Council Resolution 1487). These Resolutions controversially drew on Article 16 of the Rome Statute and came on the heels of a US threat to veto the renewal of UN peacekeeping operations. In contrast, requests by the Kenyan Government to defer the Kenyan investigations and by the African Union to defer the case against Al-Bashir were unsuccessful. While there may be good reasons for refusing these requests to defer, the refusal risks appearing problematic when read alongside the previous adherence to the US demand for a deferral.

The Security Council's powers to refer and to request a deferral, coupled with the veto, can protect member states and their friends from ICC jurisdiction.[69] This is evident in the Russian and Chinese veto of a referral of Syria in 2014. Finally, although it was not based on a Security Council referral, it is worth noting in connection with a discussion about Security Council powers that the eventual authorisation on appeal of the investigation of crimes allegedly committed in connection with the situation in Afghanistan extended to US personnel. Although it is currently unlikely that this aspect of the investigation will proceed, the decision is unparalleled in its recognition of the potential to investigate individuals from the global north, and a permanent member of the Security Council at that.[70]

D. Admissibility

Even when the ICC has jurisdiction, it must still be considered whether a particular situation or case is admissible. The ICC was not intended to replace national jurisdiction: the preamble to the Rome Statute recognises 'the duty of every State to

---

[68] See further, eg, C Stahn, 'The Ambiguities of Security Council Resolution 1422' (2002) 14(1) *European Journal of International Law* 85.

[69] See further, eg, Cowell (n 2) 682.

[70] See also on the potential for 'a move toward greater criminalization and "judicialization" of counter-insurgency and counter-terrorism measures', TO Hansen, 'Accountability for British War Crimes in Iraq? Examining the Nexus between International and National Justice Responses' in M Bergsmo and C Stahn, *Quality Control in Preliminary Examination*, vol I (Torkel Opsahl, 2018) 399, 450.

exercise its criminal jurisdiction over those responsible for international crimes'.[71] The 'Court is not meant – or equipped – to address any and all scenarios where the most serious international crimes might have been committed'.[72] As the first ICC Chief Prosecutor Luis Moreno-Ocampo famously remarked, a successful Court would have a low case load. Accordingly, Article 17 provides:

> Having regard to paragraph 10 of the Preamble and article 1, the Court shall determine that a case is inadmissible where:
>
> (a) The case is being investigated or prosecuted by a State which has jurisdiction over it, unless the State is unwilling or unable genuinely to carry out the investigation or prosecution;
> (b) The case has been investigated by a State which has jurisdiction over it and the State has decided not to prosecute the person concerned, unless the decision resulted from the unwillingness or inability of the State genuinely to prosecute;
> (c) The person concerned has already been tried for conduct which is the subject of the complaint, and a trial by the Court is not permitted under article 20, paragraph 3;
> (d) The case is not of sufficient gravity to justify further action by the Court.

Thus, the Court will only exercise jurisdiction if the requirements of complementarity are met and the case is sufficiently grave. As a legal principle, complementarity requires the ICC to act only in the absence of national proceedings, or in circumstances where the national state is unwilling or unable to investigate or prosecute.[73] The application of these criteria has given rise to several concerns

i. Complementarity

Complementarity is central to admissibility. It ensures deference to sovereign states. Although the emphasis accorded to it has varied, the ICC has adopted an approach known as positive complementarity. This aims to encourage national proceedings where feasible, although it does not involve the Court in capacity building.[74] The problem is that, as we shall see, complementarity limits the space for an alternative non-criminal approach to justice after atrocity,[75] such as truth

---

[71] Rome Statute, preamble, para 6.

[72] Afghanistan Article 15 decision (n 53) para 90.

[73] Beyond the legal, there are other understandings of complementarity. On the legal, political, relational and developmental aspects of complementarity and the dominance of the former in ICC practices, see Clark (n 49) 33.

[74] See further, eg, Y Shereshevsky, 'The Unintended Negative Effect of Positive Complementarity' (2020) 18 *Journal of International Criminal Justice* 1017, 1021; SMH Nouwen, *Complementarity in the Line of Fire: The Catalyzing Effect of the International Criminal Court in Uganda and Sudan* (Cambridge University Press, 2013); Hansen (n 70) 449.

[75] SMH Nouwen and WG Werner, 'Monopolizing Global Justice' (2015) 13 *Journal of International Criminal Justice* 157, 174; N Sekhon, 'Complementarity and Post-Coloniality' (2013) 27 *Emory International Law Review* 799, 824–25: 'Complementarity is largely preoccupied with how to best configure the division of labor between the ICC and domestic courts so as to maximize the number of ICL prosecutions conforming to due process. This all makes good sense if one accepts that more prosecutions mean less impunity, which in turn means more justice. While this logic is impeccable within the world of legal professionals, this does not mean that it will register as such in subaltern spaces.'

and reconciliation commissions. This is problematic to the extent that a one-size-fits all approach after atrocity is undesirable. Moreover, Sekhon has suggested, 'insisting that a criminal trial is the only acceptable form of justice ritual may be reminiscent of colonial impositions of the not so distant past'.[76]

To determine whether the conditions for complementary jurisdiction are satisfied, it must first be determined whether a case is being investigated[77] or prosecuted. If it is, then a case is not admissible before the ICC unless the state is 'unwilling or unable genuinely to carry out the investigation'. To decide whether a situation or case is being investigated or prosecuted, the relevant situation or case must first be identified. At the situation stage the test is a more general one, but at the case stage the Court looks to see whether the same person and substantially the same conduct is being prosecuted. The problem with this approach, Heller explains, is that 'a state can ensure the inadmissibility of a particular case only by deferring to the OTP's choice of incidents to investigate', or by guessing 'which incidents the OTP will ultimately decide to prosecute'.[78] For example, in what Mégret and Samson describe as a 'textbook case of abusive complementarity', Thomas Lubanga, a militia leader in the DRC, and the first individual to be convicted at the ICC in 2012, was transferred to face a war crimes trial for conscripting and enlisting child soldiers under the age of 15 and using them to participative actively in hostilities. Prior to being transferred to the ICC, Lubanga had been in custody in the DRC, where he had been initially arrested on broader grounds including crimes against humanity and genocide.[79] However, the arrest warrants did not refer to the conscription and enlisting of child soldiers, and therefore the DRC was not 'acting in relation to the specific case before the Court'.[80] It follows that it was not necessary for the Pre-Trial Chamber to determine the question of unwillingness or inability.[81] Of course, we cannot know what would have happened if the case had proceeded nationally. However, the eventual case against Lubanga at the ICC was criticised for being too narrowly framed. From this perspective, then, the legal tests of admissibility adopted by the ICC contributed to the situation where an opportunity may have been missed for a broader prosecution at the national level.

Once it is determined that a situation or case is being investigated or prosecuted, the question of whether a state is unwilling or unable to prosecute arises.

---

[76] Sekhon (n 75) 815.

[77] Which requires 'concrete and progressive investigative steps': *Prosecutor v Francis Kirimi Muthaura, Uhuru Muigai Kenyatta and Mohammed Hussein Ali*, Judgment on the Appeal of the Republic of Kenya against the decision of the pre-trial Chamber II of 30 May 2011 entitled 'Decision on the Application by the Government of Kenya Challenging the Admissibly of the Case Pursuant to the Article 19(2)(b) of the Statute', 30 August 2011, ICC-01/09-02/11-274, para 81.

[78] KJ Heller, 'Radical Complementarity' (2016) 14 *Journal of International Criminal Justice* 637, 648.

[79] F Mégret and MG Samson, 'Holding the Line on Complementarity in Libya: The Case for Tolerating Flawed Domestic Trials' (2013) 11 *Journal of International Criminal Justice* 571, 588. *Prosecutor v Thomas Lubanga Dyilo*, Decision on the Prosecutor's Application for a Warrant of Arrest, 10 February 2006, ICC-01/04-01/06-1-Corr-Red.

[80] *Prosecutor v Lubanga*, Decision (n 79) para 39.

[81] ibid para 40.

Whether a state is unwilling or unable is determined according to the factors listed in Article 17(2) and (3) of the Rome Statute. Thus, in determining whether a state is unwilling, the Court considers whether:

(a) The proceedings were or are being undertaken or the national decision was made for the purpose of shielding the person concerned from criminal responsibility for crimes within the jurisdiction of the Court ...

(b) There has been an unjustified delay in the proceedings which in the circumstances is inconsistent with an intent to bring the person concerned to justice;

(c) The proceedings were not or are not being conducted independently or impartially, and they were or are being conducted in a manner which, in the circumstances, is inconsistent with an intent to bring the person concerned to justice.

In determining inability,

the Court shall consider whether, due to a total or substantial collapse or unavailability of its national judicial system, the State is unable to obtain the accused or the necessary evidence and testimony or otherwise unable to carry out its proceedings.

One controversial question that has arisen is whether the failure of national proceedings to adhere to international due process standards renders a state unwilling to prosecute. In *Al-Senussi*, it was held that only if proceedings are 'so egregious that the proceedings can no longer be regarded as being capable of providing any genuine form of justice' would they be 'inconsistent with an intent to bring the person to justice', and therefore it could be considered that the state was unwilling to investigate or prosecute.[82] On the one hand, it might be thought that an opportunity was lost here to affirm the importance of international due process standards. This decision was criticised by several international (but not so much grass roots) human rights groups.[83] On the other hand, it may be that concerns about human rights are best addressed in a forum other than the ICC[84] and that, as Sekhon has observed, 'the prospect of a European-based court making political judgments about the quality of justice available in post-colonial states is symbolically fraught, to say the least'.[85]

Finally, another criticism that has been levelled against the application of the principle of complementarity is that it can work in favour of states with 'well-resourced investigative services'.[86] Hansen has argued such states may enjoy

unique possibilities to utilize the complementary regime in ways that are detrimental to accountability, including by framing and directing domestic legal processes so as

[82] Judgment on the Appeal of Mr Abdullah Al-Senussi against the decision of Pre-Trial Chamber I of 11 October 2013 entitled 'Decision on the admissibility of the case against Abdullah Al-Senussi', 24 July 2014, ICC-01/11-01/11-565, paras 1–3.
[83] P Akhavan, 'Complementarity Conundrums: The ICC Clock in Transitional Times' (2016) 14 *Journal of International Criminal Justice* 1043, 1055–56. For further discussion, see, eg, Mégret and Samson (n 79).
[84] See further, eg, ibid 588.
[85] Sekhon (n 75) 816.
[86] Heller (n 78) 643.

to prolong or otherwise frustrate the pursuit of accountability for those who bear the greatest responsibility for international crimes.[87]

On 9 December 2020, the ICC decided to close a preliminary examination into the situation in Iraq/UK.[88] The question for the OTP had been whether the UK was 'unwilling or unable genuinely to carry out the investigation'. This required it to consider whether the UK had sought to shield individuals from investigation. Ten years of domestic processes, including investigations by the Iraq Historic Allegations Team (IHAT) and then the Service Police Legacy Investigations (SPLI) and decisions by the Service Prosecuting Authority (SPA), had not led to a single prosecution. The Prosecutor determined that

> the evidence available to it at this stage does not allow it to conclude that there was intent on the part of the UK authorities to shield persons under investigation from criminal responsibility.[89]

At the same time, the absence of prosecutions did not mean that claims were vexatious. The Prosecutor found that 'several levels of institutional civilian supervisory and military command failures contributed to the commission of crimes against detainees by UK soldiers in Iraq'; the fact that evidence was insufficient to mount a prosecution could be explained by the 'inadequacies of the initial investigations conducted by the British military in theatre'.[90]

Critics have argued that the Prosecutor's reasoning may encourage a lax attitude on the part of states to investigate, does little for survivors of international crimes[91] and benefits states that delay independent investigations.[92] On the one hand, the failure to investigate can be read as evidence of the uneven application of international criminal law and the reflection of the political reality within which international criminal law operates. On the other, the report could also be read as a powerful and authoritative counterpoint to narratives emanating from the

---

[87] TO Hansen, 'Opportunities and Challenges Seeking Accountability for War Crimes in Palestine under the International Criminal Court's Complementarity Regime' (2019) 9 *Notre Dame Journal of International and Comparative Law* 1, 4.

[88] See further Hansen (n 70) 445.

[89] Office of the Prosecutor, *Situation in Iraq/UK: Final Report* (OTP, 9 December 2020) para 409 at www.icc-cpi.int/itemsDocuments/201209-otp-final-report-iraq-uk-eng.pdf. Thus, for the OPT, 'the relevant test is not whether the Prosecutor or Chamber or this Court would have come to a different conclusion to that of IHAT/SPLI or the SPA on the evidence and proceeded differently, but whether the facts, on their face, demonstrate an intent to shied persons from criminal responsibility': ibid para 10.

[90] 'Statement of the Prosecutor, Fatou Bensouda, on the conclusion of the preliminary examination of the situation in Iraq/United Kingdom' (ICC, 9 December 2020) at www.icc-cpi.int/Pages/item.aspx?name=201209-otp-statement-iraq-uk.

[91] Heller argues that the OTP applied an incorrect legal standard: KJ Heller, 'The Nine Words that (Wrongly) Doomed the Iraq Investigation' *Opinio Juris* (10 December 2020) at https://opiniojuris.org/2020/12/10/the-nine-words-that-wrongly-doomed-the-iraq-investigation/. See further A Schueller, 'The ICC, British War Crimes in Iraq and a Very British Tradition' Opinio Juris (11 December 2020) at http://opiniojuris.org/2020/12/11/the-icc-british-war-crimes-in-iraq-and-a-very-british-tradition/.

[92] Amnesty International, 'ICC decision on UK Military in Iraq Rewards Obstructionism' *Amnesty International* (10 December 2020) at www.amnesty.org/en/latest/news/2020/12/icc-decision-on-uk-military-in-iraq-rewards-obstructionism/.

then British government about the conduct of the war and its responses to the concerns raised. Already, in 2017, the Prosecutor had acknowledged that there was a 'reasonable basis to believe that members of the British armed forces committed the war crimes of wilful killing, torture, inhuman/cruel treatment, outrages upon personal dignity, and rape and/or other forms of sexual violence', and the Statement of the Prosecutor in December 2020 and accompanying report affirmed this.[93] The Prosecutor also emphasised that its 'conclusion of collective failures [was] of extreme gravity in terms of its consequences for the treatment of civilians and [that it] should continue to trigger deep institutional reflection'.[94] Even without further investigation, then, there may be important expressive potential in the report. The question is what that expressive potential might come to mean, and the processes through which its meaning is made. A series of exchanges between the UK Secretary of State for Defence at the time and the Prosecutor illustrate the importance of how the report is interpreted and the ways in which its meaning gets contested and mediated.[95] Thus, this episode provides not just a fertile source to reflect on the limits and possibilities of international criminal jurisdiction, and therefore international criminal law – more specifically in the context of powerful states – but also a site to reflect upon the complexities surrounding the creation of meaning through and in international criminal law.

ii. Gravity

A case will also be inadmissible if it is insufficiently grave. However, the Rome Statute does not define 'gravity'.[96] In a much-criticised response to multiple communications under Article 15, which detailed war crimes allegedly committed by British soldiers in Iraq, the ICC Prosecutor announced that whilst there was a 'reasonable basis to believe' that wilful killing and inhuman treatment of less than 20 individuals had been committed, the situation did not satisfy the gravity requirement under the Rome Statute. A key and, again, much-criticised part of the Prosecutor's reasoning lay in the number of victims, which 'was of a different order than the number of victims found in other situations under investigation or analysis by the Office'.[97] The ICC must inevitably be selective, and an analysis that

---

[93] 'Statement of the Prosecutor, Fatou Bensouda' (n 90). See further, OTP, 'Situation in Iraq/UK: Final Report' (n 89) para 113.

[94] ibid para 371.

[95] They can be found at ICC, 'Preliminary Examination: Iraq/UK' at www.icc-cpi.int/iraq.

[96] The Prosecutor has set out a series of relevant factors, including 'the scale of the crimes; the nature of the crimes; the manner of commission of the crimes; and the impact of the crimes': Office of the Prosecutor, *Report on Prosecutorial Strategy* (OTP, 14 September 2006) 5 at www.icc-cpi.int/sites/default/files/NR/rdonlyres/D673DD8C-D427-4547-BC69-2D363E07274B/143708/ProsecutorialStrategy20060914_English.pdf, 8–9.

[97] Office of the Prosecutor, 'Response to Communications Received Concerning Iraq' (OTP, 9 February 2006) 9 at www.icc-cpi.int/sites/default/files/NR/rdonlyres/04D143C8-19FB-466C-AB77-4CDB2FDEBEF7/143682/OTP_letter_to_senders_re_Iraq_9_February_2006.pdf. See further on

brings in a quantitative assessment might seem to have some superficial attraction. However, as Mégret has argued, such an approach 'risks being part of a very concrete politics that minimizes the collateral casualties of, for example technologically sophisticated Western wars'.[98] Another approach to gravity might, for example, take account of the special responsibilities P5 member states have in upholding international peace and security.[99] Since then, there has been a shift in the approach of the Prosecutor towards gravity, which now involves qualitative considerations alongside quantitative considerations.[100] In the context of Afghanistan, the Prosecutor argued, in relation to crimes allegedly committed by US forces and the CIA, that gravity was indicated by the 'level of responsibility of potential offenders, the number and the seriousness of the crimes, the possible responsibilities within the command structure, and the impact on the victims'.[101] The Pre-Trial Chamber noted

> [i]n relation to the crimes allegedly committed by the ANSF, the US forces and CIA … the gravity per se of the crime of torture, which is radically banned by international law, and the circumstances that the conducts have allegedly been committed by public officials in their functions.[102]

Section III.E turns to this decision in more detail.

E. Interests of Justice

On 12 April 2019, the ICC Pre-Trial Chamber controversially decided that it would not authorise an investigation into Afghanistan,[103] notwithstanding its view that the Court had jurisdiction and the situation was admissible. As already mentioned, this decision was later overturned by the Appeals Chamber. The Pre-Trial Chamber decision was unprecedented. It was the first time that the Court had decided that

---

gravity, Situation on the Registered Vessels of the Union of the Comoros, the Hellenic Republic and the Kingdom of Cambodia, Decision on the 'Application for Judicial Review by the Government of the Comoros', 16 September 2020, ICC-01/13-111.

[98] F Mégret, 'Beyond "Gravity": For a Politics of International Criminal Prosecution' (2013) 107 *Proceedings of the Annual Meeting of the American Society of International Law* 428, 430. For discussion of an alternative understanding of gravity in the context of 'banal' crimes, see I Kalpouzos and I Mann, 'Banal Crimes Against Humanity: The Case of Asylum Seekers in Greece' (2015) 16 *Melbourne Journal of International Law* 1, 27.

[99] Or where crimes were carried out by 'advanced democracies supposedly operating within the rule of law, notwithstanding the fact that they provoke less tangible harm'. See F Mégret, 'What Sort of Global Justice is "International Criminal Justice"?' (2015) 13 *Journal of International Criminal Justice* 77, 96.

[100] Office of the Prosecutor, 'Policy Paper on Preliminary Investigations' (ICC, November 2013) 15 at www.legal-tools.org/doc/acb906/.

[101] Afghanistan Article 15 decision (n 53) para 83.

[102] ibid para 85.

[103] ibid.

an investigation would not satisfy the interests of justice. The Appeals Chamber decision also broke ground by opening the way to an investigation into nationals of the US, a non-party state and permanent Security Council member state, for conduct committed in the territory of ICC party states, a decision that generated significant backlash from the then US Government.[104]

The Prosecutor had requested authorisation to open an investigation into crimes against humanity and war crimes allegedly committed by the Taliban and groups affiliated to it, Afghan National Security Forces (ANSF), and US armed forces and the CIA. The Pre-Trial Chamber held that an investigation would 'only be in the interests of justice if prospectively it appears suitable to result in the effective investigation and subsequent prosecution of cases within a reasonable time frame'.[105] An unfeasible investigation, one 'inevitably doomed to failure', could not be said to be in the interests of justice.[106] For the Pre-Trial Chamber, 'focusing on those scenarios where the prospects for successful and meaningful investigations are serious and substantive is key to its ultimate success'.[107] Three aspects weighed heavily: the lapse of time since the alleged conduct and the request; problems of state cooperation that the Prosecutor had experienced during the preliminary examination;[108] and, finally, the likelihood of being able to access evidence and suspects.[109] Moreover, the Chamber considered that the crimes and their context would require significant resources, which would detract resources from other situations.[110]

At first glance it might be thought that the Court's reasoning has some merit in a world of limited resources. Alternatively, it might be argued that the Court too readily equated institutional interests with those of the interests of justice. Three groups of victims and the Prosecutor sought to appeal. The Appeals Chamber considered that victims had no standing to appeal, but victims were permitted

---

[104] The then Government of Afghanistan also requested that the Prosecutor defer the investigation. With the change of authorities in Afghanistan, the ICC Prosecutor sought to resume the investigation and announced his intention to focus it on 'crimes allegedly committed by the Taliban and the Islamic State ... and to deprioritise other aspects of this investigation'. 'Statement of the Prosecutor of the ICC, International Criminal Court, Karim AA Khan QC, Following the Application for an expedited Order under Article 18(2) Seeking Authorisation to Resume Investigations in the Situation in Afghanistan' (ICC, 27 September 2021) at www.icc-cpi.int/news/statement-prosecutor-international-criminal-court-karim-khan-qc-following-application. See further, Amnesty International 'Afghanistan: ICC Prosecutor's Statement on Afghanistan Jeopardises His Office's Legitimacy and Future' (5 October 2021) at www.amnesty.org/en/wp-content/uploads/2021/10/IOR5348422021ENGLISH.pdf. The Pre-Trial Chamber authorised the Prosecution to continue with its investigation on 31 October 2022.

[105] Afghanistan Article 15 decision (n 53) para 89.

[106] ibid para 90.

[107] ibid.

[108] ibid para 94. The Chamber observed that the 'political landscape both in Afghanistan and in key States ... coupled with the complexity and volatility of the political climate still surrounding the Afghan scenario' meant that it was 'difficult to gauge the prospects of securing meaningful cooperation from relevant authorities for the future'.

[109] ibid para 91.

[110] ibid para 95.

to participate and to submit written appeal briefs.[111] The Appeals Chamber also invited, inter alia, human rights organisations to seek to participate as *amici curiae*.

The Prosecutor argued that the Pre-Trial Chamber had erred in the factors it considered in determining the interests of justice. Victims and some *amici curiae* went further, arguing that the Chamber should not have considered the question of the interests of justice at all.[112] Several reasons for desiring an investigation were put forward, which drew on the expressed interests of victims, including 'ending cycles of impunity, access to justice, positive complementarity or the possibility that an ICC investigation could act as a deterrent to parties engaged in ongoing violence in Afghanistan', all of which, it was argued, the Chamber failed to take sufficiently into account.[113] Moreover, *amici curiae* emphasised the nature of the duty to investigate as an obligation of conduct (as opposed to results).[114] This emphasis on the positive attributes of investigation might be useful for a Court that labours under limited resources and does not have a strong track record in delivering convictions. Yet whether these functions can sufficiently substitute for subsequent charge and conviction may well depend in part on the expectations generated amongst survivors of international crime.

On 5 March 2020, the Appeals Chamber held that the 'interests of justice' test in Article 53(1) of the Rome Statute was for the Prosecutor and not for the Pre-Trial Chamber to determine. As a result, the Appeals Chamber did not need to determine its meaning and parameters. However, it criticised the approach of the Pre-Trial Chamber to the 'interests of justice', which it considered was 'cursory, speculative and did not refer to information capable of supporting it'.[115] It emphasised that there was 'no indication that the Pre-Trial Chamber considered the gravity of the crimes and the *interests of victims as articulated by the victims themselves*'.[116] Taking all this together, it determined that 'the Pre-Trial Chamber did not properly assess the interests of justice'.[117]

---

[111] Situation in the Islamic Republic of Afghanistan, Reasons for the Appeals Chamber's oral decision dismissing as inadmissible the victims' appeals against the decision rejecting the authorisation of an investigation into the situation in Afghanistan, 4 March 2020, ICC-02/17-137; see, however, Dissenting opinion to the majority's oral ruling of 5 December 2019 denying victims' standing to appeal, 5 December 2019, ICC-02/17-133.

[112] See further, eg, Victims' Joint Response and Request for Reply, Situation in the Islamic Republic of Afghanistan, 22 October 2019, ICC-02/19, 5, arguing the Pre-Trial Chamber acted ultra vires in considering the interests of justice. One *amicus* brief described the Pre-Trial Chamber's approach as an 'extreme example of intrusion by the judiciary into the discretionary domain of the Prosecutor': *Amicus Curiae* Observations on behalf of Former International Chief Prosecutors, 15 November 2019 ICC-02/17, para 13.

[113] Armanshahr/OPEN ASIA, International Federation for Human Rights and others, *Amicus Curiae* Observations in Situation in the Islamic Republic of Afghanistan, 15 November 2019, ICC/-2/17-114, para 21.

[114] ibid para 22; K Mackintosh and G Sluiter, *Amicus Curiae Observations*, 15 November 2019, ICC-02/17-117, para 30; Amnesty International, *Amicus Curiae* Observations Submitted Pursuant to Rule 103 of the Rule of Procedure and Evidence, 15 November 2019 ICC-02/17-112, para 7.

[115] Afghanistan Article 15 appeal (n 39) para 49.

[116] ibid (emphasis added).

[117] ibid.

The scope of the phrase 'the interests of justice' remains unresolved after this decision. It is unclear how the test should balance the interests of parties and participants in the trial, on the one hand, and those outside it, on the other. The extent to which the interests of justice can and should be understood separately from the institutional interests of the Court also remains open.[118] The successful appeal in the Afghanistan situation demonstrates the importance of an independent prosecutor and the procedural space for the active involvement of civil society. The importance of a non-state perspective is even more evident in the work of citizens' tribunals, and section IV turns to explore their jurisdiction in more depth.

IV. Citizens' Tribunals

As already noted, citizens' tribunals are informal bodies, and are therefore without coercive power. For some, the fact that citizens' tribunals are non-state bodies precludes their legitimacy. Writing to the President of the first Russell Tribunal, Jean-Paul Sartre, Charles De Gaulle famously claimed 'I have no need to tell you that justice of any sort, in principle as in execution, emanates from the State'.[119] However, citizens' tribunals can provide some measure of justice, particularly to those who participate in their proceedings,[120] and may achieve legitimacy 'a posteriori'.[121] Citizens' tribunals typically adopt a radical perspective on jurisdiction from which law belongs to the people. In his opening statement at the World Tribunal on Iraq in Istanbul, Falk claimed that

> it is the peoples of the world and not the governments or even the UN that have been entrusted with the ultimate responsibility for upholding this renunciation of war: 'We the peoples of the United Nations'.[122]

---

[118] See, eg, the Pre-Trial Chamber's claim that the interests of justice test must be rigorously performed, 'in particular in light of the implications that a partial or inaccurate assessment might have for paramount objects of the Statute and hence the *overall credibility of the Court, as well as its organizational and financial sustainability*': Afghanistan Article 15 decision (n 54) para 88 (emphasis added).

[119] See, eg, De Gaulle as quoted in J Duffett (ed), *Against the Crime of Silence Proceedings of the Russell International War Crimes Tribunal Stockholm: Copenhagen* (O'Hare Books, 1968) 28.

[120] See, P Akhavan, 'Is Grassroots Justice a Viable Alternative to Impunity?: The Case of the Iran People's Tribunal' (2017) 39(1) *Human Rights Quarterly* 73. See further U Dolgopol, 'Civil Society's Engagement with International Criminal Law: The Role of Peoples' Tribunals' in M Bergsmo et al (eds), *Historical Origins of International Criminal Law*, vol 4 (Torkel Opsahl, 2015) 703, 711–12.

[121] L Moita, 'Opinion Tribunals and the Permanent People's Tribunal' (2015) 6(1) *Janus.Net* 30, 46.

[122] R Falk, 'Opening Speech on Behalf of the Panel of Advocates' in MG Sökmen (ed), *World Tribunal on Iraq: Making the Case against War* (Olive Branch Press, 2008) 5, 7. At the same time, as Falk observes elsewhere, while social movements provide the best chances for a more progressive normative order, it is dangerous to adopt an overly romantic idea of the people: R Falk, 'The Global Promise of Social Movements: Explorations at the Edge of Time' (1987) XII *Alternatives* 173, 175. However, Rajagopal argues that even movements that are not progressive may be a reaction against 'geo-political orders and regimes and, as such, enable a collective questioning of what went wrong': B Rajagopal, *International Law from Below: Development, Social Movements and Third World Resistance* (Cambridge University Press, 2003) 236. The need for caution is evident today in the growth of populist movements and

It follows that the legitimacy or authority of citizens' tribunals does not depend upon whether states or institutions accept or validate them. Rather, the concomitant of law's belonging to the people is that citizens' tribunals draw their legitimacy from public opinion.[123] Sartre, for example, claimed of the Russell Tribunal:

> If the masses agree with our judgment, it will become truth, and we, at the very moment when we step back so that they will become the guardians and powerful supporters of that truth, will then know that we have been legitimized.[124]

However, the 'people' are not unified, and their interests must necessarily be mediated. Nayar identifies three '"authors" of a peoples' legality' as: 'the representative voice of communities of the victimised (the subaltern) and their local support groups', which for him is the 'primary source'; 'the "transnational" activist individuals and groups working in solidarity with these communities of the victims'; and, finally, 'activist lawyers concerned to "translate" these voices into the languages of (dominant) law'.[125] The mediation between these different constituents is a complex process. For example, whether a particular citizens' tribunal should emphasise its close adherence to accepted legal principles or adopt a more overtly political approach is often vigorously debated amongst participants.[126] However, given that the practice of citizens' tribunals is based on a criticism of existing law, it is not logical to assess them only by the extent to which they adhere to law in more conventional terms. For example, even the WIWCT, which drew on the standards, ritual and language of the prevailing law,[127] did not apply the principle of *nullum crimen sine lege*, because the 'positive law of the 1940s and 50s disqualified itself due to the neglect of women's rights'.[128] The mediation between any constituencies within international criminal justice – whether in official or unofficial fora – may be fraught and may involve difficult compromises. However, it is the alternative

governments that also claim to speak for the people. See further, eg, H Krieger, 'Populist Governments and International Law' (2019) 30(3) *European Journal of International Law* 971.

[123] See further, eg, Moita (n 121) 35.

[124] J-P Sartre, 'Inaugural Statement' in K Coates, P Limqueco and P Weiss (eds), *Prevent the Crime of Silence: Reports from the Sessions of the International War Crimes Tribunal Founded by Bertrand Russell* (Penguin Press, 1971) 63, 67.

[125] J Nayar, 'A People's Tribunal against the Crime of Silence? The Politics of Judgement and an Agenda for People's Law' (2001) (2) *Social Justice and Global Development* at https://warwick.ac.uk/fac/soc/law/elj/lgd/2001_2/nayar.

[126] Compare, eg, J Nayar, 'Taking Empire Seriously: Empire's Law, People's Law and the World Tribunal on Iraq' in A Bartholomew (ed), *Empire's Law The American Imperial Project and the 'War to Remake the World'* (Pluto Press, 2006) 313, 324–25; and AJ Klinghoffer and JA Klinghoffer, *International Citizens' Tribunals: Mobilizing Public Opinion to Advance Human Rights* (Palgrave, 2002) 10.

[127] CM Chinkin, 'Peoples' Tribunals: Legitimate or Rough Justice' (2006) 24(2) *Windsor Yearbook of Access to Justice* 201, 215.

[128] S Jayasimha, 'Victor's Justice, Crime of Silence and the Burden of Listening: Judgement of the Tokyo Tribunal 1948, Women's International War Crimes Tribunal 2000 and Beyond' (2001) 1 *Law, Social Justice and Global Development Journal* at https://warwick.ac.uk/fac/soc/law/elj/lgd/2001_1/jayasimha/.

basis of authority and legitimacy that underpins citizens' tribunals that enables a different vision of international criminal justice, including conceptions of responsibility and definitions of crime examined in the previous chapters, which could never emanate from official tribunals within the current state-centric international legal order. It also enables some form of reckoning in the face of silence from 'official' international criminal law.

V. Conclusion

Understanding international criminal jurisdiction is vital to understanding the scope, possibility and limits of international criminal law. International criminal law is often criticised for the influence that powerful actors wield over its exercise and possibilities. This chapter has pointed to various constraints on jurisdiction and highlighted some of the spaces at national, international and non-state levels where international criminal jurisdiction (in its broadest sense) offers the potential of enabling actors to speak back not just to atrocity, but also to the impunity of powerful actors. International criminal jurisdiction, then, like international criminal law more generally, is complex, contested and full of creative possibilities.

Further Reading

H Arendt, *Eichmann in Jerusalem A Report on the Banality of Evil* (Penguin, 1984).

F Cowell, 'Inherent Imperialism: Understanding the Legal Roots of Anti-Imperialist Criticism of the International Criminal Court' (2017) 15 *Journal of International Criminal Justice* 667.

P Clark, *Distant Justice: The Impact of the International Criminal Court on African Politics* (Cambridge University Press, 2018).

S Nouwen, *Complementarity in the Line of Fire* (Cambridge University Press, 2013).

A O'Sullivan, *Universal Jurisdiction in International Criminal Law The Debate and Battle for Hegemony* (Routledge, 2018).

8

Doing Justice for Victims

I. Introduction

Central to the promise of international criminal justice is the claim to deliver justice to victims. There is disagreement, though, on what justice for victims means and how far a criminal trial can deliver it. International criminal legal discourse all too often has equated justice with the prosecution and conviction of an individual. This is, however, a limited approach, and problematic in the context of the relatively few numbers of international prosecutions and convictions. Increasingly, it has come to be accepted that justice also requires institutional acknowledgement of victims' suffering and agency, and some transformation of the often-desperate material conditions that survivors may face.[1] There are nevertheless significant limitations on what a court can do for survivors in the aftermath of mass violence. Translating justice for victims into an international criminal process is a complex and delicate exercise. It also demands significant resources given the numbers of victims (and potential victims) of international crime. Eligible victims are often located far away from international criminal courts, and face security concerns and ongoing desperate circumstances. In the case of the ICC, its presence on the ground may be limited, leaving it reliant on intermediaries and civil society organisations to support victims to access participation opportunities.[2] The reliance on intermediaries, which the Rome Statute did not foresee, raises critical questions for the Court, the defence, survivors and intermediaries themselves.[3]

As we shall see, there has been a marked shift in the approach of international criminal law to survivors of international crime. Specifically, the ICC

---

[1] William Schabas has observed, eg, that '[o]ne suspects that if the victims understood that many millions had been invested – mainly in professional salaries and international travel – in order to ensure the respect of their rights, they might ask if they could simply be given the money instead': cited in G Carayon and J O'Donohue, 'The International Criminal Court's Strategies in Relation to Victims' (2017) 15(3) *Journal of International Criminal Justice* 567, 587.

[2] See further, eg, N Kiswanson, 'Beyond Victim Participation during Proceedings: Outreach and Information Activities during Preliminary Examination in Palestine' in FIDH (International Federation for Human Rights), *Victims at the Centre of Justice: From 1998 to 2018: Reflections on the Promises and the Reality of Victim Participation at the ICC* (FIDH, 2018) 43, 44.

[3] See further, E Haslam and R Edmunds, 'Managing a New Partnership: Professionalization, Intermediaries and the International Criminal Court' (2012) 24 *Criminal Law Forum* 1; L Ullrich, 'Beyond the "Global-Local Divide": Local Intermediaries, Victims and the Justice Contestations of the International Criminal Court' (2016) 14 *Journal of International Criminal Justice* 543.

marked a major departure by ushering in two innovative features: victim participation and reparations. These provisions sought to shift the position of victims of international crime from 'passive object' of international criminal proceedings to 'potential subject matter'.[4] The increasing importance accorded to victims in international criminal law can also be seen in recent law-making efforts that have paid heightened attention to the position of 'complainants, victims, witnesses and their relatives'.[5] The Draft Articles on Prevention and Punishment of Crimes Against Humanity 2019 also contain provisions on victim participation (Article 12(2)) and reparation (Article 12(3)). However, as the ICC has experienced, implementing such provisions is far from straightforward. It is vital to reflect on the challenges, limitations and opportunities surrounding participation and reparation.

In practice, the ICC chambers have been developing the exact scope of participation and reparations, and their modalities.[6] Suggestions for improvements, and alternative ways to respond to the injustices that victims have suffered, are welcome and timely, as those inside and outside the Court struggle to make participation and reparations meaningful. However, this chapter does not encourage reflection just on the effectiveness of these provisions and how they might be improved,[7] but also an alertness to the assumptions about victims' legal subjectivity that underpin the interpretations of such provisions.

Critics argue that the figure of the victim in much of the ICC's rhetoric (and beyond) presumes an 'imagined'[8] or 'abstract'[9] figure that draws on 'infantilized, feminized and racialized victim stereotypes'.[10] This figure is manifested both in rhetorical and visual portrayals of victimhood.[11] Such portrayals, Schwöbel-Patel

---

[4] C Jorda and J de Hemptinne, 'The Status and Role of the Victim' in A Cassese, P Gaeta and JRWD Jones (eds), *The Rome Statute of the International Criminal Court: A Commentary*, vol 2 (Oxford University Press, 2002) 1389, 1399.

[5] Art 12, Draft Articles on Prevention and Punishment of Crimes against Humanity 2019, A/74/10, *Yearbook of the International Law Commission 2019*, vol II.

[6] See eg, Carayon and O'Donohue (n 1) 570–71. For a cautionary assessment, see further, eg, C Van den Wyngaert, 'Victims before International Criminal Courts: Some Views and Concerns of an ICC Trial Judge' (2012) 44 *Case Western Reserve Journal of International Law* 475, 494–95.

[7] For a distinction between effectiveness or 'efficiency' critiques and critical approaches, see P McAuliffe and C Schwöbel-Patel, 'Disciplinary Matchmaking Critics of International Criminal Law Meet Critics of Liberal Peacebuilding' (2018) 16(5) *Journal of International Criminal Justice* 985, 989–90.

[8] LE Fletcher, 'Refracted Justice: The Imagined Victim and the International Criminal Court' in C De Vos, S Kendall and C Stahn (eds), *Contested Justice: The Politics and Practice of International Criminal Court Interventions* (Cambridge University Press, 2015) 302.

[9] S Kendall and SMH Nouwen, 'Representational Practices at the International Criminal Court: The Gap between Juridified and Abstract Victimhood' (2014) 76 *Law and Contemporary Problems* 235.

[10] C Schwöbel-Patel, 'The "Ideal" Victim of International Criminal Law' (2018) 29(3) *European Journal of International Law* 703, 704.

[11] C Schwöbel-Patel, *Marketing Global Justice The Political Economy of International Criminal Law* (Cambridge University Press, 2021) 132–42. See further on imagery, eg, I Tallgren, 'Come and See? The Power of Images and International Criminal Justice' (2017) 17 *International Criminal Law Review* 259.

argues, result in and reflect the commodification of victims in the context of 'marketised global justice'.[12] Thinking about the construction of victims enables reflection on the taken-for-granted assumptions (that in turn reflect configurations of power) that underpin how justice for victims – and its parameters – are and might be understood. Justice for victims, then, is limited not only by practical and legal considerations but also by cultural and political assumptions, which can influence how legal provisions, such as 'the interests of justice', are interpreted and international criminal justice practices are carried out. For example, positioning victims as vulnerable subjects *can* denude them of political agency. It may then become harder for institutions to recognise critical victims and/or the interests of those victims who have a different vision of justice from that which emanates from the Court.[13] This tendency is exacerbated in a context in which the claim to deliver justice to victims is posited as a central justification for the work of the institution.[14] Thus, a key challenge for international criminal institutions is to acknowledge survivors' pain and suffering, on the one hand, and their political agency, on the other. While citizens' tribunals are not without their challenges, their practice, which takes a radically different approach to survivors, seeks to do just this. The central question that underpins this chapter, then, is what justice for victims means – and what might it mean – in international criminal law. In other words, it asks how the law constructs the figure of the victim, and how else it might do so.

Before exploring further, we need to consider terminology. On the one hand, the term 'victim' – as opposed to 'survivor' – is controversial and should be used carefully. Citizens' tribunals often adopt a different term. The WIWCT, for example, refers to 'survivors' and to 'those victimised'.[15] This language emphasises a more agentic subject than the term 'victim' suggests. On the other hand, use of the word 'victim' might be thought appropriate because – at least in the context of victim participation – it is the relevant legal term. Moreover, victim participation and reparations may provide an opportunity to deploy the term in a way that positions victims as rights holders.[16] Whichever term is adopted, the practices of

---

[12] Schwöbel-Patel (n 11) 127.

[13] E Haslam and R Edmunds, 'Victim Participation, Politics and the Construction of Victims at the International Criminal Court: Reflection on Proceedings in *Banda* and *Jerbo*' (2014) 14(2) *Melbourne Journal of International Law* 727, 743–44.

[14] See further, E Haslam, *The Slave Trade, Abolition and the Long History of International Criminal Law The Recaptive and the Victim* (Routledge 2020) 10–11.

[15] It also deployed the term 'sexual slavery' rather than 'enforced prostitution'. U Dolgopol, 'Civil Society's Engagement with International Criminal Law: The Role of Peoples' Tribunals' in M Bergsmo et al (eds), *Historical Origins of International Criminal Law*, vol 4 (Torkel Opsahl, 2015) 703, 721–22.

[16] See, eg, a call to reappropriate the term, 'allowing those who have been *objects* of violence to become *subjects* of political action, and, precisely *because* they are victims, to recognize themselves as rights-bearing individuals': T Lacerda, '"Victim": What Is Hidden behind This Word?' (2016) 10 *International Journal of Transitional Justice* 179, 180 (original emphasis). See further, eg, H Saeed, 'Victims and Victimhood: Individuals of Inaction or Active Agency of Change? Reflections on Fieldwork in Afghanistan' (2016) 10 *International Journal of Transitional Justice* 168.

recognition that it encompasses should marry as far as possible with survivors' experiences and their circumstances on the ground.[17] It is also important when thinking about terminology to remember and acknowledge that not all victims of international crime survive.

II. Before Rome: Victims and International Criminal Law

Historically, victims did not play an extensive role in international criminal proceedings. At Nuremberg and Tokyo, victims were given few chances to testify; while at the ICTY and the ICTR, victims participated as witnesses only, not in their own right. These ad hoc tribunals were not empowered to provide victims with compensation. Together these factors led to concerns that victims were effectively objects rather than subjects of international criminal proceedings, whose participation depended upon, and was framed by, the broader purposes of the trial.[18] As David Crane, former Prosecutor at the SCSL, observed, 'we simply don't think about or factor in the justice the victims seek'.[19] Commenting on this silence, Bitti searchingly asks:

> How can we explain that procedures for these crimes involving thousands or even millions of victims exclude them at the same time? Is it a problem of legal culture? Is it the fear of what they have to say or their criticism? Is it the fear of the influence they might have on these procedures? Or is the explanation to be found in the very nature of the crimes that are often committed by the most powerful among us?[20]

At Rome, NGOs and France were amongst those actively advocating for the recognition of victims' rights. As already mentioned, the ICC is widely claimed to be ground-breaking because under the Rome Statute it provides for both victim

---

[17] Dixon, writing of the enlistment of children associated with armed forces (CAAF), suggests 'For the ICC, one of the greatest challenges will be deciding how to identify and target them in ways that reflect their reality and do not risk further stigmatisation. Many CAAF, for instance do not self-identify as "child soldiers" ...': PJ Dixon, 'Reparations and the Politics of Recognition' in C de Vos, S Kendall and C Stahn (eds), *Contested Justice: The Politics and Practice of International Criminal Court Interventions* (Cambridge University Press, 2015) 326, 339. See also the suggestions that 'targeting reparations to victims of sexual violence can further stigmatise them' (ibid 341), hence the importance of 'targeting strategies that do not impose or reinforce identities that are harmful or irreconcilable with local realities, or which the intended beneficiaries themselves may reject' (ibid 342).

[18] Jorda and de Hemptinne (n 4) 1399; MB Dembour and E Haslam, 'Silencing Hearings? Victims-Witnesses at the ICTY' (2004) 15(1) *European Journal of International Law* 151; E Haslam, 'Victim Participation at the International Criminal Court: A Triumph of Hope over Experience' in D McGoldrick, P Rowe and E Donnelly (eds), *The Permanent International Criminal Court: Legal and Policy Issues* (Hart Publishing, 2004) 315, 320, 324.

[19] D Crane, 'White Man's Justice: Applying International Justice after Regional Third World Conflicts' (2006) 27 *Cardozo Law Review* 1683, 1686.

[20] G Bitti, 'A Court for Victims?' in FIDH (n 2) 6, 6.

participation (that is the possibility for victims to participate in proceedings other than as witnesses for the prosecution or defence (Articles 15(3), 19(3), 68(3)) and reparations (Article 75)). Several justifications were put forward at Rome for including victim participation at the ICC,[21] but the Rome Statute itself does not clarify the purposes of participation. Even today, scholars have doubted whether participation is supported by a clear rationale.[22] This results in uncertainty, but also – perhaps more optimistically – offers a fertile opportunity for legal contestation and development. It is easy to assume, when coming to victim participation for the first time, that victim participation enables individuals to have 'their day in court', an assumption that can feed into the view that victim participation is primarily expressive. However, as will become apparent, victim participation is subject to significant limitations, as a result of which very few victims will ever actually attend the Court in The Hague nor have one-to-one contact with their lawyers, through whom participation is exercised. Moreover, the assumption that victim participation is – or should be – primarily expressive is problematic to the extent that it detracts attention from survivors as political and agentic subjects, and can support uncritically the equation of international criminal institutions with victims' justice.

III. Victim Participation and Reparation: The Formal Position

The Rome Statute provides for victim participation at all stages of judicial proceedings. For example, under Article 19(3), victims may present observations to the Court in jurisdiction and admissibility proceedings, and Article 68(3) provides in general for the participation of victims in proceedings, subject to some important qualifiers:

> Where the personal interests of the victims are affected, the Court shall permit their *views and concerns* to be presented and considered at stages of the proceedings determined to be *appropriate* by the Court and in a manner which is *not prejudicial to or inconsistent with the rights of the accused and a fair and impartial trial.* The legal representatives of the victims may present such views and concerns where the Court considers it *appropriate*, in accordance with the rules of procedure and evidence. (emphasis added)

As is to be expected, victim participation is subject to defence rights and a fair trial. Moreover, the article only offers victims a procedural opportunity to express their 'views and concerns' but does not actually guarantee that victims' views will be considered. This places at least a theoretical brake on the recognition of victims'

---

[21] Amongst these were the establishment of the truth, reparations, and the therapeutic contribution it could potentially make for individuals and communities. Jorda and de Hemptinne (n 4) 1400–01.

[22] R Cryer, D Robinson and S Vasiliev, *An Introduction to International Criminal Law and Procedure* (Cambridge University Press, 2019) 453; Haslam (n 18) 324–25.

subjectivity. Key to victims' participation under Article 68(3) of the Rome Statute is the identification of victims' 'personal' interests, a phrase that the Statute does not define and that various chambers and judges have understood differently.[23] As I have argued elsewhere, how the Court understands personal interests reveals much about its approach to justice.[24] In the *Lubanga* confirmation hearing, the Chamber held:

> Subject to their intervention being restricted to the scope determined by the charges brought against Thomas Lubanga Dyilo, the victims may participate in the confirmation hearing by presenting their views and concerns in order to help contribute to the prosecution of the crimes from which they allegedly have suffered and to, where relevant, subsequently be able to obtain reparations for the harm suffered.[25]

From the beginning, then, the Court linked victims' participation to prosecution and reparations, even though victims' ability to access court-ordered reparations does not depend upon their having participated in proceedings. However, is not inevitable that victims will support prosecution, either in general or in the way particular prosecutions are framed. Victims have, after all, disagreed with the approach of the Prosecutor on numerous occasions at the ICC. As already mentioned, the expression 'personal interests' is not well defined, but the above quotation displays an assumption that victims' interests in international criminal prosecution lie in a prosecution perspective. This may be the case for many, but not all, victims. This narrow approach to personal interests is not necessarily a problem, so long as it is understood that the figure of the victim these provisions construct is a partial one. It is more problematic when this interpretation of the phrase 'personal interests' limits the range of survivors' voices that get heard, especially where charges are framed narrowly.[26]

The Rome Statute also provides for reparations in Article 75(1):

> The Court shall establish principles relating to reparations to, or in respect of, victims, including restitution, compensation and rehabilitation. On this basis, in its decision the Court may, either upon request or on its own motion in exceptional circumstances, determine the scope and extent of any damage, loss and injury to, or in respect of, victims and will state the principles on which it is acting.

A Trust Fund for Victims (TFV) is established under Article 79 of the Rome Statute, providing 'for the benefit of victims of crimes within the jurisdiction of the Court' and their families. The TFV has two mandates. Its assistance mandate requires it to aid victims of crimes within the Court's jurisdiction independently

---

[23] For further discussion of this article, see S Vasiliev, 'Article 68(3) and Personal Interests of Victims in the Emerging Practice of the ICC' in C Stahn and G Sluiter (eds), *The Emerging Practice of the International Criminal Court* (Brill, 2009) 635, 639.

[24] Haslam (n 18) 326. See further, Vasiliev (n 23) 676.

[25] *Prosecutor v Thomas Lubanga Dyilo*, Decision on the Arrangements for Participation of Victims a/001/06, 1/0002/06 and a/0003/06 at the Confirmation Hearing, 22 September 2006, ICC-01/04-01/06-462-tEN, 5.

[26] See further, eg, Haslam and Edmunds (n 13) 732, 737–38.

of any conviction. In this capacity, the TFV has enabled the provision of support to victims based on need.[27] In contrast, reparations, which may be individual and/or collective, and which must be proportionate,[28] derive from a finding of individual criminal responsibility.[29] Reparations are therefore based on a recognition of wrongdoing and, as such, unlike victim participation, position victims as rights holders.[30] Where defendants are indigent, the TFV can complement a reparations award. At the time of writing the TFV has been carrying out three reparations awards (*Lubanga, Katanga, Al Mahdi*).[31] The principles in *Lubanga*, which in turn drew on the UN Basic Principles of Justice for Victims of Crime and Abuse of Power and the UN Basic Principles on Reparations for Victims, established the basic approach towards reparations. Other reparations decisions followed, albeit with some divergences.[32] The Ntaganda Reparations Order issued in March 2021 brought with it more significant changes.[33] The TFV's activities are limited, however, to the extent that it depends on voluntary donations, without which victims' rights are hardly realisable.

IV. Practices of Participation

Judges of the ICC were left to determine the parameters and principles underpinning participation and reparations at the Court. At first sight, these provisions have been interpreted in a way that is generous to victims. For example, victim participants have been permitted to make oral submissions and opening and

---

[27] See further, for a critical account, RE Rauxloh, 'Good Intentions and Bad Consequences: The General Assistance Mandate of the Trust Fund for Victims of the ICC' (2021) 34(1) *Leiden Journal of International Law* 203.

[28] 'A convicted persons' liability for reparations must be proportionate to the harm caused, and inter alia, his or her participation in the commission of crimes for which he or she was found guilty, in the specific circumstances of the case': *Prosecutor v Thomas Lubanga Dyilo*, Appeals Chamber, Judgment on the Appeals against the 'Decision Establishing the Principles and Procedures to be Applied to Reparations' of 7 August 2010 with Amended Order for Reparations, 3 March 2015 (Reparation Appeal), ICC-01/04-01/06-3129, para 118.

[29] ibid para 99.

[30] See further PJ Dixon, 'Reparations, Assistance and the Experience of Justice: Lessons from Colombia and the Democratic Republic of the Congo' (2016) 10 *International Journal of Transitional Justice* 88.

[31] Trust Fund for Victims, 'Reparation Implementation' at www.trustfundforvictims.org/en/what-we-do/reparation-orders. See *Prosecutor v Thomas Lubanga Dyilo*, Judgment on the appeals against Trial Chamber II's 'Decision Setting the Size of the Reparations Award for which Thomas Lubanga Dyilo is Liable', 18 July 2019, ICC-01/04-01/06-3466-Red; *Prosecutor v Germain Katanga*, Judgment on the appeals against the order of Trial Chamber II of 24 March 2017 entitled 'Order for Reparations pursuant to Article 75 of the Statute', 8 March 2018, ICC-01/04-01/07-3778-Red-09-03-2018; *The Prosecutor v Ahmad Al Faqi Al Mahdi*, 'Reparations Order', 17 August 2017, ICC-01/12-01/15.

[32] See further, eg, Redress, *No Time to Wait: Realising Reparations for Victims before the International Criminal Court* (Redress, 2019) 11, 40–41.

[33] See, eg, M Lostal, 'The Ntaganda Reparations Order: A Marked Step towards a Victim-Centred Reparations Legal Framework at the ICC' *EJIL: Talk!* (24 May 2021) at www.ejiltalk.org/the-ntaganda-reparations-order-a-marked-step-towards-a-victim-centred-reparations-legal-framework-at-the-icc/.

closing statements, and examine witnesses. However, victim participation is rife with tensions that run through international criminal law more generally. These result in important limitations on participation. First, victim participation is inevitably selective. Not all victims of international crime will have the opportunity to participate in ICC proceedings, not least because participation and reparations are limited by the charges brought. Second, practices of participation (and reparation) must navigate the relationship between the individual and collective. This is particularly evident when considering victims' legal representation.

A. Selectivity: Participation and Reparations are Limited by the Charges Brought

Not all survivors of international crime will be permitted to participate at the ICC. Those who wish to participate must satisfy rule 85(a) of the Rules of Procedure and Evidence (RPE), which defines a victim as a natural person who has 'suffered harm as a result of the commission of any crime within the jurisdiction of the Court'. Harm may be 'material, physical and psychological',[34] and victims may be direct or indirect victims of crime. Thus, 'Harm suffered by one victim as a result of the commission of a crime within the jurisdiction of the Court can give rise to harm suffered by other victims', for example 'when there is a close personal relationship between the victims such as the relationship between a child soldier and the parents of that child'.[35]

Victim participation and reparations must be linked to the charges brought and proved, respectively. While limiting victim participation in this way provides an important check from a defence perspective, it means that victim participation and reparations depend on the prosecutor's charging practices.[36] The requirement for there to be a causal link between the harm suffered by the victim and the crime can also result in the potentially invidious situation in which some victims who are allowed to participate at the investigation stage may not be permitted to participate at later stages, when the case has been narrowed to certain crimes and particular incidents.[37] International criminal justice is necessarily selective.

---

[34] *Prosecutor v Thomas Lubanga Dyilo*, Judgment on the Appeals of the Prosecutor and the Defence against Trial Chamber I's Decision on Victims' Participation of 18 January 2008, 11 July 2008, ICC-01/04-01/06-1432 para 32. Additionally, r 85(b) provides 'Victims may include organizations or institutions that have sustained direct harm to any of their property which is dedicated to religion, education, art or science or charitable purposes, and to their historic monuments, hospitals and other places and objects for humanitarian purposes.'

[35] *Lubanga* (n 34) para 32.

[36] See, eg, in the context of reparations, L Moffett, 'Reparations for Victims at the International Criminal Court: A New Way Forward?' (2017) 21(9) *International Journal of Human Rights* 1204, 1207.

[37] See further, S Kendall and SMH Nouwen, 'Representational Practices at the International Criminal Court: The Gap between Juridified and Abstract Victimhood' (2014) 76 *Law and Contemporary Problems* 235, 241–46.

However, the rejection of victim status midway through a trial runs the risk of causing additional harm to survivors, including by prioritising victims of particular crimes over others.

B. The Individual and Collective: Representation

Legal representation is central to the achievement of effective participation at the ICC. According to rule 90 of the RPE, victims are 'free to choose a legal representative'. However, victims have no 'right to be represented by a legal representative of their choosing'.[38] Legally represented victims are permitted to participate more extensively than those who are not represented; the Court selects representatives for victims who are unable to pay for representation themselves. The ICC RPE empower the chambers to request victims to select a common legal representative or to ask the registry to do so. Given the sheer numbers of victim participants, in almost all these cases participation will take place through a lawyer who will represent multiple victims collectively. In *Katanga*, the Court stated:

> Common legal representation is the primary procedural mechanism for reconciling the conflicting requirements of having fair and expeditious proceedings, whilst at the same time ensuring meaningful participation by potentially thousands of victims, all within the bounds of what is practically possible.[39]

However, one problem is that common legal representatives can end up representing overwhelming numbers of victims. By the end of the *Bemba* trial, two lawyers represented 5,229 victims.[40] The vast numbers of victims and the geographical distance between them and The Hague challenges the ability of lawyers to provide meaningful representation for clients. The representative of individuals detained in Guantanamo, who put forward representations on their behalf in the legal process relating to the request for an investigation into the situation in Afghanistan, has explored the additional challenges of access and representation in this context.[41]

Another issue is how victims are organised into groups for the purposes of collective representation. Rule 90(4) of the RPE directs the chamber and registry to take 'all reasonable steps' to organise victims into groups that take account of their 'distinct interests', and to avoid 'any conflict of interest'. However, in practice, the presumption is in favour of one group in the absence of strong reasons

---

[38] *Prosecutor v Abdallah Banda Abakaer Nourain and Saleh Mohammed Jerbo Jamus*, Decision on Common Legal Representation, 25 May 2012, ICC-02/05-03/09-337, para 12. For discussion of how victims can be penalised when they seek to select their own legal representative, see Schwöbel-Patel, (n 11) 138–39.

[39] *Prosecutor v Germain Katanga*, Order on the Organisation of Common Legal Representation of Victims, 22 July 2009, ICC-01/04-01/07-1328, para 11.

[40] Cryer, Robinson and Vasiliev (n 22) 457.

[41] See K Gallagher, 'The Challenges for Legal Representation of Victims of US Torture on the Territory of Afghanistan and Other State Parties at the International Criminal Court' in FIDH (n 2) 29, 31–32.

otherwise.[42] Elsewhere, Rod Edmunds and I have argued that the Court seems disinclined to acknowledge that victims have distinct interests that would lead to their being represented separately (even if collectively separately).[43] For example, in *Prosecutor v Banda and Jerbo*, the Court insisted on common legal representation for Darfuri and non-Darfuri victims (former African Union peacekeepers and members of their families), considering that the interests of these two groups were insufficiently distinct to require their separate representation.[44] The chamber took this view even though these groups of victims had suffered different harms and were culturally, linguistically and nationally distinct from each other, and even though the Darfuri victims were nationals of a non-party state, with resultant special security concerns.[45]

Legal representatives must therefore navigate a common position across a range of victim participants. This is a process in which, given the numbers of victims involved, representatives may rely on intermediaries rather than direct contact with victims.[46] Of course, counsel (and the Court) are open, as they should be, to the possibility that a subsequent conflict of interest amongst victims might arise, justifying separate representation. However, as Edmunds and I have argued, '[i]n representing a large number of victims counsel is likely to face difficulties in being aware of what, and even when, interventions may be warranted to advance the personal interests of specific individuals and/or sub-groups represented'.[47] In a context in which victims are represented collectively in this way, the practices of representation at the level of rhetoric become even more important in the construction of the subject of the victim.

C. Summary

While the advent of victim participation at the ICC has generally been lauded, there are significant limitations on its extent and nature. Concerns have also been raised about the ways in which the provisions on victims have been interpreted. Specifically, that they have embodied a limited approach to victims' subjectivity. Despite this, victims have made significant contributions to international criminal law, both inside and outside the courtroom, as the litigation in the situation in Afghanistan explored in section V demonstrates. The formal legal provisions, then, are not the last word about the influence of victims on proceedings. To some

---

[42] See, eg, *Prosecutor v Laurent Gbagbo*, Decision on Victims' Participation and Victim's Common Legal Representation at the Confirmation of Charges Hearing and in Related Proceedings, 4 June 2012, ICC-02/11-01/11-138, para 40.

[43] E Haslam and R Edmunds, 'Common Legal Representation at the International Criminal Court: More Symbolic than Real?' (2012) 12(5) *International Criminal Law Review* 871, 883.

[44] *Prosecutor v Abdallah Banda Abakaer Nourain and Salah Mohammed Jerbo Jamus*, Order Inviting the Registrar to Appoint a Common Legal Representative, 6 September 2011, ICC-02/05-03/09-209.

[45] Haslam and Edmunds (n 43) 887–88.

[46] Ullrich (n 3) 543–54.

[47] Haslam and Edmund (n 43) 890.

extent it remains a political decision whether to emphasise the limitations of victim participation and the challenges in the ways in which survivors are framed, on the one hand, or the contribution of victims to international criminal law and the challenges victims pose to accepted interpretations, on the other. Both approaches operate as a critique and are not necessarily mutually exclusive. Indeed, emphasising the contributions of survivors to international criminal law, where they go well beyond what the law imagines, is an important starting point to acknowledge the agency of survivors of international crime.

V. The Interests of Justice

The Court's approach to victims' interests in the Afghanistan situation also raised issues. As we have seen, on 12 April 2019, the Pre-Trial Chamber declined to authorise an investigation into the situation in Afghanistan on the grounds that it would not 'at this stage serve the interests of justice' in accordance with Article 53(1)(c) of the Rome Statute.[48] This view was contrary to the views of most victims who had put forward a submission. In total, 699 submissions from victims were presented to the Pre-Trial Chamber, including '668 representations on behalf of 6,220 individuals; 17 representations on behalf of 1,690 families, 13 representations on behalf of several millions of victims, including 16 villages; and 1 representation on behalf of an institution'.[49] Of these submissions, 680 'welcomed the prospect of an investigation aimed at bringing culprits to justice, preventing crime and establishing the truth'.[50] The registry explained victims' reasons supporting investigation as follows:

> investigation by an impartial and respected international court; bringing the perceived perpetrators of crimes to justice; ending impunity; preventing future crimes; knowing the truth about what happened to victims of enforced disappearance; allowing for victims' voices to be heard; and protecting the freedom of speech and freedom of the press in Afghanistan.[51]

However, in deciding that the situation in Afghanistan rendered a 'successful investigation and prosecution extremely limited',[52] the Pre-Trial Chamber observed that

> it is unlikely that pursuing an investigation would result in meeting the objectives listed by the victims favouring the investigation, or otherwise contributing to it. It is worth

---

[48] Situation in the Islamic Republic of Afghanistan, Decision Pursuant to Article 15 of the Rome Statute on the Authorisation of an Investigation into the Situation in the Islamic Republic of Afghanistan, 12 April 2019, ICC-02/17-33.

[49] ibid para 27.

[50] ibid para 87.

[51] As cited in K Wigard, G Jahangiri and Z Moballegh, 'Victims' Representations in Afghanistan: Unprecedented Challenges and Lessons Learned' in FIDH (International Federation for Human Rights), *Victims at the Centre of Justice: From 1998 to 2018: Reflections on the Promises and the Reality of Victim Participation at the ICC* (FIDH, 2018) 22, 27.

[52] Decision Pursuant to Article 15 of the Rome Statute (n 48) para 96.

recalling that only victims of specific cases brought before the Court could ever have the opportunity of playing a meaningful role … in the absence of any such cases, this meaningful role will never materialize in spite of the investigation having been authorised; victims' expectations will not go beyond little more than aspirations. This, far from honouring the victims' wishes and aspirations that justice be done, would result in creating frustration and possibly hostility vis-a-vis the Court and therefore negatively impact its very ability to pursue credibly the objectives it was created to serve.[53]

Here the Chamber might be considered to have aptly summarised the difficulties of victim participation at the ICC more generally. This reasoning might apply to *many* if not *any* investigations and situations at the ICC. This apparent equation of the interests of victims with the interests of the Court also appears evident in the Concurring and Separate Opinion of Judge Antoine Kesia-Mbe Mindua, who emphasised that the Chamber had 'taken such a decision' in the victims' interests, while 'preserving the Court's credibility'.[54] Claiming that 'the decision of the Chamber does not irreparably endanger the interests of victims who are fully recognized as such in the Unanimous Decision', he observed that the investigation was not ruled out 'forever', not least because the Prosecutor might appeal.[55]

As we have seen in chapter 7, several different groups of victims challenged this decision. Amongst the arguments put forward, victims emphasised that the Chamber should have invited submissions on the question of the interests of justice, arguing that the decision was procedurally flawed:

> [T]he Decision noted that '680 out of the 699 applications welcomed the prospect of an investigation aimed at bringing culprits to justice, preventing crime and establishing the truth'. Yet the Chamber proceeded to a decision contrary to the victims' position without requesting any elaboration of their position or submissions from the Prosecution, violating a fundamental tenet of natural justice …[56]

In the request for leave to file *amicus curiae* submissions by several of the 'most active and prominent'[57] Afghan Human Rights Organisations, it was advocated 'that Afghan victims and society have a direct, public, and diverse voice in these proceedings',[58] arguing that such participation was critical precisely because a decision was made based on Article 53 (1)(c) of the Rome Statute (chapter 7):

> The Decision closed the door on Afghan victims and the whole of Afghan society to justice and truth. Claiming to do so in their interests. Those victims and the Afghan

---

[53] ibid.
[54] Concurring and Separate Opinion of Judge Antoine Kesia-Mbe Mindua, Decision Pursuant to Article 15 of the Rome Statute on the Authorisation of an Investigation into the Situation in the Islamic Republic of Afghanistan 12 April 2019, 31 May 2019, ICC-02/17-33-Anx-Corr07-06-2019, para 53.
[55] ibid para 50.
[56] Victims' Response to the Requests for Leave to Appeal filed by the Prosecution and by Other Victims, 13 June 2019, ICC-02/17-45, para 17.
[57] Request for Leave to File *Amicus Curiae* Submissions on behalf of Human Rights Organizations in Afghanistan, 10 June 2019, ICC-02/17-35, para 13.
[58] ibid para 17.

human rights community should now be permitted to openly, publicly, and directly disagree with that outcome and provide input on whether an appeal should proceed.[59]

Although the Pre-Trial Chamber's decision was overturned (chapter 7), the Chamber's reliance on the interests of justice – and the purported deployment of victims' interests – suggests how deep-seated the equation of the interests of victims with the interests of the Court can be. Identifying victims' interests was always going to be fraught. Survivors are not homogeneous and will have different views on justice and participation, and their own reasons for engaging with court processes. However, a too ready identification of the institutional interests of international criminal courts with those of survivors of international crime is problematic. Institutional interests are of course very real, but conflating institutional interests with victims' interests risks stripping the latter of independent substantive content. At the same time, while the interests of justice (Article 53) may go beyond victims' interests, the significance given to victims' interests in the Court's reasoning provides a hook for victims to speak back to the Court.

VI. Reparations

The ICC is the first international criminal court to be able to award victims reparations. Reparations are linked to the conviction of an individual. Therefore, they can only be granted to applicants who can show on the balance of probabilities that they suffered direct or indirect material, physical or psychological harm as a result of the crime for which an individual has been convicted.[60] The crime committed must be the 'actual' ('but for') and 'proximate' cause of the harm.[61] While indirect victims may receive reparations, victims of the actions of direct victims, such as child soldiers, may not.[62] While restricting reparations to harm resulting from convictions protects the rights of the convicted person, which is an essential function of an international criminal process, it means that survivors' reparations are contingent on the exigencies of first prosecution then conviction.[63] In *Lubanga*, for example, the Prosecutor failed to charge sexual violence, even though there was evidence of its widespread commission in the conflict; as a result, victims of SGBV were excluded from reparations.[64] However, in practice the Court relies on the TFV's assistance mandate to make up for its inability

---

[59] ibid para 24.

[60] *Lubanga*, Reparation Appeal (n 28). See also *Prosecutor v Ahmad Al Faqi Al Mahdi*, Judgment on the Appeal of the Victims against the 'Reparation Order', 8 March 2018, ICC-01/12-01/15A.

[61] *Al Mahdi*, Reparations Order (n 31), para 44. See further A Balta, M Bax and R Letschert, 'Trial and (Potential) Error: Conflicting Visions on Reparations within the ICC System' (2019) 29(3) *International Criminal Justice Review* 221, 227.

[62] See further Balta, Bax and Letschert (n 61) 227.

[63] Moffett (n 36) 1206–07.

[64] During the trial, the victim's legal representatives initially successfully sought a recharacterisation of the facts under reg 55 of the Regulations of the Court to include SGBV, a decision that was overturned

to order reparations in such cases.[65] Dixon calls this the 'Swiss cheese model', by which assistance fills the gaps left by reparations.[66] For example, Katanga was acquitted of crimes of sexual violence and using child soldiers, so the Chamber was unable to order reparations for these crimes. The Court invited the TFV to use its assistance mandate to support the victims of SGBV and the child soldiers. This approach might seem practical. However, assistance may not carry the same expressive function as reparations for victims.[67] The link between reparations and conviction is also challenging in the case of a successful appeal, or where cases are withdrawn. When Bemba was acquitted on appeal, reparations processes, which were almost complete, were discontinued.[68] Although the Chamber turned to the assistance mandate of the TFV,[69] victims, who had participated in proceedings for 10 years, reported a sense of being 'stabbed in the back'.[70] After the *Ruto and Sang* case was discontinued,[71] there was disagreement amongst the judges as to the extent to which reparations could be ordered in the absence of conviction. For Judge Eboe-Osuji:

> To conflate considerations of punitive justice with those of reparative justice – and say that this Court cannot entertain questions about reparation for victims when a case against the accused has been terminated – will create more confusion and anxiety about the administration of justice in this Court … For one thing, it may make it difficult for the victims and their sympathisers – a critical constituency of this Court – to accept acquittals at the ICC. And it may make it even more difficult for them to accept the idea that a case may be terminated at the ICC on grounds that the Prosecution has not made out a case for the defence to answer.[72]

on appeal. See further, on the effects on reparations of the limited indictment, eg, L Chappell, 'The Gender Injustice Cascade: "Transformative" Reparations for Victims of Sexual and Gender-Based Crimes in the *Lubanga* Case at the International Criminal Court' (2017) 12(9) *International Journal of Human Rights* 1223, 1229–33; Moffett (n 36) 1206–07; Regulations of the Court, adopted 26 May 2004, ICC-BD/01-02-07.

[65] See, eg, in *Al Mahdi*, 'Mr Al Mahdi cannot be held responsible for these broader tragedies, but the Chamber encourages the TFV to consider acting … to provide general assistance to those affected.' *Al Mahdi* Reparations Order (n 31) para 108.

[66] See further Dixon (n 30) 102.

[67] For a critical discussion of this claim, see, eg, ibid 101–02.

[68] *Prosecutor v Jean-Pierre Bemba Gombo*, Final Decision on the Reparations Proceedings, 3 August 2018, ICC-01-/05-01/08-3653. See further Moffett (n 36) 1209–11.

[69] Redress (n 32) 27.

[70] Legal Representatives of Victims' Joint Submissions on the Consequences of the Appeals Chamber's Judgment dated 8 June 2018 on the Reparations Proceedings, 12 July 2018, ICC-01/05-01/08, para 30. See further, M Douzima, E Ombeni and L El Hawl, 'Victims' Participation in Reparations Proceedings in the Bemba Case' in FIDH (International Federation for Human Rights), *Victims at the Centre of Justice: From 1998 to 2018: Reflections on the Promises and the Reality of Victim Participation at the ICC* (FIDH, 2018) 75, 78. For an argument emphasising the value of victim participation (in the Kenyan situation), see A Sehmi, 'Now That We Have No Voice, What Will Happen to Us?: Experiences of Victim Participation in the *Kenyatta* Case' (2018) 16(3) *Journal of International Criminal Justice* 571.

[71] *Prosecutor v William Samoei Ruto and Joshua Arap Sang*, Public Redacted Version of Decision on Defence Applications for Judgments of Acquittal, 5 April 2016, ICC-01/09-01/11-2027-Red.

[72] Dissenting Opinion of Judge Eboe-Osuji, ICC-01/09-01/11-2038-Anx, para 26.

For Judge Eboe-Osuji, the resulting concerns are 'avoidable simply by delinking questions of reparation from those of conviction to the extent possible'.[73] This is not an approach that has been followed so far, however, but it is an issue that is likely to reoccur. For example, an appeal was pending when the ICC ordered reparations in *Ntaganda*, raising the question of what would happen to the order in the case had an appeal against conviction been successful.[74]

A. Reparations and Representation

Consulting with victims is key to the implementation of reparations.[75] Under Article 75(3)of the Rome Statute, victims are after all amongst those whose representations the Court must take into account before it makes a reparations order. Consultation can bring its own benefits. For example, it has been claimed regarding the *Bemba* case that consultations on reparations 'allowed the long-ostracized rape victims to come forward and talk about their suffering and needs', including male victims of rape.[76] Even so, questions about representation in a broader sense remain. The question of representation is particularly evident in the tension between the individual and collective interests of victims, and more specifically who or what collectivity represents the harm and suffering caused by international crime. This is apparent in disagreement about whether reparations should be awarded on an individual or a collective basis. The TFV has typically favoured community-based reparations over individual ones. Collective reparations can avoid seeming to privilege a particular group of victims because they can benefit a wider range of recipients than can individual reparations, and this in a context in which resources are limited and in which victims who apply for reparations represent only some of the victims of international crime.[77] On the other hand, collective reparations do not have the same expressive function as individual reparations.[78] Moreover, there is concern that those who have perpetrated violence might also benefit from collective reparations, and this was amongst the

---

[73] ibid. Compare LRV, Victims' Views and Concerns on the Issue of Reparation or Assistance in Lieu of Reparation Pursuant to the Trial Chamber Decision of 5 April 2016 on the Defence Motion on 'No Case to Answer', 15 June 2016, ICC-01/09-01/11-2035, para 8; with *Prosecutor v William Samoei Ruto and Joshua Arap Sang*, Decision on the Requests regarding Reparations, 1 July 2016, ICC-01/09-01/11-2038.

[74] *The Prosecutor v Bosco Ntaganda*, Public redacted version of Judgment on the appeals of Mr Bosco Ntaganda and the Prosecutuor against the decision of Trial Chamber VI of 8 July 2019 entitled 'Judgment', 30 March 2021, ICC-01/04-02/06-2666-Red.

[75] See, eg, *Prosecutor v Thomas Lubanga Dyilo*, Decision Establishing the Principles and Procedures to be Applied to Reparations, 7 August 2012, ICC-01/04-01/06-2904, para 282.

[76] Douzima, Ombeni and El Hawl (n 70) 76–77.

[77] Balta, Bax and Letschert (n 61) 233.

[78] On the dilemmas of community reparations, see further L Moffett, 'Reparations for "Guilty Victims": Navigating Complex Identities of Victim-Perpetrators in Reparation Mechanism' (2016) 10 *International Journal of Transitional Justice* 146, 164.

reasons cited by victims seeking to withdraw in *Ruto and Sang*.[79] Survivors themselves are likely to have a range of views on individual and collective reparations.[80]

In practice, the Trial Chamber in *Lubanga* began by ordering collective reparations. On appeal, these were replaced by an order of 'collective reparations to identifiable' individuals. Since then, the Chamber, taking account of victims' views, has ordered individual reparations in addition to collective reparations. In *Katanga*, the Chamber observed that

> the order for reparations would, for the most part, be missing its mark – delivery of justice to and reparation of the harm done to the victims as a result of the crime committed by Mr Katanga – were it to disregard their almost unanimous preference, by awarding only collective reparations.[81]

While collective reparations may foster reconciliation,[82] it was also important that reparations should 'address the victims as individuals'.[83] Thus, the Court awarded collective reparations 'designed to benefit each victim' in the form of psychological support and support for housing, an income-generating activity and education,[84] and a symbolic individual award of US $250, designed to be 'meaningful to victims, but not the source of tension within the community' and 'not intended as compensation for the harm in its entirety'.[85] Similarly in *Al Mahdi*, the Chamber ordered collective and individual reparations, making it clear that the implementation of the award should prioritise individual reparations orders 'in so far as individual reparations do not hinder broader reconciliation or stigmatise individual victims *vis-à-vis* the community of Timbuktu'.[86] In contrast, the reparations order in *Ntaganda* was based on 'collective reparations with individualised components [which were] the most appropriate type of reparations, to appropriately address the harm suffered by the victims'.[87]

B. Reparations and the Ability to Make Change

A determinant of victims' justice is how far international criminal justice makes a tangible difference to people's lives after atrocity. In terms of implementation,

---

[79] *Prosecutor v William Samoei Ruto and Joshua Arap Sang*, Common Legal Representative for Victims' Comprehensive Report on the Withdrawal of Victims from the Turbo Area by Letter, 5 September 2013, ICC-01/09-01/11-896-Corr-Red, para 12. Balta, Bax and Letschert (n 61) 232–33.

[80] See further, eg, Dixon (n 17) 344–45.

[81] *Prosecutor v Germain Katanga*, Order for Reparations Pursuant to Article 75 of the Statute, 24 March 2017, ICC-01/04-01/07-3728-tENG, para 339.

[82] ibid para 289.

[83] ibid para 294.

[84] ibid, para 304. Notably, victims rejected collective reparations such as 'commemorative events, broadcast of the trial, the erection of monuments or the tracing of missing persons' (ibid para 301).

[85] ibid paras 299–300.

[86] *Al Mahdi*, Reparations Order (n 31) para 140. Al Mahdi was convicted on a guilty plea of a war crime under Art 8(2)(e)(iv), Rome Statute.

[87] *Prosecutor v Bosco Ntaganda*, Reparations Order, 8 March 2021, ICC-01/04-02/06-2659, para 186.

actualisation of reparations has been slow. To take just one example, Lubanga was convicted of conscripting and enlisting children under the age of 15 and using them to participate in hostilities in 2012. The Trial Chamber issued its first reparations decision in 2012, amended by the Appeals Chamber in 2015. The 2017 reparations award issued by the Chamber, which found Lubanga liable for collective reparations of US $10 million, was affirmed in 2019.[88] Moreover, the actual receipt of awards of reparations is dependent on available resources. Given this, the length of proceedings at the ICC and the fact that the material conditions of survivors' lives significantly impede the ICC's ability to deliver justice at all stages of its processes, significant challenges remain.

How far can reparations be used as a tool to seek to transform some of the conditions that contributed to crime in the first place, especially where more fundamental structural change looks otherwise unlikely? This is a controversial issue, as debates about the scope of transformative reparations show. In the context of gender justice, some commentators claim that reparations should be transformative. This means that they have been understood not just, as Walker explains, to seek to return victims to the status quo, but rather to 'aim at the reconstruction of the economic, social and political relations that oppress women and that are often among the cause of women's exposure to the violations they have suffered.[89] Walker criticises such a broad vision of transformative gender justice to the extent that it glosses over 'reparative justice as a distinct and distinctly victim-centred idea in favour of a different kind of justice agenda.[90] Using reparations as a mechanism to address such structural change in this way then is fraught.

Despite expansive claims about the centrality of victims to international criminal justice, from the preceding discussions it should be clear that significant problems remain with the approach of international criminal law to survivors at both the practical and conceptual levels. Here as elsewhere, then, the practice of citizens' tribunals provides a productive provocation to thinking about survivors and their role in international processes, and illustrates the significant impact that such alternative thinking can have on practice more generally.

VII. Survivors and Citizens' Tribunals

Citizens' tribunals enjoy greater procedural freedom than, for example, the ICC, and therefore can accord a less constrained role to survivors in proceedings. More than that, victims are considered central legal subjects within the citizens'

---

[88] *Prosecutor v Thomas Lubanga Dyiilo*, Judgment on the Appeals against Trial Chamber II's 'Decision Setting the Size of the Reparations Award for which Thomas Lubanga Dyilo is Liable', 18 July 2019, ICC-01/04-01/06-3466-Red.

[89] MU Walker, 'Transformative Reparations? A Critical Look at a Current Trend in Thinking about Gender-Just Reparations' (2016) 10 *International Journal of Transitional Justice* 108, 109.

[90] ibid 110. For further discussion, see Moffett (n 36) 1211–14.

tribunal movement.[91] This claim does not simply entail the recognising of victims procedurally.[92] As Jayan Nayar explains, people's law aims to amplify 'the voices of judgment and resistance of the violated, and to dignify those articulations as carrying with it the weight of law'.[93] Accordingly, the Myanmar Tribunal observed,

> the verdicts and deliberations of the PPT represent a narrative of international law as seen from the side of peoples, when their status of victims is translated into that of the only legitimate subjects to whom the public and private powers are accountable, beyond their legal impunity.[94]

This approach towards survivors generates an alternative and fruitful framing of testimony. For example, Dianne Otto observes how the unofficial Cambodian Tribunal vested control in those testifying, resulting in a more positive experience than survivors of sexual violence often report about their experiences in criminal trials. She also observed greater involvement from the audience than at the ECCC.[95] Citizens' tribunals organised by women characteristically emphasise agency and resistance, alongside harms, suffering and perspectives that official institutions have overlooked. For example, the World Courts of Women dedicate a session to 'testimonies of resistance, as distinct from testimonies of brutality and pain'.[96] So, in addition to providing a narrative platform for survivors where 'official' law is silent, the approach of citizens' tribunals to survivors can contribute to the broader alternative didactic focus that such tribunals typify. Otto also explains how the testimonies at the Cambodian Tribunal moved 'attention from justice aimed at shoring up the survival of the post-conflict state, to the continuing everyday injustices suffered by survivors of the conflict'.[97] Here as elsewhere,

---

[91] Despite this, Paulose observes that the PPT statute contains no reference to 'a framework or charter for victims', a situation she seeks to rectify through a series of recommendations. RM Paulose, 'Can you hear the people sing? Victim/survivor rights in People's Tribunals' in RM Paulose (ed), *People's Tribunals, Human Rights and the Law Searching for Justice* (Routledge, 2020) 2, 17–20.

[92] S Fraudatario and G Tognoni, 'The Participation of Peoples and the Development of International Law: The Laboratory of the Permanent Peoples' Tribunal' in A Byrnes and G Simm (eds), *Peoples' Tribunals and International Law* (Cambridge University Press, 2018) 133, 140.

[93] J Nayar, 'Thinking the "Impossible": Peoples' Law' (2003) 1 *Law, Social Justice and Global Development* at https://warwick.ac.uk/fac/soc/law/elj/lgd/2003_1/nayar2/nayar2.rtf See further, eg, K Campbell, *The Justice of Humans Subject, Society and Sexual Violence in International Criminal Law* (Cambridge University Press, 2022) 227.

[94] Permanent Peoples' Tribunal Session on State Crimes Allegedly Committed in Myanmar against the Rohingyas, Kachins and Other Groups, September 2018, Judgment, 3 at http://permanentpeoplestribunal.org/wp-content/uploads/2017/11/PPT-on-Myanmar-Judgment-FINAL.pdf.

[95] D Otto, 'Beyond Legal Justice: Some Personal Reflections on People's Tribunals, Listening and Responsibility' (2017) 5 *London Review of International Law* 225, 233. See further Akhavan, who notes that 'Notwithstanding years of experience with elite justice before international criminal tribunals at The Hague, this unprecedented victim-driven initiative has profoundly shaped my understanding of how those who have suffered irredeemable loss perceive the intimate meaning of life.' P Akhavan, 'Is Grassroots Justice a Viable Alternative to Impunity? The Case of the Iran People's Tribunal' (2917) 39(1) *Human Rights Quarterly* 73, 74.

[96] Otto (n 95) 236. For a rich discussion of the accounts of testimonial witnesses at the Bosnian Women's Court see Campbell (n 93) 219–23.

[97] ibid 239.

then, citizens' tribunals do not just fill the gaps where official international criminal law is silent. They provide a space for the expression of an alternative vision of justice for survivors. In so doing they cast a critical light not only on the claim of 'official' international criminal law to deliver justice to survivors, but also on its ability to recognise the different forms it might take.[98]

Citizens tribunals do not, however, escape the dilemmas of representation with which official tribunals must grapple. For example, Akhavan emphasises the grassroots nature of the tribunal on Iran because it did not originate from 'Western intellectual élites and activists a world away'.[99] In contrast, Suzuki notes, in connection with the use by the WIWCT of English, the 'possibility' that 'survivors' needs and interests' were 'subordinated to those of international feminist activism'.[100] If law belongs to the people, people's interests will never be totally unified. Just as with official tribunals, the representation of survivors' interests may involve difficult compromises, but the emphasis within citizens' tribunals on survivors as subjects and political agents ensures that the dilemmas attendant on representing and portraying survivors are more likely to be recognised. Further, survivors are more likely to participate in the processes by which these dilemmas are worked through.

Citizens' tribunals, as we have seen, are less wedded to individual responsibility. They have no power to order reparations, although they may recommend them. For example, the WTI recommended that coalition governments compensate Iraq for 'humanitarian, economic, ecological, and cultural devastation'.[101] However, even though they cannot enforce reparations, their alternative framing of testimony suggests that citizens' tribunals may be able to deliver victims an important form of justice, even where material relief is not available. The precise impact on survivors of participating in citizens' tribunals and the conditions under which that impact is made are nevertheless ripe for further research.

VIII. Conclusion

The claim of international criminal law to deliver justice to victims is, as has been widely observed, central to the legitimacy of international criminal law. Yet there are practical and legal limits to how international criminal law responds to

---

[98] See eg, Otto (n 95) 242 on a too ready equation of justice and individual criminal prosecution. See further D Otto, 'Impunity in a Different Register: People's Tribunals and Questions of Judgment, Law and Responsibility' in E Engle, Z Miller and DM Davis (eds), *Anti-Impunity and the Human Rights Agenda* (Cambridge University Press, 2016) 291, 315.

[99] Akhavan (n 92) 80.

[100] S Suzuki, 'Overcoming Past Wrongs Committed by States: Can Non-State Actors Facilitate Reconciliation?' (2012) 21(2) *Social and Legal Studies* 201, 211.

[101] Jury of Conscience, 'Declaration of the Jury of Conscience of World Tribunal on Iraq – Istanbul, 23–27 June 2005' in MG Sökmen (ed), *World Tribunal on Iraq: Making the Case against War* (Olive Branch Press, 2008) 492, 499.

survivors of international crime. Taking a more expansive approach to victims' interests where they are relevant to specific legal tests, as identified in this chapter, will not solve the underlying material conditions that limit victims' justice on the ground. However, a more expansive approach to victims' interests could have important expressive functions and, by enabling different voices to be heard, could widen the variety of justice outcomes under consideration. Reflecting, then, on how else international criminal law might construct survivors of international crime can disrupt the taken-for-granted framing of victims' subjectivity in international criminal law. Elsewhere, for example, I have argued that we could centre questions about distribution in the figure of the victim by considering victims less as beneficiaries than as creditors of international criminal justice.[102] Beyond such an abstract intervention, citizens' tribunals are already acting on a more multifaceted approach towards survivors of international crime. Their practice provides a vital site for delivering justice. It also demonstrates how an alternative framing of victims influences not just victims' justice but also other outcomes of the process, including the historical record produced and the didactic focus. Finally, their practice offers a provocation to 'official' international criminal law: how far is it possible to recognise a more complex survivor subject without risking the vital fair trial rights of the accused?

Further Reading

K Campbell, *The Justice of Humans Subject, Society and Sexual Violence in International Criminal Law* (Cambridge University Press, 2022).

LE Fletcher, 'Refracted Justice: The Imagined Victim and the International Criminal Court' in C De Vos, S Kendall and C Stahn (eds), *Contested Justice: The Politics and Practice of International Criminal Court Interventions* (Cambridge University Press, 2015) 302.

S Kendall and SMH Nouwen, 'Representational Practices at the International Criminal Court: The Gap between Juridified and Abstract Victimhood' (2014) 76 *Law and Contemporary Problems* 235.

C Schwöbel-Patel, 'The "Ideal" Victim of International Criminal Law' (2018) 29(3) *European Journal of International Law* 703.

E Stover, *The Witness: War Crimes and the Promise of Justice in the Hague* (University of Pennsylvania Press, 2005).

J van Wijk, 'Who is the "Little Old Lady" of International Crimes? Nils Christie's Concept of the Ideal Victim Reinterpreted' (2013) 19 *International Review of Victimology* 159.

---

[102] Haslam (n 14) 129–31.

9

Conclusion

International criminal law has a powerful attraction, and it continues to grow. The establishment and growth of international criminal institutions in the last 30 years have been remarkable. Concomitantly, we have seen an ever-increasing resort on the part of disputants to the language of international criminal law. The confidence in international criminal law is so evident that a common response to criticisms levelled against its limitations and partiality is to argue for its expansion. Belief in the possibility of – albeit transformed – international criminal justice can also be seen in the practices of citizens' tribunals and in the growing attention paid to them in the academic literature. It has become difficult to imagine international law and international relations without international criminal law.

How far this confidence in international criminal law is justified, and from whose perspective, remains doubtful though. The widespread commission of international crime challenges the belief that international criminal law reduces the incidence of atrocity. Its promise to deliver justice to the many survivors of international crime is limited by the material conditions that constrain its work, the dire conditions survivors often continue to face in their daily lives, as well as the ways in which international criminal practice constructs survivors of international crime. International criminal law responds to injustice selectively and it wields the power it has unevenly. Political partiality has been embedded in the Rome Statute through the role of the UN Security Council, and the ICC's reliance on states places an important brake on more universalist ambitions. Yet, as the critical scholars whose work we have explored in this book have demonstrated, such criticism is not addressed simply through expanding the practice of international criminal law but through more radical interrogation of the values and assumptions underpinning the discipline and practices of international criminal law and the particular vision of justice it reflects and excludes, and the political and economic ordering it supports.[1]

Thus, if it is difficult to imagine international law and international relations without international criminal justice, the future (and present) of international criminal law is – and should be – vigorously contested. What kind of justice is and might be delivered through international criminal law? Critical approaches

---

[1] See further, eg, C Schwöbel-Patel, *Marketing Global Justice The Political Economy of International Criminal Law* (Cambridge University Press, 2021).

provide useful tools to address this question by illuminating international criminal law's biases and pointing to alternative possibilities. The citizens' tribunals this book has drawn on are not the only critical approach to international criminal law – either theoretically or in practice.[2] Theoretically there are many other – and related – tools that play a vital role in interrogating and illuminating some of the assumptions underpinning international criminal justice: feminism, post-colonial and critical race theories, to name but a few. This book has emphasised citizens' tribunals because they offer a powerful provocation to the practice and theory of international criminal law. Citizens' tribunals challenge impunity, but they do more than that. They provoke consideration of how else international criminal law might look, including if it were to address more firmly the fundamental structures of violence, including by adopting a broader understanding of harm and responsibility, by addressing a wider audience and positioning survivors as truly agentic subjects. Thus, citizens' tribunals can be seen as parallel and complementary fora, providing an avenue for justice alongside more readily recognised approaches. As such, they can also be seen as a challenge to the homogenising approach to complementarity adopted elsewhere. Alternatively, they can be seen as a provocation – an alternative vision of justice, the very existence of which offers a lived critique of the conceptual limits and alternative possibilities of international criminal law. Or they might be seen as both complementary fora and provocation.[3] It is worth noting, though, that there is an inherent tension between the vision of citizens' tribunals as complementary on the one hand and a provocation on the other.

Even citizens' tribunals that self-consciously depart from 'official' international criminal law, still presume a confidence in the promise and potential of international criminal law to a greater or lesser extent, or at least a confidence in a form of tribunal, and a commitment to the avoidance of impunity, albeit understood broadly.[4] Added to which, they have not all escaped some of the criticism that official international criminal tribunals have faced, for example a western and male bias.[5] While the existence of citizens' tribunals thus illustrates the enduring attraction of international (criminal) tribunals, here as elsewhere it is important

---

[2] For an example of critical approaches to international law in practice see, eg, the work of the Global Legal Action Network (GLAN) at www.glanlaw.org/. On feminist judgment writing in international criminal law, and specifically the 'feminist judgments project', see R Grey, K McLoughlin and L Chappell, 'Gender and Judging at the International Criminal Court: Lessons from "Feminist Judgment Projects"' (2021) 34 *Leiden Journal of International Law* 247.

[3] For an argument that they should be seen as both – a 'complementary tool' and an opportunity to 'push for the development and advancement of international law' – see B Duerr, 'Political will and the people's will: The role of People's Tribunals in International Justice' in RM Paulose (ed), *Peoples Tribunals, Human Rights and the Law Searching for Justice* (Routledge, 2020) 22, 33.

[4] See further D Otto, 'Impunity in a Different Register: People's Tribunals and Questions of Judgment, Law and Responsibility' in E Engle, Z Miller and DM Davis (eds), *Anti-Impunity and the Human Rights Agenda* (Cambridge University Press, 2016) 291, 307.

[5] AJ Klinghoffer and JA Klinghoffer, *International Citizens' Tribunals: Mobilizing Public Opinion to Advance Human Rights* (Palgrave, 2002) 130–31 also observe that, during the First Russell Tribunal, there was a divide between American and European participants on the role of race, with Europeans seeking to downplay it.

to ensure that the increasing focus on citizens' tribunals does not have the effect of squeezing out other justice responses in legal and political thinking.[6]

Consequently, beyond this institutional focus, it is important to remember that even while international criminal law is often associated with international criminal institutions and institutional enforcement, the many faces of international criminal law extend beyond its institutional application. Thus, international criminal law is a historically contingent response to injustice. It is a language of contestation, a series of claims and counterclaims about individual and collective human agency for suffering, and a promise of justice. It follows that there are numerous different ways of 'doing' international criminal law in different spaces. There is thus no single unified vision of international criminal law. It is deployed in multiple ways by various state and non-state actors. In that sense, the subjects and subjectivities of international criminal law are related.

Whether international criminal law is viewed as a language and practice of states, a technocratic dialect of lawyers, an aspirational tool of non-governmental organisations, or as belonging to, and claimed by, the 'people', has consequences for the way it is approached and for how its possibilities and limitations are understood. Although this book has sought to introduce the reader to key principles of international criminal law, it has also emphasised that understanding international criminal law is not simply about assimilating legal rules. Learning about international criminal law requires considering and reflecting upon its actual and potential criss-crossing meanings. This enables an appreciation of the various usages of international criminal law in their contexts. This should in turn enable strategic ethical and political reflection about what it means to deploy international criminal law, and how to do so, in research, practice or as a responsible citizen. Decisions about how to approach international criminal law (methodology) and through which prisms to explore it (theoretical framing) are neither neutral nor power-free. They have consequences, and they and their consequences should be selected deliberately and reflectively.[7] This book has sought to illuminate some of these choices and their consequences. In so doing, it is hoped that it will provoke reflection on international criminal law, its limits and its potential, and demonstrate the importance of approaching international criminal law in as open and as participatory way as possible.

---

[6] See further SMH Nouwen and W Werner, 'Monopolizing Global Justice' (2015) 13 *Journal of International Criminal Justice* 157.

[7] AM Slaughter and S Ratner, 'The Method is the Message' (1999) 93(2) *American Journal of International Law* 410, 423 observe that the choice of method 'should be as self-conscious as possible'. See further M Burgis-Kasthala, 'Scholarship as Dialogue? TWAIL and the Politics of Methodology' (2016) 14 *Journal of International Criminal Justice* 912, 926, who observes that 'all scholars of international (criminal) law need to reflect on the politics of methodology'.

REFERENCES

Abtahi, H, 'The International Criminal Court during the Covid-19 Pandemic' (2020) 18(5) *Journal of International Criminal Justice* 1069.

Abi-Saab, G, 'The Uses of Article 19' (1990) 10(2) *European Journal of International Law* 339.

Adami, T, '"Who Will Be Left to Tell the Tale?" Recordkeeping and International Criminal Jurisprudence' (2007) 7 *Archives and Museum Informatics* 213.

Akhavan, P, 'Are International Criminal Tribunals a Disincentive to Peace?: Reconciling Judicial Romanticism with Political Realism' (2009) 31(3) *Human Rights Quarterly* 624.

——, 'Complementarity Conundrums: The ICC Clock in Transitional Times' (2016) 14 *Journal of International Criminal Justice* 1043.

——, 'Is Grassroots Justice a Viable Alternative to Impunity? The Case of the Iran People's Tribunal' (2017) 39(1) *Human Rights Quarterly* 73.

Aksenova, M, *Complicity in International Criminal Law* (Hart Publishing, 2019).

Alexander, A, 'A Short History of International Humanitarian Law' (2015) 26(1) *European Journal of International Law* 109.

Allain, J and Jones, JRWD, 'A Patchwork of Norms: A Commentary on the 1996 Draft Code of Crimes Against the Peace and Security of Mankind' (1997) 1 *European Journal of International Law* 100.

Alvarez, JE, 'Trying Hussein: Between Hubris and Hegemony' (2004) 2 *Journal of International Criminal Justice* 319.

Ambos, K, 'The Crime of Aggression after Kampala' (2010) 53 *German Yearbook of International Law* 463.

Amin, AM 'The role of the PPT in securing the right of Rohingya and other minorities in Mynamar' in RM Paulose (ed), *People's Tribunals, Human Rights and the Law Searching for Justice* (Routledge, 2020) 112.

Amin, S, 'The Militarization of Economy and the Economy of Militarization' in MG Sökmen (ed), *World Tribunal on Iraq: Making the Case Against War* (Olive Branch Press, 2008) 404.

Amnesty International, 'ICC decision on UK Military in Iraq Rewards Obstructionism' *Amnesty International* (10 December 2020).

——, 'Afghanistan: ICC Prosecutor's Statement on Afghanistan Jeopardises His Office's Legitimacy and Future' *Amnesty International* (5 October 2021).

Anders, G, 'Testifying about "Uncivilized Events": Problematic Representations of Africa in the Trial Against Charles Taylor' (2011) 24(4) *Leiden Journal of International Law* 937.

Anghie, A, *Imperialism, Sovereignty and the Making of International Law* (Cambridge University Press, 2005).

Anghie, A and Chimni, B, 'Third World Approaches to International Law and Individual Responsibility in Internal Conflict' (2004) 36 *Studies in Transnational Legal Policy* 185.

Anon, 'Developments in the Law – International Criminal Law: III. Fair Trials and the Role of the International Criminal Defence' (2001) 114 *Harvard Law Review* 1982.

Appel, BJ, 'In the Shadow of the International Criminal Court: Does the ICC Deter Human Rights Violations?' (2018) 62(1) *Journal of Conflict Resolution* 3.

Arimatsu, L, 'Universal Jurisdiction for International Crimes: Africa's Hope for Justice?' (Chatham House Briefing Paper, April 2010).

Askin, KD, 'Gender Crimes Jurisprudence in the ICTR' (2005) 3 *Journal of International Criminal Justice* 1007.

Baars, G, 'Law(yers) congealing capitalism: On the (im)possibility of restraining business in conflict through international criminal law' (PhD Thesis, UCL, 2012).

——, 'Capitalism's Victor's Justice? The Hidden Stories behind the Prosecution of Industrialists Post-WWII' in K Heller and G Simpson (eds), *The Hidden Histories of War Crimes Trials* (Oxford University Press, 2013) 163.

Bachman, JS, 'A "Synchronised Attack" on Life: The Saudi-Led Coalition's "Hidden and Holistic" Genocide in Yemen and the shared Responsibility of the US and UK' (2019) 40(2) *Third World Quarterly* 298.

Bachmann, SD and Abdelkader, Y, 'Reconciling Quasi-States with the Crime of Aggression under the ICC Statute' (2018) 33 *Emory International Law Review* 91.

Bachmann, SD and Kemp, G, 'The International Crime of Aggression in the Context of the Global "War On Terror": Some Legal and Ethical Perspectives' (2010) 2 *Journal of South African Law* 309.

Balta, A, Bax, M and Letschert, R, 'Trial and (Potential) Error: Conflicting Visions on Reparations within the ICC System' (2019) 29(3) *International Criminal Justice Review* 221.

Balthazar, S, 'Gender Crimes and the International Criminal Tribunals' (2006) 10 *Gonzaga Journal of International Law* 42.

Bannan, JF and Bannan, RS, *Law, Morality and Vietnam: The Peace Militants and the Courts* (Indiana University Press, 1974).

Bassiouni, MC, 'World War I: The War to End All Wars and the Birth of a Handicapped International Criminal Justice System' (2002) 30 *Denver Journal of International Law and Policy* 244.

Ben-Ari, R, 'Universal Jurisdiction: Chronicle of a Death Foretold?' (2015) 43(2) *Denver Journal of International Law and Policy* 165.

Benson, K, '"Kill' Em and Sort It out Later:" Signature Drone Strikes and International Humanitarian Law' (2014) 27(1) *Global Business and Development Law Journal* 17.

Beringola, AM, 'Intersectionality: A Tool for the Gender Analysis of Sexual Violence at the ICC' (2017) 9(2) *Amsterdam Law Forum* 84.

Bevernage, B, 'Transitional Justice and Historiography: Challenges, Dilemmas and Possibilities' (2014) 13 *Macquarie Law Journal* 7.

Bhagwat, N, 'The Privatization of War' in MG Sökmen (ed), *World Tribunal on Iraq: Making the Case Against War* (Olive Branch Press, 2008) 280.

Bitti, G, 'A Court for Victims?' in FIDH (International Federation for Human Rights), *Victims at the Centre of Justice: From 1998 to 2018: Reflections on the Promises and the Reality of Victim Participation at the ICC* (FIDH, 2018) 6.

Blaser, AW, 'How to Advance Human Rights without Really Trying: An Analysis of Nongovernmental Tribunals' (1992) 14 *Human Rights Quarterly* 339.

Boister, N, 'The ICJ in the Belgian Arrest Warrant Case: Arresting the Development of International Criminal Law' (2002) 7 *Journal of Conflict and Security Law* 293.

Borger, J and Fuchs, D, 'Spanish Judge to Hear Torture Case Against Six Bush Officials' *The Guardian* (19 March 2009).

Bosco, D, *Rough Justice: The International Criminal Court in a World of Power Politics* (Oxford University Press, 2014).

——, 'Palestine in the Hague: Justice, Geopolitics, and the International Criminal Court' (2016) 22 *Global Governance* 155.

Brown, G et al, 'Statement Calling for the Creation of a Special Tribunal for the Punishment of the Crime of Aggression Against Ukraine' (6 January 2023) at https://gordonandsarahbrown.com/wp-content/uploads/2022/03/Combined-Statement-and-Declaration.pdf.

Bryk, L and Saage-Maass, M, 'Individual Criminal Liability for Arms Exports under the ICC Statute' (2019) 17 *Journal of International Criminal Justice* 117.

Burgis-Kasthala, M, 'Scholarship as Dialogue? TWAIL and the Politics of Methodology' (2019) 14(4) *Journal of International Criminal Justice* 921.

Bush, JA, 'The Prehistory of Corporations and Conspiracy in International Criminal Law: What Nuremberg Really Said' (2009) 109 *Columbia Law Review* 1094.

Byers, M, 'Custom, Power and the Power of Rules' (1995) 17(1) *Michigan Journal of International Law* 109.

Byrnes, A and Simm, G, 'Reflections on the Past and Future of International Peoples' Tribunals' in A Byrnes and G Simm (eds), *Peoples' Tribunals and International Law* (Cambridge University Press, 2019) 259.

Cameron, H, 'British State Complicity in Genocide: Rwanda 1994' (2012) 1(1) *State Crime Journal* 70.

Campbell, K, *The Justice of Humans Subject, Society and Sexual Violence in International Criminal Law* (Cambridge University Press, 2022).

Carayon, G and O'Donohue, J, 'The International Criminal Court's Strategies in Relation to Victims' (2017) 15(3) *Journal of International Criminal Justice* 567.

Carlsson, I, 'The UN Inadequacies' (2005) 3 *Journal of International Criminal Justice* 837.

Cavallaro, J, Sharmas, D and Van Schaack, B, et al *Communiqué to the Office of the Prosecutor of the International Criminal Court under Article 15 of the Rome Statute: The Situation in Nauru and Manus Island: Liability for Crimes Against Humanity* (SLS Publications, 14 February 2017).

Chappell, L, 'The Gender Injustice Cascade: "Transformative" Reparations for Victims of Sexual and Gender-Based Crimes in the *Lubanga* Case at the International Criminal Court' (2017) 12(9) *International Journal of Human Rights* 1223.

Chazal, N, *The International Criminal Court and Global Society Control International Criminal Justice in Late Modernity* (Routledge, 2018).

Chinkin, CM, 'Peoples' Tribunals: Legitimate or Rough Justice' (2006) 24(2) *Windsor Yearbook of Access to Justice* 201.

Clapham, A, 'Extending International Criminal Law beyond the Individual to Corporations and Armed Opposition Groups' (2008) 6 *Journal of International Criminal Justice* 899.

Clark, JN, 'The Impact Question: The ICTY and the Restoration and Maintenance of Peace' in B Swart et al (eds), *The Legacy of the International Criminal Tribunal for the Former Yugoslavia* (Oxford University Press, 2011) 55.

Clark, P, *Distant Justice: The Impact of the International Criminal Court on African Politics* (Cambridge University Press, 2018).

Clark, RS, 'Building on Article 8(2)(b)(XX) of the Rome Statute of the International Criminal Court: Weapons and Methods of Warfare' (2009) 12(3) *New Criminal Law Review* 366.

Clarke, KM, *Fictions of Justice: The International Criminal Court and the Challenge of Legal Pluralism in Sub-Saharan Africa* (Cambridge University Press, 2009).

Clarke, KM, Knottnerus, AS and de Volder, E, *Africa and the ICC Perceptions of Justice* (Cambridge University Press, 2016).

Coates, K, Limqueco, P and Weiss, P (eds), *Prevent the Crime of Silence: Reports from the Sessions of the International War Crimes Tribunal Founded by Bertrand Russell* (Penguin Press, 1971).

Cogan, JK, 'International Criminal Courts and Fair Trials: Difficulties and Prospects' (2002) 27 *Yale Journal of International Law* 111.

Colacurci, M, 'The Draft Convention Ecocide and the Role for Corporate Remediation: Some Insights from the Monsanto Tribunal and a Recent Research Proposal' (2021) 21(1) *International Criminal Law Review* 154.

Copelon, R, 'Gender Crimes as War Crimes: Integrating Crimes Against Women into International Criminal Law' (2000) 46 *McGill Law Journal* 217.

Cowell, F, 'Inherent Imperialism: Understanding the Legal Roots of Anti-Imperialist Criticism of the International Criminal Court' (2017) 15 *Journal of International Criminal Justice* 667.

Crane, D, 'White Man's Justice: Applying International Justice after Regional Third World Conflicts' (2006) 27 *Cardozo Law Review* 1683.

Craven, M, Simpson, G, Marks, S and Wilde, R, '"We Are Teachers of International Law"' (2004) 17 *Leiden Journal of International Law* 363.

Creegan, E, 'Justified Uses of Force and the Crime of Aggression' (2012) 10 *Journal of International Criminal Justice* 59.

Cryer, R, Robinson, D and Vasiliev, S, *An Introduction to International Criminal Law and Procedure* (Cambridge University Press, 2019).

Çubukçu, A, *For the Love of Humanity: The World Tribunal on Iraq* (University of Pennsylvania Press, 2019).

Curtis, J and Robinson, T, 'The Uyghur Tribunal' (House of Commons Library, 18 January 2022).

Dallaire, R, *Shake Hands with the Devil* (Arrow, 2005).

Dallaire, R, Manocha, K and Degnarain, N, 'The Major Powers on Trial' (2005) 3 *Journal of International Criminal Justice* 861.

Dannenbaum, T, 'Why Have We Criminalized Aggressive War?' (2017) 126 *Yale Law Journal* 1242.

DeFalco, RC *Invisible Atrocities: The Aesthetic Biases of International Criminal Justice* (Cambridge University Press, 2022).

DeFalco, RC and Mégret, F, 'The Invisibility of Race at the ICC: Lessons from the US Criminal Justice System' (2019) 7(1) *London Review of International Law* 55.

De Vos, C, Kendall, S and Stahn, C, *Contested Justice The Politics and Practice of International Criminal Court Interventions* (Cambridge University Press, 2015).

Del Ponte, C and Sudetic, C, *Madame Prosecutor: Confrontations with Humanity's Worst Criminals and the Culture of Impunity* (Other Press, 2009).

Dembour, MB and Haslam, E, 'Silencing Hearings? Victims-Witnesses at the ICTY' (2004) 15(1) *European Journal of International Law* 151.

Dersso, SA, 'The ICC's Africa Problem: A Spotlight on the Politics and Limits of International Criminal Justice' in KM Clarke, AS Knottnerus and E de Volder (eds), *Africa and the ICC Perceptions of Justice* (Cambridge University Press, 2016) 61.

Dixon, PJ, 'Reparations and the Politics of Recognition' in C de Vos, S Kendall and C Stahn (eds), *Contested Justice: The Politics and Practice of International Criminal Court Interventions* (Cambridge University Press, 2015) 326.

——, 'Reparations, Assistance and the Experience of Justice: Lessons from Colombia and the Democratic Republic of the Congo' (2016) 10 *International Journal of Transitional Justice* 88.

Dolgopol, U, 'Civil Society's Engagement with International Criminal Law: The Role of Peoples' Tribunals' in M Bergsmo et al (eds), *Historical Origins of International Criminal Law*, vol 4 (Torkel Opsahl, 2015) 703.

Douzima, M, Ombeni, E and El Hawl, L, 'Victims' Participation in Reparations Proceedings in the Bemba Case' in FIDH (International Federation for Human Rights), *Victims at the Centre of Justice: From 1998 to 2018: Reflections on the Promises and the Reality of Victim Participation at the ICC* (FIDH, 2018) 75.

Drumbl, MA, *Atrocity, Punishment and International Law* (Cambridge University Press, 2007).

——, 'The Push to Criminalize Aggression: Something Lost Amid the Gains' (2009) 41 *Case Western Reserve Journal of International Law* 291.

——, 'Memorializing Dissent: Justice Pal in Tokyo' (2020) 114 *American Journal of International Law Unbound* 111.

Dubler, R, 'What's in a Name? A Theory of Crimes Against Humanity' (2008) 15 *Australian International Law Journal* 85.

Duerr, B, 'Political will and the people's will: The role of People's Tribunals in International Justice' in RM Paulose (ed), *People's Tribunals, Human Rights and the Law Searching for Justice* (Routledge, 2020) 22.

Duffett, J (ed), *Against the Crime of Silence Proceedings of the Russell International War Crimes Tribunal Stockholm: Copenhagen* (O'Hare Books, 1968).

Durney, J, 'Crafting a Standard: Environmental Crimes as Crimes Against Humanity under the International Criminal Court' (2018) 24 *Hastings Environmental Law Journal* 41.

Ediger, M, 'Prosecuting the Crime of Aggression at the International Criminal Court: Lessons from the Tokyo Tribunal' (2018) 51 *New York University Journal of International Law and Politics* 179.

Ehard, H, 'The Nuremberg Trial Against the Major War Criminals and International Law' (1949) 43 *American Journal of International Law* 223.

Elberling, B, *The Defendant in International Criminal Proceedings* (Hart Publishing, 2012).

Eslava, L, 'The Teaching of (Another) International Law: Critical Realism and the Question of Agency and Structure' (2020) 54(3) *The Law Teacher* 368.

Everest, L, 'The History of US and UK Interventions in Iraq' in MG Sökmen (ed), *World Tribunal on Iraq: Making the Case Against War* (Olive Branch Press, 2008) 35.

Fairlie, MA, 'The Hidden Costs of Strategic Communications for the International Criminal Court' (2016) 51(3) *Texas International Law Journal* 281.

Falk, R, 'The Global Promise of Social Movements: Explorations at the Edge of Time' (1987) XII *Alternatives* 173.

——, 'Opening Speech on Behalf of the Panel of Advocates' in MG Sökmen (ed), *World Tribunal on Iraq: Making the Case Against War* (Olive Branch Press, 2008) 5.

——, 'War, War Crimes, Power, and Justice: Toward a Jurisprudence of Conscience' (2013) 21(3) *Transnational Law and Contemporary Problems* 668.

Farrell, N, 'Attributing Criminal Liability to Corporate Actors' (2010) 8 *Journal of International Criminal Justice* 873.

Favez, J-C, *The Red Cross and the Holocaust* (Cambridge University Press, 1999).

Felman, S, *The Juridical Unconscious: Trials and Traumas in the Twentieth Century* (Harvard University Press, 2002).

Fineman, M, *Feminist Perspectives on Transitional Justice: From International and Criminal to Alternative Forms of Justice* (Intersentia, 2013).

Fisher, KJ, 'The Problems with the Crime of Forced Migration as a Loophole to ICC Jurisdiction' (2020) 11(2) *Journal of International Humanitarian Legal Studies* 385.

Fletcher, GP, 'The Storrs Lectures: Liberals and Romantics at War: The Problem of Collective Guilt' (2002) 111 *Yale Law Journal* 1499.

Fletcher, LE, 'From Indifference to Engagement: Bystanders and International Criminal Justice' (2005) 26 *Michigan Journal of International Law* 2013.

—— 'Refracted Justice: The Imagined Victim and the International Criminal Court' in C De Vos, S Kendall and C Stahn (eds), *Contested Justice: The Politics and Practice of International Criminal Court Interventions* (Cambridge University Press, 2015) 302.

Fraudatario, S and Tognoni, G, 'The Participation of People and the Development of International Law: The Laboratory of the Permanent Peoples' Tribunal' in A Byrnes and G Simm, *Peoples' Tribunals and International Law* (Cambridge University Press, 2018) 133.

Gallagher, K, 'The Challenges for Legal Representation of Victims of US Torture on the Territory of Afghanistan and Other State Parties at the International Criminal Court' in FIDH (International Federation for Human Rights), *Victims at the Centre of Justice: From 1998 to 2018: Reflections on the Promises and the Reality of Victim Participation at the ICC* (FIDH, 2018) 29.

Galtung, J, 'Violence, Peace and Peace Research' (1969) 6(3) *Journal of Peace Research* 167.

Garcia, A, 'Corporate Liability for International Crimes: A Matter of Legal Policy Since Nuremberg' (2015) 24 *Tulane Journal of International and Comparative Law* 98.

Garkawe, S, 'The South African Truth and Reconciliation Commission: A Suitable Model to Enhance the Role and Rights of the Victims of Gross Violations of Human Rights' (2003) 27 *Melbourne University Law Review* 334.

Garrod, M, 'Piracy, the Protection of Vital State Interests and the False Foundations of Universal Jurisdiction in International Law' (2014) 25 *Diplomacy and Statecraft* 195.

Gil, AG and Maculan, E, 'Current Trends in the Definition of "Perpetrator" by the International Criminal Court: From the Decision on the Confirmation of Charges in the *Lubanga* Case to the *Katanga* Judgment' (2015) 28 *Leiden Journal of International Law* 349.

Gilbert, G, 'The Criminal Responsibility of States' (1990) 39 *International and Comparative Law Quarterly* 345.

Glasius, M, 'Expertise in the Cause of Justice: Global Civil Society Influence on the Statute for an International Criminal Court' in M Glasius, M Kaldor and HK Anheier (eds), *Global Civil Society Yearbook 2002* (Oxford University Press, 2002) 137.

Global Diligence LLP, Communication under Article 15 of the Rome Statute of the International Criminal Court: The Commission of Crimes Against Humanity in Cambodia July 2002 to Present (2014).

Goldstone, R, 'Foreword' in M Sterio and M Scharf (eds), *The Legacy of Ad Hoc Tribunals in International Criminal Law* (Cambridge University Press, 2019) xv.

Goodman, R and Hamilton, R, 'Model Indictment for Crime of Aggression Against Ukraine: Prosecutor v President Vladimir Putin' *Just Security* (14 March 2022).

Goodrich, T, 'The Conduct of the US Army' in MG Sökmen (ed), *World Tribunal on Iraq: Making the Case Against War* (Olive Branch Press, 2008) 228.

Graff, J, 'Corporate War Criminals and the International Criminal Court: Blood and Profits in the Democratic Republic of Congo' (2004) 2 *Human Rights Brief* 23.

Graham, L, '"Austerity" Policies as Crimes Against Humanity: An Assessment of UK Social Security Policy Since 2008' (2018) 9(1) *Queen Mary Law Journal* 5.

Graubart, J and Varadarajan, L, 'Taking Milosevic Seriously: Imperialism, Law and the Politics of Global Justice' (2013) 27(4) *International Relations* 439.

Greenawalt, AKA, 'Rethinking Genocidal Intent: the Case for a Knowledge-Based Interpretation' (1999) 99 *Columbia Law Review* 2259.

——, 'International Criminal Law for Retributivists' (2014) 25 *University of Pennsylvania Journal of International Law* 969.

Greene, A, 'The Campaign to Make Ecocide an International Crime: Quixotic Quest or Moral Imperative' (2019) 30(3) *Fordham Journal of International Law* 1.

Greene, J, 'Hostis Humani Generis' (2008) 34(4) *Critical Inquiry* 638.

Grey, R, McLoughlin, K and Chappell, L, 'Gender and Judging at the International Criminal Court: Lessons from "Feminist Judgment Projects"' (2021) 34 *Leiden Journal of International Law* 247.

Grief, N, 'Legal Challenges to the United Kingdom's Nuclear Defence Policy' [1989] *Public Law* 541.

Guilfoyle, DJA, 'Responsibility for Collective Atrocities: Fair Labelling and Approaches to Commission in International Criminal Law' (2001) 64 *Current Legal Problems* 255.

——, 'The ICC Pre-Trial Chamber Decision on Jurisdiction over the Situation in Myanmar' (2019) 73 *Australian Journal of International Affairs* 2.

Gulam, H and O'Connor, M, 'Selective Conscientious Objection: The Court-Martial of Flight Lieutenant Malcolm Kendall-Smith, RAF' (2006) 7 *ADF Health* 68.

Hajjar, L, 'The Counter Terrorism War Paradigm versus International Humanitarian Law: The Legal Contradictions and Global Consequences of the US "War on Terror"' (2019) 4 *Law and Social Inquiry* 922.

Hamilton, RJ, 'State-Enabled Crimes' (2016) 41 *Yale Journal of International Law* 301.

Hansen, TO, 'Accountability for British War Crimes in Iraq? Examining the Nexus between International and National Justice Responses' in M Bergsmo and C Stahn (eds), *Quality Control in Preliminary Examination*, vol I (Torkel Opsahl, 2018).

——, 'Opportunities and Challenges Seeking Accountability for War Crimes in Palestine under the International Criminal Court's Complementarity Regime' (2019) 9 *Notre Dame Journal of International and Comparative Law* 1.

Haslam, E, 'Victim Participation at the International Criminal Court: A Triumph of Hope over Experience' in D McGoldrick, P Rowe and E Donnelly (eds), *The Permanent International Criminal Court: Legal and Policy Issues* (Hart Publishing, 2004) 315.

——, 'Writing More Inclusive Histories of International Criminal Law: Lessons from the Slave Trade and Slavery' in I Tallgren and T Skouteris, *New Histories of International Criminal Law* (Oxford University Press, 2019) 130.

——, *The Slave Trade, Abolition and the Long History of International Criminal Law: The Recaptive and the Victim* (Routledge, 2020).

——, 'Archived Bodies: The Transatlantic Slave Trade and Abolition' in D Herman and C Parsley (eds), *Interdisciplinarities Research Process, Method, and the Body of Law* (Palgrave Macmillan, 2022) 9.

Haslam, E and Edmunds, R, 'Common Legal Representation at the International Criminal Court: More Symbolic than Real?' (2012) 12(5) *International Criminal Law Review* 871.

Haslam, E and Edmunds, R, 'Managing a New Partnership: Professionalization, Intermediaries and the International Criminal Court' (2012) 24 *Criminal Law Forum* 1.

Haslam, E and Edmunds, R, 'Victim Participation, Politics and the Construction of Victims at the International Criminal Court: Reflection on Proceedings in *Banda* and *Jerbo*' (2014) 14(2) *Melbourne Journal of International Law* 727.

Hathaway, OA, 'The Case for Creating an International Tribunal to Prosecute the Crime of Aggression Against Ukraine' *Just Security* (20 September 2022).

Hazan, P, *Justice in a Time of War* (Texas A&M University Press, 2004).

Heller, KJ, 'Radical Complementarity' (2016) 14 *Journal of International Criminal Justice* 637.

——, 'The Nine Words that (Wrongly) Doomed the Iraq Investigation' *Opinio Juris* (10 December 2020).

Hodgson, N, 'International Criminal Law and Civil Society Resistance to Offshore Detention' (2020) 26(3) *Australian Journal of Human Rights* 449.

Howard, J, 'Invoking State Responsibility for Aiding the Commission of International Crimes – Australia, the United States and the Question of East Timor' [2001] *Melbourne Journal of International Law* 2.

Howard, M, Andreopoulos, GJ and Shulman, MR, *The Laws of War: Constraints on Warfare in the Western World* (Yale University Press, 1994).

Human Rights Council, '"They Came to Destroy": ISIS Crimes Against the Yazidis', 15 June 2016, A/HRC/32/CRP.2.

Hutchinson, JG, *Champions of Charity: War and the Rise of the Red Cross* (Westview Press, 1996).

International Commission of Inquiry on Darfur, *Report to the United Nations Secretary-General Pursuant to SCR 564 of 18 September 2004*, 25 January 2005.

International Commission of Jurists Expert Legal Panel on Corporate Complicity in International Crimes, *Corporate Complicity and Legal Accountability*, vol 2: *Criminal Law and International Crimes* (International Commission of Jurists, 2008).

International Committee of the Red Cross, 'International Humanitarian Law and the Challenges of Contemporary Armed Conflicts' EN 321C/15/11 (ICRC, October 2015).

International Conference on Military Trials, London, 1945 (Department of State Publication No 3080, 1949).

International Criminal Court, 'Guidelines for the Judiciary Concerning the Holding of Court Hearings during the COVID-19 pandemic' (23 June 2020).

International Criminal Tribunal for the Former Yugoslavia, *Final Report to the Prosecutor by the Committee Established to Review the NATO Bombing Campaign Against the Federal Republic of Yugoslavia* (United Nations International Criminal Tribunal for the former Yugoslavia nd)

Jacobson, KR, 'Doing Business with the Devil: The Challenges of Prosecuting Corporate Officials whose Business Transactions Facilitate War Crimes and Crimes Against Humanity' (2005) 56 *Air Force Law Review* 167.

Jain, N, 'Individual Responsibility for Mass Atrocity: In Search of a Concept of Perpetration' (2013) 61(4) *American Journal of Comparative Law* 831.

Jalloh, CC, 'What Makes a Crime Against Humanity a Crime Against Humanity?' [2013] *American University International Law Review* 381.

Jayasimha, S, 'Victor's Justice, Crime of Silence and the Burden of Listening: Judgement of the Tokyo Tribunal 1948, Women's International War Crimes Tribunal 2000 and Beyond' (2001) 1 *Law, Social Justice and Global Development Journal* 35.

Jessberger, F, 'On the Origins of Individual Criminal Responsibility under International Law for Business Activity' (2010) 8 *Journal of International Criminal Justice* 783.

Jochnick af, C and Normand, R, 'The Legitimation of Violence: A Critical History of the Laws of War' (1994) 25 *Harvard International Law Journal* 49.

Johnson, DHN, 'The Draft Code of Offences Against the Peace and Security of Mankind (1955) 4 *International and Comparative Law Quarterly* 455.

Jonas, S, McCaughan, E and Martinez, ES, *Guatemala Tyranny on Trial Testimony of the Permanent Peoples' Tribunal* (Synthesis Publications, 1984).

Jones, A, *Genocide, War Crimes and the West* (Zed Books, 2004).

Jones, CA, 'Lawfare and the Juridification of Late Modern War' (2016) 40(2) *Progress in Human Geography* 221.

Jorda, C and de Hemptinne, J, 'The Status and Role of the Victim' in A Cassese, P Gaeta and JRWD Jones (eds), *The Rome Statute of the International Criminal Court: A Commentary*, vol 2 (Oxford University Press, 2002) 1387.

Jordash, W and Aysev, UY, 'Victim Participation in the Pre-Situation Phase: Insights from the Pre-Trial Chamber's Rohingya decision' in FIDH (International Federation for Human Rights), *Victims at the Centre of Justice: From 1998 to 2018: Reflections on the Promises and the Reality of Victim Participation at the ICC* (FIDH, 2018) 13.

Jørgensen, NHB, 'Complicity in Torture in a Time of Terror: Interpreting the European Court of Human Rights Extraordinary Rendition Cases' (2017) 16 *Chinese Journal of International Law* 11.

Jury of Conscience, 'Declaration of the Jury of Conscience of World Tribunal on Iraq – Istanbul, 23–27 June 2005' in MG Sökmen (ed), *World Tribunal on Iraq: Making the Case Against War* (Olive Branch Press, 2008) 492.

Kaeb, C, 'The Shifting Sands of Corporate Liability under International Criminal Law' (2016) 49 *George Washington International Law Review* 351.

Kalpouzos, I, 'International Criminal Law and the Violence Against Migrants' (2020) 21 *German Law Journal* 571.

Kalpouzos, I and Mann, I, 'Banal Crimes Against Humanity: the Case of Asylum Seekers in Greece' (2015) 16 *Melbourne Journal of International Law* 1.

Kastner, P (ed), *International Criminal Law in Context* (Routledge, 2017).

Keenan, PJ, 'Conflict Minerals and the Law of Pillage' (2014) 14(2) *Chicago Journal of International Law* 524.

Kendall, S and da Silva, C, 'Beyond the ICC: State Responsibility for the Arms Trade in Africa' in KM Clarke, AS Knottnerus and de Volder (eds), *Africa and the ICC: Perceptions of Justice* (Cambridge University Press, 2016) 407.

Kendall, S and Nouwen, SMH, 'Representational Practices at the International Criminal Court: The Gap between Juridified and Abstract Victimhood' (2014) 76 *Law and Contemporary Problems* 235.

Kersten, M, 'No Justice Without Peace, But What Peace is on Offer? Palestine, Israel and the International Criminal Court' (2020) 18(4) *Journal of International Criminal Justice* 1001.

Kiswanson, N, 'Beyond Victim Participation during Proceedings: Outreach and Information Activities during Preliminary Examination in Palestine' in FIDH (International Federation for Human Rights), *Victims at the Centre of Justice: From 1998 to 2018: Reflections on the Promises and the Reality of Victim Participation at the ICC* (FIDH, 2018) 43.

Kiyani, A, 'International Crime and the Politics of Criminal Theory: Voices and Conduct of Exclusion' (2015) 48(1) *New York University Journal of International Law and Politic* 129.

——, 'Group-Based Differentiation and Local Repression: The Custom and Curse of Selectivity' (2016) 14 *Journal of International Criminal Justice* 939.

Kiyani, A, Reynolds, J and Xavier, S, 'Foreword: Third World Approaches to International Criminal Law' (2016) 14 *Journal of International Criminal Justice* 915.

Klabbers, J, *International Law* (Cambridge University Press, 2020).

Klinghoffer, AJ and Klinghoffer, JA, *International Citizens' Tribunals: Mobilizing Public Opinion to Advance Human Rights* (Palgrave, 2002).

Knottnerus, AS and de Volder, E, 'International Criminal Justice and the Early Formation of an African Criminal Court' in KM Clarke, AS Knottnerus and E de Volder (eds), *Africa and the ICC Perceptions of Justice* (Cambridge University Press, 2016) 376.

Kontorovich, E, 'The Piracy Analogy: Modern Universal Jurisdiction's Hollow Foundation' (2004) 45(10) *Harvard International Law Journal* 183.

Kopelman, S, 'Ideology and International Law: Dissent of Indian Justice at the Tokyo War Crimes Trial' (1991) 23 *New York University Journal of International Law and Politics* 373.

Koskenniemi, M, 'Between Impunity and Show Trials' (2002) 6 *Max Planck Yearbook of United Nations Law* 1.

——, *From Apology to Utopia: The Structure of Legal Argument* (Cambridge University Press, 2006).

Kramer, A, 'The First Wave of International War Crimes Trials? Istanbul and Leipzig' (2006) 14(4) *European Review* 441.

Kress, C, 'The Iraqi Special Tribunal and the Crime of Aggression' (2004) 2 *Journal of International Criminal Justice* 347.

——, 'Time for Decision: Some Thoughts on the Immediate Future of the Crime of Aggression: A Reply to Andreas Paulus' (2010) 20 *European Journal of International Law* 1129.

——, 'On the Activation of ICC Jurisdiction over the Crime of Aggression' (2018) 16(1) *Journal of International Criminal Justice* 1.

Krever, T, 'International Criminal Law: An Ideology Critique' (2013) 26(3) *Leiden Journal of International Law* 701.

Krieger, H, 'Populist Governments and International Law' (2019) 30(3) *European Journal of International Law* 971.

Kyriakakis, J, 'Corporations before International Criminal Courts: Implications for the International Criminal Justice Project' (2017) 30(1) *Leiden Journal of International Criminal Law* 221.

Lacerda, T, '"Victim": What Is Hidden behind This Word?' (2016) 10 *International Journal of Transitional Justice* 179.

Langer, M and Eason, M, 'The Quiet Expansion of Universal Jurisdiction' (2019) 30(3) *European Journal of International Law* 779.

Lawrence, JC and Heller, KJ, 'The First Ecocentric Environmental War Crime: The Limits of Article 8(2)(b)(iv) of the Rome Statute' (2007–08) 20 *Georgetown International Environmental Law Review* 61.

Leebaw, B, 'Justice and the Faithless: The Demand for Disobedience in International Criminal Law' (2018) 24(2) *European Journal of International Relations* 344.

Legge, D and Brooman, S, 'Reflecting on 25 Years of Teaching Animal Law: Is It Time for an International Crime of Animal Ecocide?' (2020) 41 *Liverpool Law Review* 201.

Lemkin, R, *Axis Rule in Occupied Europe* (Carnegie Endowment for International Peace, Division of International Law, 1944).

Lingaas, C, 'The Crime Against Humanity of Apartheid in a Post-Apartheid World' (2015) 2 *Oslo Law Review* 86.

——, 'The Elephant in the Room: The Uneasy Task of Defining "Racial" in International Criminal Law' (2015) 15 *International Criminal Law Review* 485.

——, 'Imagined Identities: Defining the Racial Group in the Crime of Genocide' (2016) 10(1) *Genocide Studies and Prevention: An International Journal* 79.

Lippman, M, 'Nuremberg: Forty Five Years Later' (1991) 7 *Connecticut Journal of International Law* 1.

——, 'Liberating the Law: The Jurisprudence of Civil Disobedience and Resistance' (1994) 16(2) *San Diego Justice Journal* 299.

Lostal, M, 'De-Objectifying Animals: Could They Qualify as Victims before the International Criminal Court?' (2021) 19(3) *Journal of International Criminal Justice* 583.

——, 'The Ntaganda Reparations Order: A Marked Step towards a Victim-Centred Reparations Legal Framework at the ICC' *EJIL: Talk!* (24 May 2021).

Luban, D, 'A Theory of Crimes Against Humanity' (2004) 29 *Yale Journal of International Law* 85.

Lubell, N and Derejko, N, 'A Global Battlefield? Drones and the Geographical Space of Armed Conflict' (2013) 11 *Journal of International Criminal Justice* 65.

Lynch, A, 'Comfort Women' *Encyclopedia Britannica* (15 February 2023) at www.britannica.com/topic/comfort-women.

Macleod, C, 'Towards a Philosophical Account of Crimes Against Humanity' (2010) 21(2) *European Journal of International Law* 28.

Manfredi, Z, 'Sharpening the Vigilance of the World: Reconsidering the Russell Tribunal as Ritual' (2018) 9(1) *Humanity* 75.

Manirakiza, P, 'A Twail Perspective on the African Union's Project to Withdraw from the International Criminal Court' (2018) 23 *African Year Book of International Law* 391.

Mankowski, E, 'Conflict Minerals and Crimes Against Humanity in the DRC: How to Hold Individual Corporate Officers Criminally Liable' (2019) 94 *Notre Dame Law Review* 1453.

Mansell, W and Openshaw, K, *International Law: A Critical Introduction* (Hart Publishing, 2013).

Martinez, JS, *The Slave Trade and the Origins of International Human Rights Law* (Oxford University Press, 2012).

Max-Neef, MA, 'The good is the bad that we don't do: economic crimes against humanity: a proposal' (2014) 104 *Ecological Economics* 152.

McAuliffe, P and Schwöbel-Patel, C, 'Disciplinary Matchmaking Critics of International Criminal Law Meet Critics of Liberal Peacebuilding' (2018) 16(5) *Journal of International Criminal Justice* 985.

McDonald, GK, 'Problems, Obstacles and Achievements of the ICTY' (2004) 2 *Journal of International Criminal Justice* 558.

Meernik, J, 'The International Criminal Court and the Deterrence of Human Rights Atrocities' (2015) 17 *Journal of Civil Wars* 318.

Mégret, F, 'From "Savages" to "Unlawful Combatants": a Postcolonial Look at International Humanitarian Law's "Other"' in A Orford (ed), *International Law and its Others* (Cambridge University Press, 2006) 265.

——, 'Civil Disobedience and International Law: Sketch for a Theoretical Argument' (2008) 46 *Canadian Yearbook of International Law* 143.

——, 'The Problem of an International Criminal Law of the Environment' (2011) 36 *Columbia Journal of Environmental Law* 195.

——, 'Beyond "Gravity": For a Politics of International Criminal Prosecution' (2013) 107 *Proceedings of the Annual Meeting of the American Society of International Law* 428.

——, 'What Sort of Global Justice is "International Criminal Justice"?' (2015) 13(1) *Journal of International Criminal Justice* 77.

——, 'The Laws of War and the Structure of Masculine Power' (2018) 19(1) *Melbourne Journal of International Law* 200.

——, 'Bring Forth the Accused: Defendant Attitudes and the Intimate Legitimacy of the International Criminal Trial' (2019) 36(3) *Arizona Journal of International and Comparative Law* 397.

Mégret, F and Samson, MG, 'Holding the Line on Complementarity in Libya: The Case for Tolerating Flawed Domestic Trials' (2013) 11 *Journal of International Criminal Justice* 571.

Mehta, S and Merz, P, '"Ecocide" – A New Crime Against Peace' (2015) 17(1) *Environmental Law Review* 3.

Michels, JD, 'Compensating Acquitted Defendants for Detention before International Criminal Courts' (2010) 8(2) *Journal of International Criminal Justice* 407.

Milanovic, M, 'Establishing the Facts about Mass Atrocities: Accounting for the Failure of the ICTY to Persuade Target Audiences' (2016) 47 *Georgetown Journal of International Law* 1321.

Minkova, LG, 'Expressing What? The Stigmatization of the Defendant and the ICC's Institutional Interests in the Ongwen Case' (2021) 34(1) *Leiden Journal of International Law* 223.

Moffett, L, 'Reparations for "Guilty Victims": Navigating Complex Identities of Victim-Perpetrators in Reparation Mechanism' (2016) 10 *International Journal of Transitional Justice* 146.

——, 'Reparations for Victims at the International Criminal Court: A New Way Forward?' (2017) 21(9) *International Journal of Human Rights* 1204.

Moita, L, 'Opinion Tribunals and the Permanent People's Tribunal' (2015) 6(1) *Janus.Net* 30.

Morris, PS, 'Economic Genocide under International Law' (2018) 82(1) *Journal of Criminal Law* 18.

Moynihan, H, *Aiding and Assisting: Challenges in Armed Conflict and Counterterrorism* (Chatham House, Royal Institute of International Affairs, 2016).

Murphy, SD, 'The International Law Commission's Proposal for a Convention on the Prevention and Punishment of Crimes Against Humanity' (2018) 50 *Case Western Reserve Journal of International Law* 249;

Mutua, MW, 'Africans and the ICC Hypocrisy, Impunity, and Perversion' in KM Clarke, AS Knottnerus and E de Volder (eds), *Africa and the ICC Perceptions of Justice* (Cambridge University Press, 2016) 47.

Nayar, J, 'A People's Tribunal Against the Crime of Silence? The Politics of Judgement and an Agenda for People's Law' (2001) 2 *Social Justice and Global Development* at https://warwick.ac.uk/fac/soc/law/elj/lgd/2001_2/nayar.

——, 'Thinking the "Impossible": Peoples' Law' (2003) 1 *Law, Social Justice and Global Development* at https://warwick.ac.uk/fac/soc/law/elj/lgd/2003_1/nayar2.

——, 'Taking Empire Seriously: Empire's Law, People's Law and the World Tribunal on Iraq' in A Bartholomew (ed), *Empire's Law The American Imperial Project and the 'War to Remake the World'* (Pluto Press, 2006) 313.

Neff, SC, 'International Law and Nuclear Weapons in Scottish Courts' (2002) 51 *International and Comparative Law Quarterly* 171.

Nesiah, V, 'Local Ownership of Global Governance' (2016) 14 *Journal of International Criminal Justice* 985.

Nollkaemper, A, 'Introduction' in A Nollkaemper and H van der Wilt (eds), *System Criminality in International Law* (Cambridge University Press, 2009) 1.

——, 'Complicity in International Law – Some Lessons from the US Rendition Program' (2015) 109 *American Society of International Law Proceedings* 177.

Nolte, G and Aust, HP, 'Equivocal Helpers: Complicit States, Mixed Messages and International Law' (2009) 58 *International and Comparative Law Quarterly* 1.

Normand, R and Jochnick af, C, 'The Legitimation of Violence: A Critical Analysis of the Gulf War' (1994) 35(2) *Harvard International Law Journal* 387.

Norwojee, B, '"Your Justice Is Too Slow" Will the ICTR Fail Rwanda's Rape Victims?' (United Nations Research Institute for Social Development, 2005).

Nouwen, SMH, *Complementarity in the Line of Fire: The Catalyzing Effect of the International Criminal Court in Uganda and Sudan* (Cambridge University Press, 2013).

Nouwen, SMH and Werner, W, 'Doing Justice to the Political: the International Criminal Court in Uganda and Sudan' (2011) 21(4) *European Journal of International Law* 941.

Nouwen, SMH and Werner, WG, 'Monopolizing Global Justice' (2015) 13 *Journal of International Criminal Justice* 157.

O'Keefe, R, *International Criminal Law* (Oxford University Press, 2017).

Office of the Prosecutor, Communications Received by the Office of the Prosecutor of the ICC (OTP, 16 July 2003).

——, *Report on the Activities Performed during the First Three Years: June 2003–June 2006* (OTP, 12 September 2006).

——, 'Policy Paper on Preliminary Investigations' (ICC, November 2013).

——, Policy Paper on Case Selection and Prioritisation (OTP, 15 September 2016).

——, *Situation in Iraq/UK: Final Report* (OTP, 9 December 2020).

——, *Report on Preliminary Examination Activities 2020* (OTP, 14 December 2020).

Orakhelashvili, A, 'The High Court and the Crime of Aggression' (2018) 5(1) *Journal on the Use of Force and International Law* 3.

O'Sullivan, A, *Universal Jurisdiction in International Criminal law The Debate and the Battle for Hegemony* (Routledge, 2019).

Otto, D, 'Performing Legal Order: Some Feminist Thoughts on International Criminal Law' (2011) 11(3) *International Criminal Law Review* 409.

——, 'Impunity in a Different Register: People's Tribunals and Questions of Judgment, Law and Responsibility' in K Engle, Z Miller and DM Davis (eds), *Anti-Impunity and the Human Rights Agenda* (Cambridge University Press, 2016) 291.

——, 'Beyond Legal Justice: Some Personal Reflections on People's Tribunals, Listening and Responsibility' (2017) 5 *London Review of International Law* 225.

Palmer, N, *Courts in Conflict: Interpreting the Lawyers of Justice in Post-Genocide Rwanda* (Oxford University Press, 2015).

Panel of Experts on the Illegal Exploitation of Natural Resources and other Forms of Wealth of the Democratic Republic of the Congo, *Final Report*, 16 October 2002, S/2002/1146.

Paulose, RM, 'Can you hear the people sing? Victim/survivor rights in People's Tribunals' in RM Paulose (ed), *People's Tribunals, Human Rights and the Law Searching for Justice* (Routledge, 2020) 2.

—— (ed), *People's Tribunals, Human Rights and the Law Searching for Justice* (Routledge, 2020).

Pereira, R, 'After the ICC Office of the Prosecutor's 2016 Policy Paper on Case Selection and Prioritisation: Towards an International Crime of Ecocide?' (2020) 31 *Criminal Law Forum* 179.

Permanent Peoples' Tribunal, 'Workers and Consumers Rights in the Garment Industry' (PPT & International Clean Clothes Campaign, 1998).

Permanent Peoples' Tribunal, 'Global Corporations and Human Wrongs' (PPT, March 2000).

——, 'Permanent Peoples' Tribunal on Global Corporations and Human Wrongs, University of Warwick, 22–25 March 2000, Findings and Recommended Action' (2001) 1 *Law, Social Justice and Global Development Journal (LGD)* at https://warwick.ac.uk/fac/soc/law/elj/lgd/2001_1/ppt/.

——, *The EU and Transnational Corporations in Latin America* (PPT, 2010).

——, *Session on Agrochemical Transnational Corporations* (PPT, 2011).

——, 'Free Trade, Violence, Impunity and Peoples' Rights in Mexico (2011–2014)' (PPT, November 2014).

——, *Peoples' Tribunal on Sri Lanka 7–10 December 2013* (PPT & International Human Rights Association, 2014).

——, *Sessions on Transnational Corporations in Southern African* (PPT, 2016–2018).

——, 'State Crimes Allegedly Committed in Myanmar Against the Rohingyas, Kachins and Other Groups' (University of Malaya, Faculty of Law, 18–22 September 2017).

Peters, C, 'The Impasse of Tibetan Justice: Spain's Exercise of Universal Jurisdiction in Prosecuting Chinese Genocide' (2015) 39 *Seattle University Law Review* 165.

Pinzauti, G and Pizzuti, A, 'Prosecuting Aggression against Ukraine as an "Other Inhumane Act" before the ICC' (2022) 20 *Journal of International Criminal Justice* 1061.

Plomp, C, 'Aiding and Abetting: The Responsibility of Business Leaders under the Rome Statute of the International Criminal Court' (2014) 4 *Utrecht Journal of International and European Law* 4.

Rajagopal, B, 'International Law and Social Movements: Challenges of Theorizing Resistance' (2003) 41 *Columbia Journal of Transnational Law* 397.

——, *International Law from Below: Development, Social Movements and Third World Resistance* (Cambridge University Press, 2003).

Rauxloh, RE, 'Good Intentions and Bad Consequences: The General Assistance Mandate of the Trust Fund for Victims of the ICC' (2021) 34(1) *Leiden Journal of International Law* 203.

Redress, *No Time to Wait: Realising Reparations for Victims before the International Criminal Court* (Redress, 2019).

Reggio, A, 'Aiding and Abetting in International Criminal Law: The Responsibility of Corporate Agents and Businessmen for "Trading with the Enemy" of Mankind' (2005) 5 *International Criminal Law Review* 623.

Reydams, L, 'The ICTR Ten Years On: Back to the Nuremberg Paradigm?' (2005) 3 *Journal of International Criminal Justice* 977.

Reynolds, J and Xavier, S, '"The Dark Corners of the World": TWAIL and International Criminal Justice' (2016) 14 *Journal of International Criminal Justice* 959.

Robinson, D, 'Inescapable Dyads: Why the International Criminal Court Cannot Win' (2015) 28 *Leiden Journal of International Law* 323.

Rogo, R 'People's Tribunals and truth commissions' in RM Paulose (ed) *People's Tribunals, Human Rights and the Law Searching for Justice* (Routledge, 2020) 40.

Rosenne, S, 'State Responsibility and International Crimes: Further Reflection on Article 19 of the Draft Articles on State Responsibility' (1997) 30 *New York University Journal of International Law and Politics* 145.

Roy, A, 'Opening Speech of the Spokesperson of the Jury of Conscience' in MG Sökmen (ed), *World Tribunal on Iraq: Making the Case Against War* (Olive Branch Press, 2008) 1.

Rubio-Marin, R, *The Gender of Reparations: Unsettling Sexual Hierarchies while Redressing Human Rights Violations* (Cambridge University Press, 2009).

Rumney, PNS, 'Getting away with Murder: Genocide and Western State Power' (1997) 60 *Modern Law Review* 594.

Ruys, T, 'Criminalizing Aggression: How the Future of the Law on the Use of Force Rests in the Hand of the ICC' (2018) 29(3) *European Journal of International Law* 887.

SáCouto, S, Sadat, LN and Sellers, PV, 'Collective Criminality and Sexual Violence: Fixing a Failed Approach' (2020) 33(1) *Leiden Journal of International Law* 207.

Sadr, S 'From painkillers to cures: Challenges and future of Peoples Tribunals' in RM Paulose (ed) *People's Tribunals, Human Rights and the Law Searching for Justice* (Routledge, 2020) 177.

Saeed, H, 'Victims and Victimhood: Individuals of Inaction or Active Agency of Change? Reflections on Fieldwork in Afghanistan' (2016) 10 *International Journal of Transitional Justice* 168.

Sagan, A, 'African Criminals/African Victims: The Institutionalised Production of Cultural Narratives in International Criminal Law' (2010) 39(1) *Millennium Journal of International Studies* 3.

Sander, B, 'International Criminal Justice as Progress: From Faith to Critique' in M Bergsmo et al (eds), *Historical Origins of International Criminal Law*, vol 4 (Torkel Opsahl, 2015) 749.

——, 'The Expressive Turn of International Criminal Justice: A Field in Search Of Meaning' (2019) 32 *Leiden Journal of International Law* 851.

Sartre, J-P, 'Inaugural Statement' in K Coates, P Limqueco and P Weiss (eds), *Prevent the Crime of Silence: Reports from the Sessions of the International War Crimes Tribunal Founded by Bertrand Russell* (Penguin Press, 1971) 63.

——, 'On Genocide' in K Coates, P Limqueco and P Weiss (eds), *Prevent the Crime of Silence: Reports from the Sessions of the International War Crimes Tribunal Founded by Bertrand Russell* (Penguin Press, 1971) 350.

Schabas, WA, *Genocide in International Law* (Cambridge University Press, 2000).

——, 'Conjoined Twins of Transitional Justice? The Sierra Leone Truth and Reconciliation Commission and the Special Court' (2004) 2 *Journal of International Criminal Justice* 1082.

Scharf, M and Sterio, M, 'Introduction' in M Sterio and M Scharf (eds), *The Legacy of Ad Hoc Tribunals in International Criminal Law* (Cambridge University Press, 2019) 1.

Schueller, A, 'The ICC, British War Crimes in Iraq and a Very British Tradition' *Opinio Juris* (11 December 2020).

Schwarzenberger, G, 'Judgment of Nuremberg' (1946–47) 21 *Tulane Law Review* 329.

Schwöbel, C, *Critical Approaches to International Criminal Law* (Routledge, 2014).

Schwöbel-Patel, C, 'Spectacle in International Criminal Law: The Fundraising Image of Victimhood' (2016) 4(2) *London Review of International Law* 247.

——, 'The "Ideal" Victim of International Criminal Law' (2018) 29(3) *European Journal of International Law* 703.

——, *Marketing Global Justice The Political Economy of International Criminal Law* (Cambridge University Press, 2021).

Scobbie, I, 'Assumptions and Presuppositions: State Responsibility for System Crimes' in A Nollkaemper and H Van der Wilt (eds), *System Criminality in International Law* (Cambridge University Press, 2009) 270.

Scott, D, *Conscripts of Modernity: The Tragedy of Colonial Enlightenment* (Duke University Press, 2004).

Sehmi, A, 'Now That We Have No Voice, What Will Happen to Us?: Experiences of Victim Participation in the *Kenyatta* Case' (2018) 16(3) *Journal of International Criminal Justice* 571.

——, 'Judicializing Economic Violence as Means of Dismantling the Structural Causes of Atrocity in the Democratic Republic of Congo' (2020) 14 *International Journal of Transitional Justice* 423.

Sekhon, N, 'Complementarity and Post-Coloniality' (2013) 27 *Emory International Law Review* 799.

Sellars, K, 'Delegitimizing Aggression: First Steps and False Starts after the First World War' (2012) 10 *Journal of International Criminal Justice* 7.

Scharf, M and Sterio, M, 'Conclusion' in M Sterio and M Scharf (eds), *The Legacy of Ad Hoc Tribunals in International Criminal Law* (Cambridge University Press, 2019) 357.

Shelton, D, 'The Participation of Nongovernmental Organisations in International Judicial Proceedings' (1994) 88 *American Journal of International Law* 611.

Shereshevsky, Y, 'The Unintended Negative Effect of Positive Complementarity' (2020) 18 *Journal of International Criminal Justice* 1017.

Simm, G, 'The Paris Peoples' Tribunal and the Istanbul Trials: Archives of the Armenian Genocide' (2026) 29 *Leiden Journal of International Law* 245.

Simpson, G, *Law, War and Crime War Crimes Trials and the Reinvention of International Law* (Polity Press, 2007).

——, 'Men and Abstract Entities: Individual Responsibility and Collective Guilt in International Criminal Law' in A Nollkaemper and H Van der Wilt (eds), *System Criminality in International Law* (Cambridge University Press, 2009) 69.

——, 'The Conscience of Civilisation, and its Discontents: A counter history of international criminal law' in P Kastner (ed), *International Criminal Law in Context* (Routledge, 2017) 11.

Skogly, SI, 'Crimes Against Humanity Revisited: Is There a Role for Economic and Social Rights? (2001) 5(1) *International Journal of Human Rights* 58.

Skouteris, T, *The Notion of Progress in International Law Discourse* (TMC Asser Press, 2010).

Slaughter, AM and Ratner, S, 'The Method is the Message' (1999) 93(2) *American Journal of International Law* 410.

Smith, L and Friedlaender, C, 'Collective Agent and Global Structural Injustice: An Introduction to the Special Issue' (2021) 38(1) *Journal of Applied Philosophy* 1.

Stahn, C, *A Critical Introduction to International Criminal Law* (Cambridge University Press, 2019).

——, 'Confronting Colonial Amnesia' (2020) 18 *International Journal of Transitional Justice* 793.

Stewart, JG, 'Overdetermined Atrocities' (2012) 10 *Journal of International Criminal Justice* 1189.

——, 'The Turn to Corporate Criminal Liability for International Crimes: Transcending the Alien Tort Statute' (2014) 47(1) *New York University Journey International Law and Politics* 121.

Stolk, S, 'The Record on Which History Will Judge Us Tomorrow: Auto-History in the Opening Statements of International Criminal Trials' (2015) 28 *Leiden Journal of International Law* 993.

Stop Ecocide Foundation, *Independent Expert Panel for the Legal Definition of Ecocide* (2 June 2021).

Stover, E and Weinstein, HM, 'Conclusion: A common objective, a universe of alternatives' in E Stover and HM Weinstein (eds), *My Neighbor, My Enemy: Justice and Community in the Aftermath of Atrocity* (Cambridge University Press, 2004).

Suzuki, S, 'Overcoming Past Wrongs Committed by States: Can Non-State Actors Facilitate Reconciliation?' (2012) 21(2) *Social and Legal Studies* 201.

Szpak, A 'National, Ethnic, Racial and Religious Groups Protected Against Genocide in the Jurisprudence of the Ad Hoc International Criminal Tribunals' (2012) 23(1) *European Journal of International Law* 155.

Tallgren, I, 'We Did it? The Vertigo of Law and Everyday Life at the Diplomatic Conference on the Establishment of an International Criminal Court' (1999) 12 *Leiden Journal of International Law* 683.

——, 'The Sensibility and Sense of International Criminal Law' (2002) 13(3) *European Journal of International Law* 561.

——, 'Come and See? The Power of Images and International Criminal Justice' (2017) 17 *International Criminal Law Review* 259.

——, 'Watching *Tokyo Trial*' (2017) 5(2) *London Review of International Law* 291.

Tayler, L and Epstein, E, 'Legacy of the "Dark Side": The Costs of Unlawful US Detentions and Interrogations Post-9/11' (Watson Institute & Brown University, January 2022).

Tefferi, YK, 'The Genocide Convention and the Protection of "Political Groups" Against the Crime of Genocide' (2017) 5 *Mekelle University Law Journal* 29.

Terrell, F, 'Unofficial Accountability: A Proposal for the Permanent Women's Tribunal on Sexual Violence in Armed Conflict' (2005) 15 *Texas Journal of Women and the Law* 107.

Thörn, H, *Anti-Apartheid and the Emergence of a Global Civil Society* (Palgrave Macmillan, 2006).

Tladi, D, 'The Immunity Provision in the AU Amendment Protocol' (2015) 13 *Journal of International Criminal Justice* 3.

Trahan, J, 'Examining the Benchmarks by Which to Evaluate the ICTYs Legacy' in M Sterio and M Scharf (eds), *The Legacy of Ad Hoc Tribunals in International Criminal Law* (Cambridge University Press, 2019) 25.

Trial International, *Universal Jurisdiction Annual Review 2020: Terrorism and International Crimes: Prosecuting Atrocities for What They Are* (Trial International, 2020).

Tromp, N, 'The right to tell The Sarajevo Women Court in search for a feminist approach to justice' in RM Paulose (ed), *People's Tribunals, Human Rights and the Law Searching for Justice* (Routledge, 2020) 77.

Tsagareishvili, N, 'The ICC Investigation into the Situation of Georgia: Lack of Victims' Involvement and Related Challenges' in FIDH, *Victims at the Centre of Justice: From 1998 to 2018: Reflections on the Promises and the Reality of Victim Participation at the ICC* (FIDH, 2018) 64.

Ullrich, L, 'Beyond the "Global-Local Divide": Local Intermediaries: Victims and the Justice Contestations of the International Criminal Court' (2016) 14 *Journal of International Criminal Justice* 543.

United Nations, *Report of the Secretary-General on the Rule of Law and Transitional Justice in Conflict and Post-Conflict Societies*, UN Doc S/2004/616 (2004).

Van der Wilt, H, 'Joint Criminal Enterprise and Functional Perpetration' in A Nollkaemper and H Van der Wilt (eds), *System Criminality in International Law* (Cambridge University Press, 2009) 158.

——, 'Corporate Criminal Responsibility for International Crimes: Exploring the Possibilities' (2013) 12 *Chinese Journal of International Law* 43.

Van den Wyngaert, C, 'Victims before International Criminal Courts: Some Views and Concerns of an ICC Trial Judge' (2012) 44 *Case Western Reserve Journal of International Law* 475,

Van Sliedregt, E, 'System Criminality at the ICTY' in A Nollkaemper and H Van der Wilt, *System Criminality in International Law* (Cambridge University Press, 2009) 183.

——, 'International Criminal Law: Over-Studied and Underachieving?' (2016) 29 *Leiden Journal of International Law* 1.

Van Sliedregt, E and Yanev, LD, 'Co-Perpetration Based on Joint Control over the Crime' in J de Hemptinne, R Roth and E Van Sliedregt (eds), *Modes of Liability in International Criminal Law* (Cambridge University Press, 2019) 85.

van Wijk, J, 'Who is the "Little Old Lady" of International Crimes? Nils Christie's Concept of the Ideal Victim Reinterpreted' (2013) 19 *International Review of Victimology* 159.

Vasiliev, S, 'Article 68(3) and Personal Interests of Victims in the Emerging Practice of the ICC' in C Stahn and G Sluiter (eds), *The Emerging Practice of the International Criminal Court* (Brill, 2009) 635.

Vervaet, L, 'The Guantánamo-isation of Belgium' (2015) 56(4) *Race and Class* 26.

Vukušić, I, 'The Archives of the International Criminal Tribunal for the Former Yugoslavia' (2013) 98 *History* 623.

Walker, MU, 'Transformative Reparations? A Critical Look at a Current Trend in Thinking about Gender-Just Reparations' (2016) 10 *International Journal of Transitional Justice* 108.

Wanjiru, SM, *Black Iconography and Colonial (Re)production at the ICC: (In)dependence Cha Cha Cha?* (Routledge, 2022).

Wesche, P, 'Business Actors, Paramilitaries and Transitional Criminal Justice in Columbia' (2019) 13(3) *International Journal of Transitional Justice* 478.

Wheeler, CH, 'Re-Examining Corporate Liability at the International Criminal Court through the Lens of Article 15 Communication Against Chiquita Brands International' (2018) 19 *Melbourne Journal of International Law* 369.

Whiting, A, 'An Investigation Mechanism for Syria: The GA Steps into the Breach' (2017) 15(2) *International Journal of Criminal Justice* 231.

Wigard, K, Jahangiri, G and Moballegh, Z, 'Victims' Representations in Afghanistan: Unprecedented Challenges and Lessons Learned' in FIDH (International Federation for Human Rights), *Victims at the Centre of Justice: From 1998 to 2018: Reflections on the Promises and the Reality of Victim Participation at the ICC* (FIDH, 2018) 22.

Williams, PR and Larkin, K, 'Twenty-Four Years On: The Yugoslav and Rwanda Tribunals' Contributions to Durable Peace' in M Sterio and M Scharf (eds), *The Legacy of Ad Hoc Tribunals in International Criminal Law* (Cambridge University Press, 2019) 326.

Williams, S and Woolaver, H, 'The Role of State *Amici Curiae* in the Article 18(3) ICC Statute Proceedings: Friends or Distraction' (2020) 18(4) *Journal of International Criminal Justice* 891.

Williams, T and Pfeiffer, D, 'Unpacking the Mind of Evil: A Sociological Perspective on the Role of Intent and Motivations in Genocide' (2017) 11(2) *Genocide Studies and Prevention: An International Journal* 72.

Wisner, SC, 'Criminalizing Corporate Actors for Exploitation of Natural Resources in Armed Conflict' (2018) 16 *Journal of International Criminal Justice* 963.

Womack, A, 'The Latest Nuclear War: Does the Use of Depleted Uranium Armaments and Armors Constitute a War Crime?' (2016) 41 *Vermont Law Review* 405.

Yanev, LD, 'Joint Criminal Enterprise' in J de Hemptinne, R Roth and E Van Sliedregt (eds), *Modes of Liability in International Criminal Law* (Cambridge University Press, 2019) 121.

Zacklin, R, 'The Failings of Ad Hoc International Tribunals' (2004) 2 *Journal of International Criminal Justice* 541.

Zahar, A, 'Command Responsibility of Civilian Superiors for Genocide' (2001) 14 *Leiden Journal of International Law* 591.

Zelter, A, 'Civil Society and Global Responsibility: The Arms Trade and East Timor' (2004) 18(1) *International Relations* 125.

Zimmermann, A and Teichmann, M, 'State Responsibility for International Crimes' in A Nollkaemper and H Van der Wilt (eds), *System Criminality in International Law* (Cambridge University Press, 2009) 298.

Zunino, M, 'Subversive Justice: The Russell Vietnam War Crimes Tribunal and Transitional Justice' (2016) 10 *International Journal of Transitional Justice* 211.

INDEX

Roy, Arundhati, 19–20
Russell Tribunal (Bertrand Russell Peace
Foundation (BRPF)), 3, 39–40
Sartre's statement on genocide accepted by,
61–2
Rwanda, tribunal for, establishment and
progress of, 42–3

Security Council, 124–6
'destruction of Iraqi infrastructure', 108
'loss of civilian life', 108
power to request ICC to defer investigation,
125–6
referrals to ICC, 124–5
Service Prosecuting Authority (SPA), 130
sexual and gender-based violence (SGBV),
47
genocide, considered as, (*Akayesu* case), 56
international crime and, 51
Nuremberg and Tokyo Tribunals' neglect
of, 35
sovereignty, violation of, and abduction,
113–14 (case law)
Special Court for Sierra Leone (SCSL), 11, 44
Stanford International Human Rights Clinic,
123–4
state-centrism, 78–9
state responsibility and individual criminal
responsibility considered together,
107
state responsibility:
states' support for other states, challenge to,
107
wrongful acts against states, for, 104
states:
aid cessation and Article 16, 106–7
ICC, withdrawal from, 119
international crime, obliged not to aid and
assist in, 104–5
investigative services and complementarity,
129–30
support to other states, challenge to and
Article 16, 107
universal jurisdiction, approach to, 116
unwillingness or inability to prosecute, 128–9
(case law)
wrongful acts against, state responsibility
for, 104
Statute of the African Court of Justice and
Human and Peoples' Rights, 45
structural harm, 52, 53
CAH and, 65–6

structural violence, 52, 54
international crime and, 51
international criminal law, not addressed by,
25–6
survivors and citizens' tribunals, 154–6
system crimes, 53, 54

Tadić case, 91–2
Taliban, the, 133
Third World Approaches to International Law
(TWAIL), 5–6
Tokyo:
Charter and judgments, 33–4
trials, 36
victims at, 141
Tokyo Tribunal, 30, 31–2, 33, 35, 107
SGBV, neglect of, 35
transatlantic slave trade and international
criminal law, 30
transnational crimes and international crimes
distinguished, 11
truth-telling, and international criminal
tribunals, 22–4

Ukraine, aggression in, 78
United Nations Charter, 40–1
United States:
ICC and, 46
Universal Declaration of the Rights of Peoples
(the Algiers Declaration), 41
universal jurisdiction, 115
in absentia, 115–16 (case law)
international crimes and, 114–15
'no safe haven' approach, 116–17
states' approach to, 116
Universal Jurisdiction Annual Review, 115
Uyghur Tribunal, 2021 judgment, 24

victim participation:
reparations dependent on prosecutor's
charging practice and, 145
Rome Statute, in, 142–3
victim reparations, 143–4
Lubanga principles and, 144
victims:
actions of direct victims and reparations, 150–2
Afghanistan situation, submission in, 148
collective representation of, 146–7 (case law)
Darfuri and non-Darfuri, 147 (case law)
definition, 145
gravity and, 131–2
harm and, 145